THE SORROW AND THE LOSS

Martin Dillon worked as a BBC journalist for eighteen years, producing award-winning programmes for television and radio, and has won international acclaim for his unique, investigative books on the Ireland conflict. Conor Cruise O'Brien, the renowned historian and scholar, described him as 'our Virgil to that inferno'.

THE SORROW AND THE LOSS

The Tragic Shadow Cast by the Troubles on the Lives of Women

MARTIN DILLON

First published in 2025 by
Merrion Press
10 George's Street
Newbridge
Co. Kildare
Ireland
www.merrionpress.ie

© Martin Dillon, 2025

978 1 78537 541 5 (Paper)
978 1 78537 542 2 (eBook)

A CIP catalogue record for this book is available from the British Library.

All rights reserved. No part of this publication may be reproduced, stored in a retrieval system, or transmitted, in any form or by any means (electronic, mechanical, photocopying, recording or otherwise), without the prior written permission of both the copyright owner and the publisher of this book.

Typeset in Minion Pro 11.5/17 pt

Cover design by Fiachra McCarthy

Merrion Press is a member of Publishing Ireland.

CONTENTS

List of Abbreviations   vii

Preface   ix

1. Dublin's 9/11: 'The Accident'   1
2. Always Seven and a Half   12
3. A Never-ending Tragedy   23
4. Lost & Lost Forever   35
5. Bride of 'Top Gun'   53
6. Addicted to Death   70
7. Loss of a Young Soldier Husband   95
8. The Fierce Campaigner for Justice   107
9. Judges' Daughters Remember   124
10. Marked for Death   142
11. The 'Beauty Queen' Bomber   157
12. Death on the Front Lines   172
13. Grieving Without a Body   184
14. Mothers and Executioners   199
15. A Political Firebrand   226
16. The Cenotaph Massacre   258

LIST OF ABBREVIATIONS

CID	Criminal Investigation Department
FRU	Force Research Unit
HET	Historical Enquiries Team
INLA	Irish National Liberation Army
IRA	Irish Republican Army
IRSP	Irish Republican Socialist Party
ISU	Internal Security Unit
LVF	Loyalist Volunteer Force
MP	Member of Parliament
MRF	Military Reaction/Reconnaissance Force
NATO	North Atlantic Treaty Organization
OOB	Out of Bounds
PD	People's Democracy
PSNI	Police Service of Northern Ireland
PTSD	Post-traumatic stress disorder
RUC	Royal Ulster Constabulary
SAS	Special Air Service
SDLP	Social Democratic and Labour Party

SEFF	South East Fermanagh Foundation
SLR	Self-loading rifle
TA	Territorial Army
UDA	Ulster Defence Association
UDR	Ulster Defence Regiment
UFF	Ulster Freedom Fighters
UVF	Ulster Volunteer Force
UWC	Ulster Workers' Council

PREFACE

AS AN INVESTIGATIVE WRITER, I authored books that focused on the Northern Ireland conflict and its major players – the men in arms from both sides of the political divide. In retrospect, I overlooked the role of women in the conflict until I realised that understanding the nature of that conflict also required considering the various roles women played in it. Whether political activists, lawyers, campaigners for justice, terrorists, or the wives, mothers and daughters of victims, women of the Troubles deserve our attention. During the tumultuous years of war 321 women lost their lives and many were injured but little is known about their identities, beliefs, aspirations, dreams, suffering and the price they paid.

My intention in writing this book is to give voice to a diverse group of women from different backgrounds – Catholics (nationalist, republican) and Protestants (loyalist, unionist). They shared with me their first-hand experiences, painful memories and political beliefs. Some were directly, or indirectly, involved in violence as members of paramilitary organisations or as sympathisers. Many witnessed gruesome killings, leaving an indelible mark on their psyches that shaped their lives. All these women were deeply affected by the violence and its aftermath, but what do we truly know about their lives, motivations and political beliefs? Can we comprehend the deep pain when they describe memories of brutal killings, or the anger when killers were given well-paid jobs due to post-conflict legislation? I urge readers to ask these questions before forming an opinion.

PREFACE

The narratives of the women who confided in me remain as raw as they were decades ago. Violence has a cascading effect and the war in Ireland and Britain left many women psychologically damaged. In some cases, their trauma motivated lifelong crusades to find the truth about the murders of their loved ones. I consider these women innocent victims of the conflict.

The term 'collusion' surfaced frequently in my conversations with women on both sides of the political divide. Some used the term after they were denied vital information in their search for truth. Many of the murders were never solved, not necessarily due to police incompetence but due to the secret role British intelligence services played in protecting terrorists who were also agents of the State. This aspect of the dirty war, in which the intelligence services ran paramilitary agents, many of whom were permitted to commit terrorist attacks, was a well-known governmental practice and prevented proper investigations of major crimes. This does not prove the argument that terrorist agents were an unnecessary element of the counterterrorism war. On the contrary, terrorist agents were often a vital tool in the defeat of the Irish Republican Army (IRA) and they saved many lives. Nevertheless, allowing and encouraging agents to commit terrorist acts to improve their status within paramilitary organisations crossed moral boundaries.

I have investigated and written about notorious double agents, including IRA interrogator/torturer Frederick Scappaticci, codenamed 'Stakeknife', and the paedophile IRA commander Brendan 'Ruby' Davison, aka MI5's 'Agent Ascot'. I am convinced that the British government knows that opening files which would further expose how British intelligence used men like these as paid agents throughout the conflict will lead to demands for redress. It could result in major political and financial costs.

In the past, the need for answers led the British government to create, and then disband, the Historic Enquiries Team (HET) of detectives from across the UK, which investigated 3,269 cold cases. Many women in this book labelled the HET as 'incompetent', since it lacked the investigative resources required to unpack many of the murders in which collusion was a potential factor. The HET's limitations were due to a lack of access to critical intelligence files held by MI5, British Military Intelligence and Special Branch. These agencies, if they have not already 'scrubbed' many of their highly sensitive, compromising files, have been unwilling to share information even with police and ombudsman investigators.

Special Branch often labelled sensitive and classified material as 'NDD', meaning no downward dissemination or sharing with investigators. They also used the label 'Slow Waltz' on documents as an instruction to share information in 'slow time'. In other words, do not respond immediately, or wait for a reasonable amount of time before supplying information after a request is made. This lack of information-sharing impacted investigations, possibly costing lives. I believe a decision was made in Whitehall after 2000 to wrap up the past, fearing the exposure of compromising stories about sectarian murders, innocent lives lost, political machinations and networks of agents and double agents involved in terror attacks on civilians.

When I interviewed women for this book, their determination to seek truth and justice impressed me. Many had navigated for years the British government's jurisdictional system and opposed legacy law legislation, seeing it as an attempt by the British government to limit access to information about past crimes. They rightly deduced that it would stymie truth-seekers, ending any chance of fair investigations into the thousands of unsolved murders of the Troubles era. For Whitehall, legacy law legislation was economically sound, but those promoting it ignored a complex reality: that it would face stubborn resistance. Similar laws in post-Franco Spain were introduced, aimed at capping the past and erasing Franco's role in Spain's brutal Civil

War. However, today Spain is still dealing with demands for answers to unsolved crimes by the State in that war.

The British government's efforts to hide disturbing truths concealed in highly classified intelligence dossiers has left many relatives of victims helpless and vulnerable to conspiracy theories. Too often they have felt cheated and have been lied to by the very authorities empowered to bring culprits to justice. They have come to realise that their pain will never be alleviated and the truths which they are seeking will continue to be denied to them. This leaves them wondering why a fully-fledged Truth Commission was never established during the Good Friday Agreement to provide open access to police, intelligence, military and IRA interrogation files. After all, what is there to protect, even now, if a deal can be struck in which truth buys immunity from prosecution for all the combatants?

Finally, I must admit that I faced some obstacles when writing the book. Most, but not all of the women I contacted were willing to share their personal stories. Some explained how they were emotionally unable to revisit the past; others said their memories were too personal to share with a stranger. A few hinted that their spouses were opposed to them speaking to me. It was as if their husbands felt that the pain their wives experienced was part of a life best left in the past, since they had moved on. I understood that these women did not wish to create personal conflict in their marriages. In one case, a prominent political figure appeared willing to share her story but her participation was cut short by her party bosses. They did not want her upsetting the status quo so she bailed out of the project. Privacy was another reason for some women not to contribute to the project. They did not wish to be part of a public narrative, and one or two argued that they had never seen themselves central to the story of those they had lost. It was, I felt, their way of creating an emotional barrier between the past and the present.

The majority of those who refused to contribute still encouraged me to write the book. Overall, most of the women who participated in the project appear to have benefited from involvement with support groups and organisations that provided them with a much-needed service not available decades ago. I came away with the utmost respect for all the women I spoke to. They were honest, a little apprehensive at times but always eager to supply me with the smallest detail about their lives. They had all paid a price for being victims or participants in a bloody conflict.

As one woman reminded me, the pain begins after the murder and it never ends.

1

DUBLIN'S 9/11: 'THE ACCIDENT'

ON THE MORNING OF FRIDAY, 17 May 1974, the media's focus throughout the British Isles was on Northern Ireland, where day two of a modern rebellion of sorts was taking place: the Ulster Workers' Council (UWC) strike. This was how I later described it: 'A self-elected provisional government of Protestant power workers, well-armed private armies and extreme politicians organised a strike that almost broke up the fabric of civilised life in Ulster. They deprived most of the population for much of the strike of food, water, electricity, gas, transport, money, and any form of livelihood.'

Although it was a significant political event, most people watching the strike unfold, with loyalist paramilitary groups at the cutting edge, were unaware that one of those paramilitary bodies, the Ulster Volunteer Force (UVF), was about to rain down hell on innocent shoppers in the Irish Republic.

By 1 May 1974 the UVF had decided that Dublin would be its next target, although it had bombed the city twice before. On Friday, 1 December 1972, bombs exploded in the early evening near Liberty Hall on Eden Quay and at Sackville Place, off O'Connell Street. Two people were killed and twenty-seven injured. There were rumours that the explosions were timed to coincide with proposed anti-terror legislation in the Dáil aimed specifically at targeting the IRA. A second attack on the Irish capital came on 20 January 1973, leaving one person dead and seventeen injured. The bombings were planned by the UVF leadership in the Shankill area of west Belfast.

While the Shankill was undoubtedly the beating heart of the UVF – it was where its modern founders, such as Gusty Spence, lived and where the Shankill Butchers would later ply their grisly trade – it was not its only strategy centre. Many UVF killings and bombings were planned in mid-Ulster's so-called 'Murder Triangle', encompassing the towns of Lurgan, Portadown and Armagh. Indeed, despite some journalists and political commentators being inclined to consider Belfast as the core of the UVF's murderous activities, its most efficient killing machine operated from a farm in Glenanne, a townland in Armagh. It was there that an assortment of vicious gunmen, most linked to the UVF, established a tightly run militia known as the Glenanne Gang. Their common goal was to kill Catholics, envisaging such a murderous enterprise as the ideal means of driving a wedge between Catholics and the IRA. The theory was that if the UVF could prove that the IRA was unable to protect Catholics, this would damage the IRA's standing in the nationalist community and Catholics would blame the IRA for loyalist attacks. It was a rather naive concept, since the effect of killing Catholics only drove more of them into the arms of the IRA, but the UVF, and those associated with this strange militia, were not always sophisticated political thinkers, and nor were those members of the State security apparatus in their ranks.

As well as killing Catholics, the Glenanne Gang planned attacks on the Irish Republic. This goal did not come exclusively from the UVF. It originated with a core group within the militia of seasoned UVF killers and others who were members of the Royal Ulster Constabulary

(RUC) Special Patrol Group and the Ulster Defence Regiment (UDR). Several figures in the militia leadership were secret assets of Special Branch, MI5, British Military Intelligence and, in the case of one, MI6. The militia even had a few Ulster Defence Association (UDA) killers in its ranks.

Some of the British intelligence agents linked to this violent militia had close ties to the Irish police, An Garda Síochána, especially its upper ranks. MI6 had made it a policy, beginning in 1970, to infiltrate the gardaí. MI6 also tried to expand its influence to the whole of Ireland, which contravened its brief as a foreign intelligence agency with no legal remit inside the United Kingdom. It tried to recruit covert British Military Intelligence agents on the ground in Northern Ireland, which led to an internecine political war with MI5, which MI5 won, so MI6 backed off, but not very far. It secretly retained some assets in Northern Ireland, including one within the Glenanne Gang. MI6 felt that it needed to know if Northern Ireland loyalists were planning acts of terror within the Irish Republic, which MI6 considered its domain.

On 17 May 1974 the UWC strike in Northern Ireland was a world away as far as sixteen-year-old Bernie O'Hanlon was concerned. It was a normal Friday in north Dublin, where she lived with her dad, Joe, her mum, Rose, and seven siblings. Anyway, she paid no attention to politics and usually on Fridays she had her eyes firmly on the weekend, when she could get together with her friends. Her dad was strict, so she was not allowed to be out late at night. She had only been to two discos. Nowadays she smiles when she recalls that they were held at a boys' school for the blind in Drumcondra on Friday evenings between 8 and 11 p.m. When she told people the disco was called 'The Blind', they thought she was joking. The school organised the discos to provide young people with entertainment and it was a safe venue. Bernie always left the disco early because her father insisted that she be at home by 11 p.m. and 'his word was law'. 'I was anxious to grow up, but we were innocent kids,' she explained. 'We never did any harm or did anything that was unacceptable. My dad ran a tight ship.'

After breakfast on 17 May, Bernie made her way to O'Neill's shoe shop on Talbot Street, close to the junction with Gardiner Street, in the centre of Dublin. She had begun working there the previous summer after leaving school. O'Neill's was a large, successful shop. It was divided into two sections: one for men and boys, the other for women and girls. It had two large display windows separated by a big, heavy Georgian door that led to a hallway for people who lived in the apartments above the store. The staff could access both parts of the store via the hallway.

It was a lovely day as Bernie walked up Talbot Street. There had been a city bus strike for weeks, but it had not limited the numbers of shoppers. It was also First Communion Day for young boys and girls, and many of them were enjoying an outing in the city with parents and relatives. A lot of people were heading to Connolly Station to get trains because of the bus strike.

By 5.30 p.m. Bernie was anxious to go home, happy that the shop closed at 6 p.m., leaving one person to lock up. At that moment, she was asked to go to the underground storeroom to fetch a pair of sandals for a lady customer. She was not happy about this because the storeroom was 'dark and creepy'. She was on her way back upstairs when she heard an explosion, which she would later learn was a car bomb going off in Parnell Street.

'I hadn't a clue what damage a bomb might do,' says Bernie. 'I had no experience of the devastation it would cause. I came up a flight of stairs, carrying the sandals, and saw Mary McKenna, who lived in one of the flats above our store. She had also heard the bomb go off and rushed downstairs. She was standing in the hallway at the Georgian door, which was open to the street. Mary worked in Clery's department store on O'Connell Street, but that day she was off work because its staff was on strike.'

Mary caught sight of Bernie and asked her if she had heard the explosion. 'I told her it sounded like a bomb, but I couldn't be sure,' remembers Bernie.

Suddenly, Bernie's boss, Joe O'Neill, appeared in the hallway. Originally from Northern Ireland, he was staring at an empty car with Northern Irish licence plates parked across the street. As a shop owner, he was familiar with advice from the gardaí to report abandoned cars. For him, one with a Northern registration spelled danger. He shouted to Mary to close the door to the street. As she did so, Bernie stepped back slightly.

'Right away, there was a big flash of lightning in the sky,' says Bernie. 'I thought lightning had hit me, but I never lost consciousness. The ground was vibrating and whether it was thirty seconds or less I don't know. It just seemed like a long time. I was thinking, *Why is nobody helping me?* It was as if my skeleton was rattling inside my flesh. That's the only way I can explain it because the vibration was so strong. Things settled and I got up off my knees and heard somebody groaning.'

The groans were coming from the lady shopper who had wanted the pair of sandals. It was clear to Bernie that this lady was very weak, but there was so much dust it was difficult to see anything clearly. Nevertheless, she reached out to find the woman and called to her to make more noise so she could best locate her, but the woman was too weak to respond. Bernie was unaware that the poor lady was dying.

Unable to move around, Bernie would later compare her surroundings to a demolition site because of the debris in the hallway. She somehow got to her feet only to realise that she was sightless. Within minutes, the sight had returned to her left eye like 'a grey sheet being lifted'. She did not know, however, that her right eye had been badly damaged, believing instead that it was impaired by dust in the air. Looking across Talbot Street, Bernie saw a fireman removing what she thought was a mannequin from a blown-out shop-window display. When he put it over his shoulder and turned towards her, she realised that it was a dead body.

One man and thirteen women died in Talbot Street. Mary McKenna had been closing the Georgian door when the car across the street exploded; she died instantly. John Joe O'Neill survived, albeit with severe stomach wounds.

A third bomb exploded in Leinster Street. In all, three no-warning bombs detonated within six minutes. Two hours later, a bomb exploded in Monaghan, killing five people. The four bombs killed thirty-four people, most of them women, and injured 258. It was Dublin's 9/11, and the highest casualty atrocity of the Troubles. One of the dead, Collette Doherty, was nine months pregnant.

Covered in blood, Bernie was taken to hospital an hour after the explosion. She still did not know what damage had been done to her right eye or that she had gashes to her thigh and head, which required stitches. She was about to walk out of the hospital to go home, worried that her parents, who had no home phone for her to contact them, would be searching for her, when nurses quickly detained her. A friend was persuaded to get in contact with her loved ones. After her wounds were stitched and her damaged eye examined, she was transferred to the Royal Victoria Eye & Ear Hospital at Adelaide Road, where she spent six weeks undergoing several surgeries, with a promise from specialists that they would eventually return the sight to her eye. Twenty-four years after the bombing, following decades of treatment and multiple surgeries, they removed her right eye.

Bernie manages to laugh about the fact that she was forty years old when she finally had her eye removed. Her eighty-year-old mother accompanied her to provide moral support. Nevertheless, Bernie still calls it a 'traumatic event' because it finally confirmed that her sight would never be made whole and, at the same time, it would not end future hospital visits.

Months after the explosion, she returned to work as a sales assistant at O'Neill's. In 1989 she married John McNally, and a year later left work and became a housewife with the birth of the first of their four children. She now has five grandchildren. Irrespective of her courage, she has never dismissed the impact the 1974 bombing had on her life. Here is how she explains some of the ways it affected her: 'I have had multiple reconstructive surgeries, and it just doesn't end. When you are sixteen, it's a very delicate age, and I suppose looking back it affected my self-esteem. I always felt very ashamed of how I looked. Self-conscious would be another way to describe how I felt.'

When she took her children to school, their friends would stare at her and ask what happened to her eye. Once, her daughter Lorna came home from school and proudly showed Bernie a crayon drawing she made for a class project. It was of Lorna accompanied by two adults with spikey hair to represent her parents.

'Which one is me?' asked Bernie.

'The one with the broken eye,' Lorna replied, pointing to a figure with one eye drawn as a circle and the other eye a triangle.

Bernie told me that she often felt 'ashamed' at being linked to the bombing. When I asked her why, she couldn't explain it but provided a description of the event that shocked me. I had never heard the atrocity described in this manner: 'I can't understand why I felt ashamed,' she began, 'but the bombing was always referred to as "The Accident". I remember going to a solicitor with my dad and letters from the solicitor to my dad about me referred to "The Accident". I called it an accident for so long and so did others. In 1998, after I had my eye removed and joined the group Justice for the Forgotten, I learned how the bombing was planned and carried out. Everybody referred to the tragedy as "The Accident". I don't know why.'

She heard a story about a man who lost his daughter to the bombing and he also called it 'The Accident'. When he attended a commemoration Mass for victims of the bombings, someone present asked him: 'Why are you saying that? People were murdered.' The grieving father was shocked and later remarked that he had always called the atrocity 'The Accident'. He had never known it as anything else.

Bernie does not know the origin of this absurd phrase, which was used to describe the horrific slaughter. It left me somewhat confused. I suspect that efforts to conceal the truth of the event, as well as the failure of politicians to hold a major public inquiry and the inability of the media to unpack who was behind the bombings that day led to false claims that warnings about the bombs were ignored, making the atrocity seem like an unplanned event. This would perhaps account for the slaughter being considered an accident rather than a deliberate example of mass murder. Still, this does not fully explain the use of 'The Accident' by victims.

Joining Justice for the Forgotten in 1998 brought Bernie into contact with other survivors of the 1974 bombings, as well as relatives of the dead. She was impressed by the organisation's founder, Margaret Irwin, who possessed an acute knowledge of all the Dublin bombings of the 1970s. It was during conversations with her that Bernie learned a lot about the failures of the authorities, north and south of the border, to fully investigate the 1974 attack and bring the perpetrators to justice.

Bernie often looks back on her life, grateful that she survived. She has deep compassion for all those who died on that bright May day and for the families who are missing parents and loved ones. According to her, when she thinks of what others lost she is encouraged to feel blessed that she lived to have a loving husband, four children and five grandchildren. Still, it breaks her heart every time she remembers those who were 'cut down so horrifically'. Like most of the women in this book, she cannot forget the past. Over time, she has grown to feel that there is blame to be laid at the door of authorities on both sides of the border and of the security agencies, which accuse each other of refusing to open secret intelligence files to get to the truth of the slaughter. It bothers her that neither side is willing to make a difference. Instead, everything, in her opinion, 'has been swept under the carpet'.

She is upset that after fifty years, the Irish and the British governments continue to use the excuse of 'national security', claiming this prevents them revealing what they know about Dublin's 9/11. She credits former Irish Taoiseach Bertie Ahern with being the only politician who made a serious effort to answer calls for justice.

There was undoubtedly political confusion in the Irish Republic after the May 1974 tragedy, with many blaming the IRA's bombing campaign in the North for the mass slaughter in Dublin and Monaghan. Declan Costello, the Republic's attorney general, laid the blame at the door of the IRA, while some commentators noted a lack of general anger in Ireland. The *Irish Press* wondered why blame was being attributed to a range of 'actors' but not to those who planted the car bombs. The singular focus on IRA terror as the catalyst for the Monaghan–Dublin attacks might have inspired a belief in the Republic that this was payback for events like Bloody Friday in Belfast in 1972.

It was nevertheless inexcusable for the Irish government of the day to neglect to launch a major inquiry into the attacks. An Garda Síochána refused to reveal what it knew about the perpetrators. It should have been obvious to the gardaí that the planned attacks on Monaghan and Dublin, timed for 17 May, were known to British intelligence agencies and elements of the RUC. Within weeks, the perpetrators' identities had been shared among senior security figures in Northern Ireland. Critical information about them was buried, however, in part because some of those involved directly or indirectly in the planning or delivery of the bombs to Dublin and Monaghan were State intelligence assets.

A retired member of Special Branch who worked closely with MI5 shared with me that the gardaí were tipped off by its Special Branch contacts in early 1974 to expect something big. It is possible, though not proven, that one of those contacts was Superintendent Harry Breen, who maintained regular contact with senior garda figures. He often drove to Dundalk and Drogheda to meet garda and Irish Special Branch personnel to discuss mutual security matters. Breen was considered an expert on the IRA but his real depth of knowledge related to loyalists in mid-Ulster, especially the UVF/UDA. He was familiar with the activities of the Glenanne Gang and had drinks from time to time with prominent UVF figures in the gang, in particular Robin 'The Jackal' Jackson. It is not clear how much of his insider knowledge was shared with his RUC bosses and MI5 or with his counterparts in the Irish Republic.

No one has been charged with Dublin's 9/11 slaughter and the likelihood is that no one ever will be. It was planned by a loyalist militia with roots deep in the British security architecture in Northern Ireland. A security source told me that to unravel the origins and activities of the militia would be akin to peeling an onion. I think that it would be like peeling an entire basket of onions.

Bernie O'Hanlon was a courageous teenager when she fell victim to a massacre. She tends to minimise the physical and mental hurt she has suffered, but her memories of the horror still trouble her. Nowadays, she is articulate and knowledgeable about what she once called 'The Accident'. Like other women who continue to pay a price for the Troubles, she devotes her time to advocating for justice for those she refers to as the 'forgotten victims'.

Her selflessness is remarkable. Even with partial vision, she has never complained about the difficulties she went through. Nowadays, she downplays her suffering and focuses on helping others. Her quest for justice is an integral part of her being and she insists that she will not be satisfied until she sees the terrorists behind bars.

2

ALWAYS SEVEN AND A HALF

MOST LITTLE GIRLS LOVE THEIR fathers and it is hard for those of us who didn't lose our dads when we were seven to imagine what it is like for someone to live the rest of their lives frozen, to some degree, in the year they did. For Serena Graham, her world felt like it had ended when she was seven and a half. She has never forgotten the date, the month or the year. It was 15 March 1977. Life would never be the same. A precious part of her life was cruelly snatched away, never to be replaced. She was left with cherished memories of her father, feelings of despair and a conviction that members of her community betrayed her and him.

'I always say seven and a half because the half matters. At least I got an extra half a year with my daddy when I was seven,' Serena likes to remind people.

She recalls lying on a sofa at home when she learned that he had died, just ten days after he was shot by two IRA gunmen. 'I cried for hours,' she says. 'I thought, I am not gonna see my daddy again. He'll never give me a hug again. He's not gonna be there for me ever again. I stopped living as a child that day.'

As she grew up, Serena was terrified by the prospect of his killers coming back to murder her. 'They knew us. They had watched my daddy, so they must have watched us too. It was horrific. It was like they had a hold on us,' she admits.

Her father was David Graham, born in 1938 in the rural townland of Cohannon/Tamnamore in County Tyrone. In March 1964 he married his childhood sweetheart, Eileen McMinn. They had met at a dance hall in Dungannon and he took her for a ride on his motorcycle. She was impressed by his caring nature and his gentle, quiet demeanour. He enjoyed gardening and growing flowers, having been raised in a rural environment. After their marriage they moved to Coalisland, a town with a mixed community of Catholics and Protestants. One of the first things David did was to create his own garden. In 1966 they had their first child, Derrick, followed two years later by Alan; Serena was born in 1970.

David missed the countryside but he compensated by expanding his vegetable patch and growing his favourite pink roses. He also bred and trained greyhounds. Ireland breeds more of these graceful dogs than anywhere in the world. Some of them can run at speeds of up to 64km/h. I recall seeing men walking greyhounds through the Falls area of Belfast when I was a child. They would often lead them up Divis mountain to exercise them in large open spaces. Some of those dogs were bred to sell but most owners raced them. It was an industry that went into decline during the Troubles because greyhound breeders and owners feared walking their dogs at night or in the early morning in remote areas where they might be vulnerable to terrorists. A feature of greyhound racing was the illegal racing of the dogs against live hares. A cruel, despicable activity, David Graham wanted no part of it. He loved his greyhounds, treated them like he did his roses and bred them to run like the wind. He sold his most prized dog, which later broke a track record in a major racing event in England, to give his family a special holiday in County Mayo in the west of Ireland.

A family man, David worked in a cement factory, a five-minute stroll from his home. He would get up early every morning and stand in his kitchen drinking tea, admiring his garden. No one in his family circle remembers him being political, though he was an energetic member of his local Orange Lodge, LOL 513. It was part of his tradition, as was his membership of the RBP No. 4, part of the Royal Black Preceptory or the Royal Black Institution. Catholics considered it another form of the Orange Order, but there were significant differences. It had a smaller membership and based much of its reason for existing on the need for members to study scripture and support charitable funding. It was perceived as a more conservative institution than the Orange Order, not tainted with a history of partisan behaviour. Members had to pass certain tests to become what was called a Sir Knight. Its ritualism did not appeal to the rank and file of the Orange Order.

In 1972, two years after Serena was born, David joined the UDR as a part-time member. For many young Protestant men, the UDR was a way to supplement their earnings. For others, it was a means to play a role in the defence of Protestant, unionist values. There was also a minority within the regiment who were bitterly anti-Catholic, some of whom were members of loyalist paramilitary bodies. For them, the UDR offered military training, access to weapons and the ability to use military roadblocks to spy on nationalists and republicans. As members of foot and motorised patrols, they were able to build files on Catholics considered to be the enemy by their UVF or UDA bosses. The UDR replaced the B Specials and it was perhaps inevitable that this military inherited some of its predecessor's sectarian prejudices, especially in rural border areas where Protestants lived in fear of republican militants. There is sufficient evidence to show that some

UDR soldiers carried out murders for the UDA and UVF. However, it would be incorrect to label the UDR a terrorist organisation, as some republicans have done, or to claim that most of its members were 'dirty'.

The infiltration of the UDR by loyalist paramilitaries cannot, however, be underestimated. In 1977 a British Army investigation of two UDR companies based in Girdwood Barracks, Belfast, identified seventy UDR soldiers with UVF links. Some officers were connected to thefts of money from UDR funds which found their way into UVF coffers. Members of the UVF were even drinking in the UDR Mess at Girdwood. However, only two of the seventy identified by army investigators as being linked to the UVF were dismissed. In retrospect this is a shocking indictment of the UDR's leadership. The investigation was quickly closed after representations were made to senior UDR figures that public exposure of the infiltration of the regiment would only serve to damage morale in its ranks. In other words, a decision was reached at a very high political/military level to paper over serious flaws in the regiment. It was exactly this kind of behaviour that damaged its reputation. It could be argued that the failure of the British government to deal decisively with this issue led to the UDR being branded a sectarian force and contributed to the deaths of the 200 UDR soldiers murdered by the IRA during the Troubles and others who were murdered after they retired from the regiment.

David Graham had no links to paramilitarism. According to his friends, he believed that UDR membership was his contribution to defending his country and it supplemented his weekly cement-factory wage packet. Even before joining the UDR, he had been a part-timer in the Territorial Army (TA), which had the nickname 'Saturday Night Soldiers'. But after joining the UDR in 1972, it would have been apparent to him that this was not 'Saturday Night soldiering'. He was now a potential IRA target. If he had done his due diligence, he would have discovered that many UDR soldiers were shot while going to and from work or when getting into their cars outside their homes in the early morning hours. Some of the UDR's part-time soldiers even committed suicide due to the stress that they were under, or developed a dependence on alcohol and drugs.

The year 1972 was brutal in the history of the Troubles and the scale and horror of it was not lost on David Graham. He confided to his wife, Eileen, that he had made enquiries about emigrating to Australia. This suggests, though he never admitted it to her, that he recognised the IRA threat to him and, potentially, to his loved ones. Serena later concluded from things that were said within her family that Coalisland had been affected by tribal bitterness and this worried him too. David believed it was no longer the mixed Catholic–Protestant community he fell in love with back in 1964. It was now more nationalist–republican in character. Irrespective of the truth of this belief, he was sufficiently concerned that he moved his family back to the townland of his birth, Cohannan, a ten-minute car ride from Coalisland and from his workplace. The prospect of emigrating to Australia was never raised again after the family settled into their new home.

The first thing David did was to create a new vegetable garden with a secluded space for his pink roses. According to Serena, he felt safer in Cohannan. It was a predominantly Protestant locality and some of his fellow UDR soldiers lived there. Before long he was back in his routine, tending his garden, breeding greyhounds and working in the cement factory. Just as he did in his previous home, he stood in the kitchen in the mornings, humming a tune while gazing out of the window into his garden. Before his children left for school he would put his lunch box under his arm and go out to his car.

Serena has wonderful memories of the lunch box because of how he used it to play games with his children. 'When he came home from work he would leave the lunch box in the kitchen and we would rummage through it because he often left little gifts of sweets like Smarties and the like in it. When there were none, he would laugh and we knew that he had hidden them in the house, so we would have to go in search of them,' she recalled.

David was a religious man who took his family to church regularly. He was also strict, insisting that his children were mannered. He made them sit at the table for meals, using knives and forks and never their fingers.

Serena has spent decades talking to friends and relatives, hoping to learn more about her father. She says that she decided a long time ago that it was important for her to know exactly what she lost when he was taken from her.

In March 1972 David Graham was a UDR corporal, in line to be made sergeant. He could have joined the regiment as a full-time member, but he liked his lifestyle and the fact that he had extra time to spend in his garden and with his family. Five years later, on the morning of 15 March 1977, he left home for work, unaware that the IRA had him under surveillance. While he was driving, two IRA gunmen rounded up the staff at the cement factory and locked them in a room. On arriving at the factory, David walked towards the canteen to leave his lunch box there. Suddenly, two gunmen emerged from a doorway. One was armed with a pump-action shotgun, the other with a .45 Colt pistol. They shot David at point-blank range, then stood over him when he collapsed and continued shooting. Police concluded that one of the shooters must have been young and nervous because of the spray pattern of the bullets. He is thought to have been the one with the shotgun, which was so close to David that wadding from the cartridges lodged in his wounds.

Miraculously, he was found alive, lying on his back moaning, as a workmate rushed to him and placed a cushion under his head. Bernard, another worker, then arrived on the scene.

'Bernard, Bernard, what happened?' David whispered. Bernard assured him that he was going to be okay.

David was transported to a local hospital before being flown by helicopter to the Royal Victoria Hospital in Belfast. His wife, Eileen, made the journey to Belfast and stayed by his side. Meanwhile, Serena and her brothers were looked after by relatives.

'I was sitting with my brothers, Derrick and Alan, in a relative's home,' remembers Serena, 'and Derrick asked, "What if Daddy dies?" Alan told him, "He's not gonna die." I asked, "What would we do without our daddy?"'

Their mother came home after eight days but she had to rush back to Belfast when she received a call to say that David's condition was worsening. He died on the tenth day of his hospital stay. Before he passed, he only said one word: 'Eileen!'

'It was so, so sad for our mum,' says Serena. 'He was shot the day before their wedding anniversary.'

Serena will never forget the day her mother came home and told her that her father was dead. 'She was wearing a cerise-coloured suede coat with fur round the collar. I hated that coat since it was associated with the end of my daddy. I always linked that coat with his death. I hated it so much I would scream seeing my mother wearing it.'

Serena also remembers her father's remains being brought home and placed in her bedroom for the wake. 'The adults did not realise when they laid my daddy to rest in my bedroom how this would trouble me in the years to come. I struggled with it. As a child, it scared me to death.'

Not long after David's murder, Eileen joined the UDR and served in the regiment for eleven years. Throughout all that time, she and her children were upset by the lack of police progress in solving David's murder. They felt that there were too many unanswered questions and insufficient leads to advance the investigation. Nevertheless, it is notable that two weeks before he was murdered, the RUC had a report of two gunmen wearing balaclavas running across a field behind the cement factory where David worked, yet he was unaware of this, as were his workmates.

On the morning of the murder, David was due to pick up two workmates on his way to the factory but one of them did not turn up. It appears that he was ill. Another workmate was ill that day too and was not at work. He was Ian Frederick Beattie, David's UDR sergeant, who had previously survived a murder attempt by the IRA. One must consider whether he was the intended target on the day David was killed, or perhaps both men were.

Before his death, David was known to the IRA. Months earlier, he had been on a traffic stop in Dungannon that yielded an IRA weapons cache. As a result, he was required to give evidence in court about the find. He also had to identify the men in possession of the weapons.

Still, one of the most puzzling aspects of this murder is why the police never informed David or his UDR colleague, Beattie, about the gunmen seen in the field behind their workplace. Police surely knew that David and Beattie were the only Protestant employees in the factory and were prime targets because they were part-time UDR soldiers. Surely security could have been put in place to prevent David's murder?

Years later, David's widow, Eileen, still serving in the UDR, insisted on meeting members of the HET investigating Troubles cold cases. She asked to meet them in the company of the secretary of state for Northern Ireland, determined to get answers about her husband's shooting. When the meeting took place, the secretary of state's deputy was present. Serena says her mother, who was accompanied by two family members, told her about the meeting: 'The HET detectives walked into the room with a wee, wee, tiny file and we all laughed.'

By then, Eileen, with the help of some UDR colleagues, had learned the names of her husband's killers. Better still, she had discovered that a witness spoke to police two weeks before David's murder confirming the sighting of two gunmen in balaclavas in the field behind the factory. When Eileen mentioned this and the names of the killers, the HET detectives nodded knowingly at each other. They refused, however, to verbally confirm or deny her evidence.

Eileen had also learned that the .45 Colt pistol from her husband's murder was subsequently recovered in 1984, after the British Army ambushed an IRA unit on its way to bomb a factory in Ardboe in County Tyrone. The gun was found on the person of IRA operative William Alfred Price, who was killed in that ambush. Forensics linked it to another murder after David Graham's and to two attempted murders and five shooting incidents.

Eileen wanted more answers but she was denied them. Many aspects of her husband's murder puzzled her, including how the shotgun used by one of the killers was found by a soldier thirty minutes after the murder. She tracked down the soldier but he had only a vague recollection of finding the gun.

Like so many families who suffered a tragic event, Eileen and her children were not spared the trauma. According to Serena, her mother had a difficult life but, like her late husband, she never complained. She served eleven years in the UDR and did other jobs to earn money. She nevertheless found time to look after her elderly parents, her aunts and an uncle. At the time of writing, she is in care but still very sharp, and she insists to friends that she would hate to lose her memory.

One cameo of her life, which she has never forgotten, was the morning David left for work for the last time. He was in the kitchen whistling, as he always did at breakfast time, before he started talking to himself, loud enough for her to hear, about his plans for the garden. He was still the country boy she fell in love with, who had a passion for growing vegetables and pink roses.

Eileen, like many of the women in this book, opposed the British government's legacy legislation aimed at capping future attempts by families to seek justice.

Nowadays, Serena believes that the death of her father came at a terrible price for her and her two brothers. She says the pain never ended in what was left of her world after her father was taken from her. Her mother had to deal with the fact that she knew one of the two killers of her husband. He passed her often in the street in Coalisland and even greeted her once.

'I have seen this killer over the years,' says Serena, 'and so has my mother and we are certain that he recognised us as the family of a man he murdered.'

Serena has never been able to shake off her deeply held suspicion that some Catholic neighbours her family had known in the Coalisland community betrayed her father. The killers were from the town and townspeople knew their identities.

Serena joined the TA Reserve, serving in it for nine years, starting in 1987. 'I knew that it held risks but I felt it was the right thing to do. It helped me focus. I also joined victims' aid groups.' She worked in a factory, got married and had children, but she developed cardiac issues and had to have a heart transplant in 2022.

Serena has always tended to focus less on herself, trying to help others who have suffered a similar loss. Though she was the youngest in her family, she understood from an early age that her brothers too never came to terms with the loss of their father. According to her, they 'struggled mentally' and became 'angry and bitter'. While Derrick was talkative, Alan was quiet and morose. Later, he was involved in petty crime and served time in prison.

'Alan did stupid things,' says Serena, who understands the dangers facing those who are left emotionally vulnerable. She says that she faced the same risk but managed to control her emotions.

'I could have been sucked into the paramilitary thing but I wasn't,' she admits.

She loved her brothers and knew that they needed professional help, but they never got it. Her greatest concern was their vulnerability to being recruited and exploited by loyalist paramilitaries. Police believed that a hoax bomb was left at Derrick's house after he refused to do a favour for a loyalist paramilitary outfit.

Like Serena, Derrick later developed cardiac issues. In May 2022 Serena took him aside and told him that he had never come to terms with the loss of their father and it was time to put this right by going into therapy. He agreed with her, but seven months later he died of cancer.

'Alan was always a lost soul,' Serena confesses sadly about her other brother. 'He just never got the psychological help he needed.'

Once, after he was arrested by police and questioned about a matter for which he was never charged, Serena confronted him and, after reminding him about what it was like to lose a father, she warned that if he ever did anything bad, she would never talk to him again. At the start of the Covid pandemic he suffered a stroke.

Serena and her brothers were not the only children of UDR members to lose a parent in 1977 and for Serena it is important that they are all remembered, along with the terrible loss this caused their loved ones.

3

A NEVER-ENDING TRAGEDY

MARY KANE NEVER KNEW HER father, but fifty-two years after his untimely death, not a day goes by when she does not look at the photos of him on her mantelpiece. When she was old enough to walk alone to school, she would pass the bombed-out ruins of McGurk's Bar on Belfast's North Queen Street in the New Lodge area where her father was murdered. Her brothers too were reminded of him every day when they passed that spot on their way to school.

The Kanes lived in a part of Belfast known for murders, riots and gun battles. The bombing of McGurk's, in which fifteen people were killed and dozens injured, was one of the worst atrocities of the Troubles. Later, Mary learned from relatives that they had searched for hours in the rubble of the bar for her father's body after the bomb exploded.

McGurk's proper name was the Tramore Bar but locals called it McGurk's because it was owned and run by Patrick and Philomena McGurk, who lived with their four children in a flat above the bar. All the regulars knew each other and if a stranger entered the premises, he would have been closely scrutinised. On 4 December 1971 everyone in the bar knew about the heavy police and army presence in the area, following the escape of three republican prisoners from Crumlin Road Gaol, half a mile away. They were also aware that between 1 September and 4 December five Belfast pubs frequented by Catholics and Protestants had been bombed. It seems bizarre that, knowing the risks, people still went out for a drink.

Due to the heavy security presence in the New Lodge–North Queen Street area, people may have had a false sense of well-being on 4 December, which drew them to McGurk's. Most of the regulars were older Catholic men from the local community and, according to British intelligence files, the pub was not frequented by the Provisional IRA. Suddenly, in the early evening, army and police checkpoints in the area were removed. Files related to security forces activity, or lack of it, at that time are no longer available. It is therefore difficult, if not impossible, to establish the exact time that security cordons were lifted. Efforts by a police ombudsman in 2010 to locate records of vehicle checkpoints for the area that evening proved fruitless.

Close to 8.30 p.m. an eight-year-old local boy spotted three men in a car in McCleery Street, adjacent to McGurk's. He saw a 'wee Union Jack' on the rear window of the car and watched a man get out of the vehicle with a parcel. The man walked to McGurk's and placed the parcel inside a small vestibule doorway. He then ran back to the car, which quickly drove off. The boy's attention was drawn back to the parcel because there were now sparks coming from it. He ran to a man passing and warned him that a bomb had been left at the bar. This man later corroborated seeing the boy and praised him for helping him escape certain death. A massive explosion of 50lbs of gelignite went off, collapsing the two-storey building. Most of the bar's patrons were buried under the rubble.

Locals, police and soldiers rushed to the scene. Ambulances arrived too, but the Fire Service took control because there were small fires burning in the debris. Hours passed before any of the dead and injured were pulled from the rubble. The Provisional IRA, meanwhile, took advantage of the situation and instigated a riot between local youths and the British Army, while people continued to work on the rubble heap and a large mechanical device was used to gently shift some of it. Soon the rioting led to a gun battle in which four civilians and two police officers were shot and wounded and an army officer was shot dead.

Mary's father and fourteen others were dead in the ruins of the bar, including the bar owner's wife, Philomena, and Maria, their fourteen-year-old daughter. What makes the McGurk's tragedy especially horrific is the lasting impact it had on the lives of the families of the victims. Their trauma after five decades still lingers.

The eight-year-old boy's testimony should have been sufficient, together with corroboration from the local man he spoke to and eyewitness testimony from a woman who saw the bomber sprint from the bar to the parked car with its engine running, to suggest that this bombing was carried out by loyalists. Yet, from the moment the bomb went off, some senior RUC officers and the British military decided that the bombing was what they called an IRA 'own goal'; that it had been a bomb in a suitcase carried into the bar by a member of the IRA and had exploded prematurely. This bogus theory, emanating from police and military sources, angered the local population. It implied, as reporters were quick to suggest, that among the elderly regulars of McGurk's there had been a member of the IRA with a bomb. The RUC insisted that the bomb exploded inside the bar and not, as the boy testified, in the small vestibule-like side entrance. The tabloid media theory was that the suitcase bomb was in transit.

The sheer bias of police investigators ensured from the outset that there would be no serious investigation of the facts, especially of the eyewitness testimony. Senior police officers and their staff were willing to dismiss eyewitness accounts. One leading police officer not only challenged the veracity of their testimony but suggested that the evidence provided by the woman was deliberately concocted to suggest the bombing was carried out by loyalists. Considering what we now know, this was shocking. It highlighted a deep prejudice within all levels of the RUC. The officer in question was later quoted as having claimed that the female witness 'was thrown into the breach' to corroborate the boy's testimony and this was a 'somewhat sinister twist to the allegation that this was a loyalist paramilitary bombing'. This deeply biased and flawed analysis suggested that locals were part of a plot to shift the blame for the explosion from the IRA to loyalists. Since this was stated publicly, written, proposed and repeated by senior police and British military and intelligence figures, it was inevitable that the true story of the bombing of McGurk's would be buried with the dead. A police ombudsman's report in 2011 quoted a British Army officer's statement that the bomb exploded inside the bar and this was supported by a police investigation in the aftermath of the tragedy.

Not a single loyalist paramilitary terrorist was arrested or questioned about the bombing until five years later, when suspicion fell on UVF gunman Robert Campbell – but only after he was arrested for another crime. He admitted to bombing McGurk's but refused to implicate his four accomplices. It is unclear if they were arrested and questioned. The UVF in west Belfast, of which Campbell was a member, had Special Branch assets in its ranks, so it would have been easy for the authorities to investigate Campbell and his accomplices. Yet, aside from him, no one else was charged with the atrocity, even though he explained to police how he had received the bomb and how he and his associates used three cars to transport it to the bar. According to him, McGurk's was not their primary target and they settled on it out of convenience.

Someone dropped the ball in the subsequent investigation of the atrocity, for reasons which remain murky. It would not be unreasonable to conclude that someone in Campbell's inner circle was an intelligence asset who could not be prosecuted, so the need for a major investigation of him and his accomplices was dismissed.

Despite Campbell's own admission that the bombing was a UVF operation, no effort was made over the years to correct the lies that locals were the bombers. Blame for this must be placed squarely on the security forces. Their silence left a lot of locals who were injured or lost loved ones feeling betrayed. Mary Kane and her mother spent decades battling for truth and justice, to no avail. Their pain at the loss of a father and husband was worsened by the British government's failure to right a wrong. Blaming victims for the tragedy was an appalling and immoral act of political manipulation.

Unfortunately, the evidence surrounding the police investigation of the McGurk's bombing exposed deep flaws in the RUC's ability at a senior level to be fair and balanced. I was told that the British Army Information Policy outfit was behind the way in which the media was briefed with bogus information about the bombing. I have wondered since if someone in the intelligence architecture at the time had prior knowledge of the bombing, allowed it to proceed and stymied efforts to find the perpetrators. I developed this suspicion because evidence about security-force activities at the time of the bombing vanished, the cover-up was concerted, and the subsequent lack of a proper investigation raised many red flags of a type I recognised in other episodes in which collusion was part of the operation.

Kevin Winters, the lawyer representing families of those who died in the McGurk's bombing, has pointed out that the police ombudsman, in a 2011 report into the tragedy, withheld important information, namely the fact that fingerprint evidence was subsequently found on a vehicle believed to be the one the bomber was seen running towards. This means that the bombers' car was located and 'dusted down' by forensics. But the curious thing is that while files confirm that police examined the car and lifted two fingerprints from it, as well as fingerprints from evidence taken from the bombing scene, the information trail ended there. Writer and Troubles investigator Ciarán MacAirt has done a lot of investigative work for the families, using freedom of information requests, and this is why we know more today.

When we think of a tragedy of this magnitude, we must never ignore the impact it had and continues to have on those who lost loved ones and on the children deeply traumatised by loss who carried the pain into adulthood. Bridget Kane was the twenty-four-year-old mother of four young children – Eddie (5), Billy (4), Mary (3) and Carol (16 months) – when she lost her husband, Edward (29), a hardworking bricklayer. He was a quiet and non-political man, who often had a pint in McGurk's on his way home from work. He was liked by the pub regulars because he was probably the youngest person to frequent the bar. After all, as his daughter, Mary, later said, 'It was a pub for old men,' with the best Guinness in the neighbourhood.

On the fateful evening, Bridget was getting the children ready for bed after eight o'clock, certain her husband would not be home for dinner until nine. At 8.30 p.m. she heard an explosion, but she paid it no heed. It was not as loud as some she had heard in the past. When neighbours arrived at her door an hour later and told her that McGurk's had been bombed, she assumed that Edward was probably fine. 'He's likely on his way home,' she told a neighbour. Perhaps her mind would not let her consider the possibility of him being one of the victims.

When he did not return by midnight, fear set in, but Bridget could not leave her young children, and she had to depend on locals and family to keep her informed. Anyway, it would have been dangerous for her to undertake the five-minute walk to McGurk's because there had been rioting and gunfire in the streets of the New Lodge. Friends assured her that they would look for her husband, who was probably at the pile of rubble helping search for injured bar regulars. In the early morning hours there was still no news of him, but Bridget remained convinced that he would come home soon.

Until I began researching this story I was unaware of the bizarre events that unfolded that night. Imagine the fear, pain and confusion Bridget might have felt when she heard a loud banging on her front door at 4 a.m. on 5 December. At first, she thought it must be her husband or someone with good news about him. To her horror, when she opened her door, she was confronted by armed soldiers and a police–army search team. They ordered her to get her children out of their beds. It was a cold, wintry morning and she tried to dress them as quickly and as best she could. She was made to stand with her small children in the street while their home was literally pulled apart. She was given no reason for the search.

Edward Kane's body had not been found in the rubble of McGurk's by the time the army arrived at his home. So why was this search carried out? The answer to that question is unknown. He had no criminal record and was not involved with Irish republicanism. There was no army or police intelligence file linking him to political or terrorist activities. Did the authorities know that he was a regular in McGurk's? Had people within the security apparatus, hours after the explosion, fingered him as an IRA bomber whom they would claim had a suitcase bomb in the bar? Why was he was being considered as the culprit at such an early stage in the investigation? Did Military Intelligence and Special Branch personnel, who would undoubtedly have been at the bomb site, hear people say that they were looking for Edward Kane? After all, there were friends and family members searching the debris for him. Someone, or some grouping within the security–intelligence framework, decided before midnight on 4 December that this atrocity would be labelled an 'IRA own goal' and they needed a culprit. I believe that the search of the Kane home signalled from this early point that the IRA would be blamed, irrespective of evidence to the contrary.

This decision would have ramifications for the innocent and would lead to a policy of false statements and lost files.

In fingering Edward Kane, the authorities singled out his family too and this would have long-term consequences. His body was recovered before lunchtime on 5 December but it was not released to his family for a considerable time. The explanation was that it had to be tested for explosives residue. In fact, his body was so badly damaged that he was only identified by a pair of socks that had a particular colour of thread and the type of stitching used by Bridget. This was the man, she would say, 'who left for work and never came home'. The fact that his remains arrived home days later in a sealed coffin led Bridget to develop a phobia about his absence. According to Mary, because her mother could never view his remains, she began to fantasise that he was not dead because he left and never came home. There was, in her mind, nothing to convince her that he was one of the McGurk's bomb victims.

It was not long before people in the New Lodge area made up their own minds about the identity of the perpetrators. They knew about the boy's evidence of seeing the bomber running to the car with a 'wee Union Jack' on the back window. They believed the denials from both wings of the IRA and laid the blame at the door of loyalist paramilitaries. Because army checkpoints had been withdrawn from the New Lodge shortly before the bombing and there had been no sustained effort to find and prosecute the culprits, locals alleged that there had been collusion between the bombers and the security forces.

Because the security authorities were convinced that it was an IRA 'own goal', as they told the media, it followed that they were unwilling to consider alternative evidence and theories. As a result, they failed to search for the real culprits, creating deep suspicion among Catholics of their motives. One could argue that this points to the following possible factors: collusion, institutional bias, downright incompetence or a policy to exploit the bombing for a political objective, namely damaging the IRA's standing in its own community. While proving collusion would require prima facie evidence, I think a combination of these other factors was definitely in play.

Two years after the tragedy, its effects were being manifested in the Kane family. Bridget remained busy tending to her children but friends noticed that she suffered from bouts of depression. Eddie, her eldest, now seven years old, began to cry a lot and draw gory images of blood-spattered coffins. Bridget suspected that he was upset because, on his way to and from school each day, he passed the bomb site. He would tell Mary and Billy that he imagined going into the pub to save his father. Billy cried a lot too and began smearing excrement over his bedroom walls. Mary says that she was sad that other kids had fathers and she had none. Bridget decided that it would be best if she moved her children to schools outside the area, which did not require them to pass the place where their father died. Eventually the children were all admitted for a mental health evaluation and received counselling.

According to Mary, as they grew older, she noticed how Eddie developed an intense hatred of the British Army, the RUC and loyalist paramilitaries. He blamed all of them for his father's death. Billy became a street thug, throwing bottles and bricks at British Army foot patrols. He was involved in many street battles with the army and was noted as a prominent rioter in police and army files. He was often stopped by army patrols as he walked through the New Lodge and was ordered to take off his socks and shoes to humiliate him. When he refused, as he always did, they roughed him up, and if he resisted, they arrested him but released him after a few hours. He was told that, before long, 'You'll be pushing up the daisies with your da.'

In Mary's opinion, rioting was Billy's way of dealing with his emotional pain. She never asked him why he did not join the IRA, but she suspected that, like his closest friends, who liked rioting, they did not want to be under IRA control. They would riot and then go to one of their houses to watch television and drink beer. Eddie, on the other hand, became attached to the Irish National Liberation Army (INLA). To this day, Mary is unsure if he was a member or just a helper.

Mary remembers that when her sister Carol was at primary school, she was asked why she could not spell 'father'. She replied that it was because she had never had a father. Carol, like her siblings, also underwent therapy.

By the time the children were in their teens, their mother, Bridget, had tried several times to commit suicide and had to go into treatment. She had never managed to come to terms with losing her husband and she did not know how to deal with the emotional chaos in her children's lives. Her friends and neighbours admired her steadfastness and her commitment to her children, but they did not see the inner turmoil with which she was dealing. She was so depressed she rarely left her home.

By the mid-1980s Billy was out of the rioting business but the new army regiments, as they rotated into the New Lodge area, clearly had his file handed to them each time they arrived to patrol the district. Eddie, on the other hand, had moved out of the area. Soldiers would often tell Billy that his days were numbered and he received a bullet in the post. He lived at home with his mother, within sight of a large army surveillance 'bunker' on top of Templar House, a large block of flats in the centre of the New Lodge. The bunker had a sniper's nest, powerful cameras and a list of homes to be kept under constant watch.

In 1988 Billy was unemployed, but it did not bother him much. He was home for meals every evening. On 15 January, in the late afternoon, Eddie arrived at the family home in Upper Meadow Street in the New Lodge. He did not stay long, explaining that he had to go home to see his children. After 4 p.m., Billy arrived, took off his pullover and fell asleep on a couch in the living room. The youngest of the Kane children, Carol, then eighteen years old, arrived home at

5 p.m. and, seeing Billy's large pullover, wrapped it round herself and joined him on the couch.

At 5.50 p.m. Bridget was in the kitchen cooking, with Mary's fourteen-year-old daughter beside her, when she heard a strange noise. She stepped out of the kitchen into the living room in time to see three gunmen, one of them standing over Billy with his weapon pointed at him. He shot Billy several times. The gunmen were about to leave when one of them asked his companions, 'Did you shoot him?' pointing to Carol, who had short hair and was wearing a male pullover.

Bridget shouted, 'Please don't! She's a girl. She's a girl.'

Carol was frozen with fear but the gunman ignored her and shot Billy again, several times, although he was already dead.

The gunmen, members of the UVF, fled into a darkened street because all the lights were out in Upper Meadow Street. Conveniently, it was the only unlit street in the New Lodge that evening. The street lights were not turned back on until the next day. No explanation was ever given for the lights being off in a street where someone was murdered. It made it easier for the killers to make their escape without being seen by neighbours.

The shock of this murder had a big impact on Carol, on Bridget and on Mary's fourteen-year-old daughter, who suffered so much trauma that years later she could still not remember the episode. According to her therapist, her mind had somehow blocked out the terrible experience. In psychology, this is known as dissociative amnesia.

Bridget blamed herself for the death of her son, for not trying to fight off the gunmen, but was nevertheless grateful that Mary, who was due to visit her, had gone to do chores at her grandmother's and was not in the house when Billy was murdered.

Mary is convinced that if she had been at home when the three gunmen arrived, she would have launched herself at them. 'I was very close to Billy. I would have given my life to save him,' she told me. 'His death affected us all more than our father's. We had not really been old enough to know our dad but we all lived together with Billy and shared our pain together. Billy's death had a dreadful effect on all of us.'

Two of the gunmen were later apprehended and pleaded guilty but not the third gunman or the person who drove them to the New Lodge. Was Billy their target or was it Eddie? One is inclined to believe that it was Billy, who lived at his mother's home. The house must have been under surveillance for the gunmen to know that Billy was at home. Since the New Lodge was a republican stronghold, one must wonder who was doing the watching.

After Billy's death, the Kane family demanded to see the police file on his murder, but it was missing. After some legal pressure, it was found with Billy's father's 1971 file. Why it was logged with a 1971 file and who ordered it to be placed with such a dated file remains a mystery to this day.

Eddie could not withstand the psychological pressure and subsequently became an alcoholic, which led to his death in 2019.

The story of the Kane family is not unique, but it mirrors the fate of many other Catholic and Protestant families who survived the horrors of the Troubles. It is an example of the way violence has a cascading impact on all the victims who witness the brutal killing of loved ones or have been indirectly affected by their loss. Stressful traumatic experiences left them all with feelings of anger, despair, sadness, pain and sometimes guilt that they were survivors. The victims/survivors had to find ways to cope with their dysfunctional world. Many, without the aid of therapy or counselling groups, turned to alcohol and drugs to dull the pain. It is interesting to note that the survivors I spoke to have one thing in common that is fundamental and unifies them, namely their quest for truth. They all want answers about the loss of loved ones and most have a desire to bring the perpetrators to justice.

4

LOST & LOST FOREVER

THOSE OF US WHO DID not lose loved ones to the violence of the Troubles are inclined to think that the pain victims continue to feel is confined to a singular, tragic event. The truth is that their pain lurks in cascading sequences of memories, some joyful and others sad and painful.

In talking to many of the women whose stories are featured in this book, I realised that they had all tried to bring some order to their painful past. The past only made sense by reliving it, but this meant enduring the trauma again. Some, fearing they could not cope with revisiting the past, refused to talk to me. I respected their decision. The wounds were still raw and the pain was acute. Others were prepared to talk to me because theirs was a constant battle with a past they did not choose. They wanted their stories to be heard, hoping that by sharing them they might bring understanding and support in their crusades for justice for their lost loved ones – for forgotten victims.

These women wanted the opportunity to remind society of the senseless violence that took the lives of their family members and the need for a fair judicial system to bring the perpetrators to justice for their crimes. The fight for justice was not over.

I was struck by their enduring courage and determination, sometimes over decades, to keep the focus on this issue of accountability. I was grateful for their willingness to speak to me, though I often felt unease when I asked them to re-enter a space filled with darkness, despair and terrible loss. As women from whom the Troubles exacted a terrible price, I hope that they all find closure in whatever terms they choose to define it.

When I contacted Paula Fox on the advice of a friend, she was happy to talk to me because, according to her, no one had shown any interest in her story. For years she had tried to get answers about who murdered her father in 1988. She wanted to know why no one was brought to justice for the crime and if there had been collusion between the security forces and paramilitaries in his murder. Her quest to find the truth was not unlike efforts made by relatives of other victims, Catholic and Protestant, many of whom alleged or suspected collusion. I was keen to find out what drove this forty-eight-year-old woman to devote over three decades of her life to seeking answers to an unsolved mystery; a mystery for which she might never get the answers she expected. To grasp the nature of her determination to unlock the past, I asked her to revisit all the memories she lived with, many of them still as vivid today as when the tragedy unfolded.

Paula's father, Leonard Joseph Fox, was born in 1952, one in a family of six children. They lived in a tiny house in Lurgan, but by the mid-1960s they had moved to the Mountainview housing estate there, one of several similar housing complexes that sprang up throughout the United Kingdom at that time. The houses offered indoor toilets, tiny gardens and a sense of uniformity. Mountainview housed Catholics and Protestants and, according to Paula, there was harmony until the Troubles began. Her father's family, like most Catholics, were forced to leave the estate when it became dominated by UVF and UDA gangs. It remains so to this day, she claims.

The Fox family moved to Taghnaven, another housing estate in Lurgan with a Catholic, nationalist majority. In November 1971 Paula's father, then aged nineteen, married seventeen-year-old Anne Breen. She was from a rural community outside Lurgan where her devout Catholic parents had many Protestant friends among their neighbours. According to Paula, Anne was a quiet girl who was 'naive' about Northern Ireland politics. Before long, the young couple set up home in a two-up-two-down house on a quiet Lurgan street. In 1973 their first child, Leonard Jr, arrived, and Paula was born the following year. By that time the couple had moved house, after a bomb exploded in their street.

According to Paula her father joined the IRA in 1972, shortly after he was married. Here is how she described him: 'My dad joined the IRA in March 1972, having lost great friends to the violence. He was not pressured at all. It was instilled in his heart to help free Ireland. That is just the man he was – a gentleman, quiet, brave, lovable, funny, but do not push him too far or you would hear his word. He loved Ireland, loved our heritage and our history and it was a combination of all this that made him join the Provisional IRA.'

Leonard Fox's entry into the IRA during one of the most violent years of the Troubles had serious consequences for his family. 'Life was never going to be the same again for my mum and dad and for me and my brother,' says Paula.

It is understandable that her memory of early childhood, with parents in their mid-twenties, may well be a construct of a kind, because she was born in 1974. Therefore, what she describes as personal recollections about the period were likely shaped by details supplied by adults in her family circle. Nevertheless, what is shocking is that she can describe this period in her childhood as though she remembers living through it, like in the following account provided to me.

'It wasn't too long after we moved home in 1974 that our home started to get raided, sometimes three to four times a week, ripping the house apart each time. I remember men, probably IRA, coming in after each raid to check the attic and other places to make sure the RUC or the British soldiers had not planted anything in the house. This was normal life for us, front door always kicked in during the night – it never happened during the day, not ever – my brother and I being taken out of bed, brought down to the living room to sit with my mother while my dad followed the police into every room. They searched everywhere. Sometimes it would last for hours, other times for 30 minutes. It just depended on which cop was on duty and if they knew my dad or not. Things continued like this, the trauma never-ending, the mental torture even when we were stopped in the car at a checkpoint, taken out for the car to be searched and we were searched, my mother too. Then, on 1 July 1976, the door was put in again, only this time it was a punishment beating for my dad. He was put into handcuffs and taken away. We saw all of this and I will never forget even though I was so young; it's instilled into my memory forever. My father was taken to Gough Barracks, where they questioned and tortured him for three days. He was charged with being a member of the Provisional IRA and with possessing explosive charges. He was remanded to Crumlin Road Gaol until his conviction and sentencing in 1977. He got twenty years but ended up serving ten in Long Kesh jail. It was the beginning of our new family life – a visit to Long Kesh once a week.'

Her reference to IRA men coming to her home to check if the police or army had bugged it or left ammunition in rooms during searches was something many republicans worried about, fearing they might be set up for a later arrest. The men who arrived in her home after security forces left were more than likely her father's IRA associates.

The vivid way Paula described life in the Fox family is evidence of how she constantly relives the past. Her account is probably familiar to many girls of her generation, Catholic and Protestant, who experienced house searches and the sudden arrest and detention of a parent in the middle of the night or early morning. It happened more frequently within the Catholic population, especially with the introduction of internment without trial in August 1971.

The internment operation was directed almost exclusively at Catholics, as well as trade unionists and some student activists. They were dragged from their homes, many of them beaten and detained in old Nissen huts, like the ones seen in *The Great Escape*, on a disused airfield called Long Kesh. A small number of them were taken to a secret Military Intelligence site to be subjected to specific in-depth interrogation techniques. Out-of-date Special Branch files used in the internment operation meant that many of those arrested had no links to violent republicanism.

Leonard Fox was known to the authorities when they arrested him in 1976, a month after his twenty-fourth birthday. By then he had spent two years in the IRA's ranks and was considered an experienced operator. Paula's recollections of his arrest and the searches of their home are fractured memories of a troubled childhood, knitted together with the experiences of other family members. After his arrest, he was transported to Gough Barracks in Armagh, a fortified military site where republican suspects were subjected to rough treatment and sometimes to brutality bordering on torture. After three days of interrogation, he was charged with IRA membership and possessing firearms and explosives. His wife, Anne, only twenty-three years old and with two young children on her hands, had to fend for herself.

The first thing Anne did was to visit her mother, who was displeased by the news that her son-in-law was a convicted IRA bomber.

Her advice to her daughter was, 'If you burn your ass, you have to sit on the blister.' She never offered her daughter any sympathy, but for the next decade she provided financial support.

Paula says her mother thought that with her husband in prison, the family would be free from the stress of police and military searches of her home, but they continued. 'My mum thought we would be left alone. There would be no more house raids in the middle of the night and no more mental stress for me and my brother. Oh, how she was wrong! The raids continued, not as often, but they continued. It became the norm for us as we grew up. It would be like, "Ach, not again. Here we go." Up from 4 a.m., a two-hour search and then get ready for school and carry on as normal.'

One of Paula's most disturbing and sad memories was the weekly trip with her mother and brother to visit their father in what she continues to call Long Kesh. From 1976 on, it became the newly built Maze Prison, also called the H-Blocks, but nationalists and republicans, as a political ploy, insisted on referring to it by the old internment-era name, Long Kesh. The trips became what Paula calls her 'normal', and by then she was old enough to know where she was going and what happened during those visits. Like many other little girls who visited the prison, she was subjected to considerable stress.

'Travelling to Long Kesh became the normal too,' she recalls. 'As time went on, a new routine would start with checkpoints set up just around the corner from the prison as a stalling tactic to make us late for visits. Our minibus was stopped and searched and all of us searched again before entering the prison. We would be too late for the visit and two or three weeks would pass before we could see Dad. It was so hard, but my mum put her smile on her face and tried to cover up the disappointment of no visit again. The job of getting into the prison on time was horrific, especially our mum getting strip-searched. Me and my brother were poked and prodded at such a young age, but as I have said numerous times, it was normal to us. I remember those visits like it was yesterday. They have never left my mind in over forty years. Another tactic which sticks in my mind is that we would be sitting waiting on my dad to arrive for our visit. If after ten minutes he had not shown up, we knew the reason. The screws would have tried to strip-search him, totally naked, mirrors used, squatting forced upon him, beaten up, black eyes covered in bruises, so he would refuse the visit just to protect us from seeing him that way. He didn't want us to be upset by seeing what had been done to him. The inhumane treatment got worse the older I got, or maybe I just understood more. As I say, it was our normal.'

On 25 September 1983 the Maze Prison saw the largest breakout of prisoners in British criminal history. Thirty-eight IRA men escaped and though eighteen were quickly recaptured, nineteen made it to the safety of the Irish Republic. The episode had a particular relevance for Paula because she claims, with justification, the authorities over-reacted after the escape. Convinced that her father and other prisoners were on lockdown and being roughly treated took a mental and physical toll on her as she was now aged twelve. The worst part was that her father was moved to another prison.

'Things got a lot worse for my dad and the inmates,' she explained. 'It also got worse for all the families who had someone in Long Kesh. After the escape, the men who were inside were tortured, beaten to a pulp. There were twenty-four-hour lock-ups and no visits. It was horrendous. We did not see Dad for weeks. Then my mum got a phone call to say my dad had been moved to Magilligan Prison in Derry. While Long Kesh was about twenty minutes away from Lurgan where we lived, Magilligan was over a two-hour drive away. Our visits were cut to once a fortnight. I wasn't a very good traveller and the joke used to be, "Nobody sits beside Paula because she'll throw up all over you."

The travelling up and back to Magilligan was a full day. It was so hard on us as a family.'

In autumn 1985 the family learned that her father would be released in 1986, having served ten years behind bars. Paula was ecstatic. She would have her 'lost daddy' back. By then, her mother had a new partner and had left her marriage to Leonard. According to Paula, her mother still idolised her father, but the stress of being a young mum living through his imprisonment had taken an emotional toll. Nevertheless, she cared for Leonard Jr and Paula, who were respectively thirteen and twelve years old.

The marriage break-up did not trouble Paula, who insists that she, Leonard Jr and her mum had been a tight-knit unit for ten years. The 'critical issue' was her father's release. Would it happen or would something intervene to keep him behind bars? What Paula did not know then was that while in the Maze, her father had severed ties with the IRA. He was finished with militant republicanism. He would later say that he had decided to focus all his energies on his family.

'The last couple of months of waiting for my dad's release dragged on,' Paula recalls. 'I remember me and my brother talking, then laughing that it seemed years for the last couple of weeks to come round. The day finally arrived and I was so excited but nervous too, worrying that when we went to collect my daddy the screws would not let him go. I had nightmares about this for a few nights beforehand. I prayed to God everything would be okay. I was twelve and Leonard was thirteen and my uncle collected us at 9 a.m. because dad's release time was noon on 1 July 1986. The gates opened and out he came out. I will never forget the moment. All he had was a brown paper bag with clothes in it and his guitar, which was his pride and joy because he self-taught the guitar in jail along with the Irish language. He was a fluent Irish speaker now and by God did we know about it. We ran as fast as we could and he swung us round and round. He cried and we cried. I never left his side. I kept touching him the whole way back to Lurgan. I was afraid to let go of his hand in case I lost him again. His life as a free man was awaiting him.'

Paula's euphoria over getting her father back would not last. After her father was freed, he moved in with his mother. Within six weeks he had met his future wife at a party held in his honour. He remarried within a year, living a street away from his ex-wife, who was still caring for their children. Paula remembers him as a loving father who was funny and good at delivering 'one-liners'. After he bought a car, he often took her and her brother on day trips. He also visited his ex-wife to seek advice about personal and work matters. 'They got on well,' Paula recalls, but for the little girl who lost her father once, she was about to lose him again a year after he left prison. She was now thirteen years old and anxious to make up for lost time with her dad but it was not to be.

'His new wife did not like me,' Paula claims. 'She told me … that she resented me sitting on my father's knee. I guess she also wanted to forget the past and make a new life with him.'

Things came to a head one day when her father's wife had harsh words for her. Paula ran home and cried in her mother's arms. Her mother put on her coat and went to her ex-husband's house and complained. Paula says that after this altercation, she never talked again about her unhappiness to her mother, grandmother or her father. 'I kept it to myself, even when it was bad. I did not want to cause trouble for everyone,' she says.

Six years later after leaving prison, on 24 September 1992, Leonard Fox, now forty years old, was working as a bricklayer, alongside his son, Leonard Jr. Father and son were employed by a Lisburn company, which was refurbishing public sector houses on the Ballybeen estate, a predominantly loyalist neighbourhood in east Belfast. It was an area with a heavy UDA presence where a former IRA prisoner would not have been welcome, yet the Fox father and son had been working there for eight months. Perhaps this fact convinced them that they were not potential targets. Leonard Sr was not from Belfast and may not have fully understood the sectarian geography of the city. Perhaps his employers assured him that he would be safe. It is hard to explain why he was prepared to take this risk to support his new family, which included two children and a stepchild. Throughout the Troubles, however, people, often to their cost, downplayed risks or believed that they were immune to the violence.

Whatever his mindset, he was made fully aware of the danger facing him after receiving a home visit from police on 24 August. They told him and his second wife, Elizabeth, that they knew of a threat directed specifically at him. The threat, however, was from Banbridge, where he had worked six months earlier, and not from any group in the Ballybeen estate in Belfast where he was presently employed. A police inspector explained that an anonymous caller, representing the UVF, identified Leonard Sr by name, warning that 'he had better be taken off the work, or else he would be shot during the week'. It could well be that Leonard dismissed this threat since it did not appear to be related to his Belfast workplace. It was, nevertheless, a threat which ought to have alerted him that loyalist terrorists had been watching him.

He was on sick leave at this time, but after consulting his employer, he chose to return to work at Ballybeen two weeks later, on 7 September. In retrospect, the decision seems reckless but given that no one in Ballybeen had threatened him, he may have felt safe. Nevertheless, he was naive if he believed that, as former IRA, he could work safely in a loyalist stronghold like Ballybeen.

On the morning of 24 September he began work as usual inside 21 Kilmuir Avenue, with his son and three other men. He was rebuilding a fireplace in the downstairs lounge. Just before 11 a.m. a lady in a house nearby saw two young men in their late teens or early twenties, one with a gun, running towards Kilmuir Avenue. Minutes later, she heard three loud bangs and then saw the same men sprint past her home.

At 11 a.m. sharp, Leonard was standing on a stool plastering the fireplace in the lounge of no. 21 when two men entered the house. One of them shot him in the back three times with a .357 Magnum. Leonard was seen to arch his back as the bullets struck him and then fall to the floor. The other gunman then shot him at close range.

The murder was a targeted killing, since the killers must have known that his son was also in the house yet they made no attempt to shoot him. It is likely that Leonard Fox Sr was identified as a former member of the IRA when his car was stopped from time to time at security force roadblocks on his way to and from Belfast and when entering and leaving the Ballybeen estate. His car's number plate and his name would have been fed into the massive military/police database of republican suspects, which would have returned information about his political history. This would have sealed his fate if the data was leaked to loyalists by a dirty policeman or a member of the UDR. The possibility that a workmate was a loyalist paramilitary who alerted the UDA or UVF that two Catholics were working with him seems unlikely because no attempt was made to target Leonard Jr. Had it been a typical sectarian murder, the killers would have murdered both father and son. Here, there was a single, specific target with an IRA history.

The .357 Magnum used to murder Leonard Fox had been used months earlier to kill Jack Kielty, a Catholic businessman and music promoter, who was father of the well-known broadcaster Patrick. His murder was carried out by three members of the South Down UVF, with assistance from the Shankill UVF. Kielty was selected to die because he was a prominent Catholic and an easy target. He was not, as some commentators alleged, shot because he was giving information to a TV investigation into the leading loyalist killer and criminal James 'Pratt' Craig. All the conspiracy theories about the motives of the Kielty assassins were false. The killing was purely sectarian. Kielty was a highly respected figure with no links to republican politics. On the contrary, he was admired for his moderate views, yet he was shot six times. His killers included Delbert Watson, a former member of the UDR, and William Bell, an ex-Royal Marine.

According to Paula, she had lost her father a second time when he remarried and now, his death represented 'a third loss' and it meant that there were so many things she would never be able to ask him, nor would he have the chance to play with her two children after they were born.

She blames developing the condition fibromyalgia on her loss. Fibromyalgia produces widespread muscular pain with tiredness, as well as memory and mood issues. When she revealed this to me in July 2024, she had just passed fifty years of age. It hurt too that she had lived longer than her father. People, she says, hear about a murder but never fully understand its effects or that those left behind are deprived forever of relationships they had planned to cherish. 'People do not realise that the pain begins after a murder and it never stops. I had two mental breakdowns and lost my marriage,' she told me.

There are some issues which I find troubling about the Leonard Fox killing and this concerns theories and claims about who killed him. Paula Fox found these troubling too. One would assume that it was the UVF which carried out the killing, as one of the shooters used the same weapon that killed Jack Kielty. However, immediately following Leonard's death, the UDA's Ulster Freedom Fighters (UFF) outfit of assassins, and not the UVF, claimed the murder, pointing out that Leonard had been an IRA man convicted for having explosives and firearms and that he had ignored warnings to stay out of loyalist areas. Police investigators also noted the peculiar linkage of the UVF and UFF, since these were separate groups and did not normally share weapons or franchise targeted killings to each other. Another curious detail was that the phoned-in threat about Leonard had come from the UVF, not the UFF, so why did the latter claim the killing?

When they examined the murder in 2005, HET investigators concluded: 'The Investigation Team attributed the murder to the UFF from the outset. As with most murders involving paramilitary organisations, investigators were confronted with a degree of organisation, and a terrorist support network unmatched in other policing environments. To counter this challenge, security forces relied heavily on intelligence to direct investigations, and on specific legislation designed to support them. As a result of intelligence, five UFF members were arrested in the first week of November 1992, and their homes were searched with a negative result. Three of these suspects maintained their right to silence and refused to answer any questions during several interviews.'

Investigators identified a dozen other men in the following year who they believed were linked to Leonard Fox's murder by their close association with the original five men arrested and questioned. One can see from this that those detectives had their eyes firmly fixed on the UDA/UFF as the culprits. One other factor that convinced them they were on the right trail was the arrest of the UDA/UFF quartermaster in Ballybeen. This came after a tip-off led police to a cache of weapons, ammunition and a woollen balaclava. Forensic analysis of a hair on the balaclava led to him. Under interrogation, he admitted that the night before Leonard Fox was shot, he supplied two handguns to a UFF member whom he refused to name but who was also a member of Ballybeen G Company, UDA. He understood the guns were to be used to kill a Catholic. He admitted that he supplied guns to kill other Catholics. On legal advice, he subsequently retracted these admissions, claiming that he had lied. He was tried for the Leonard Fox murder and found guilty, but on appeal a judge tossed out his conviction, ruling that it was based on admissions in police custody that were unreliable. Nevertheless, he received a sentence of between seven and twenty years for other terrorist offences. He was released in July 2000.

The UDA/UFF knew who Leonard was and where he was working and it was on their territory in Belfast. How they discovered this is open to speculation, but we know from his son that he and his father were stopped and searched at security checkpoints at least weekly for six months when driving to and from Lurgan and Belfast. We also know that his photo and details about his earlier IRA membership were on a noticeboard in an army base in County Down. Soldiers from that base would have been involved in checkpoints in east Belfast. Why was this not part of the HET report? The answer lies in the fact that HET investigators did not spend a lot of time re-examining cases and relied too heavily on some, but not all, of the documentation from over a decade earlier. It is not known if the RUC was aware that the British Army had its eyes on Leonard Fox, and presumably also the UDR, whose members operated out of army bases. Members of the UDR could have passed information about Fox's working patterns to the UFF in Ballybeen.

Another detail missing from the HET report, yet revealed during a 1993 inquest into the murder, was that one of Leonard Fox's killers missed his target with one of his shots, hitting the wall above the fireplace that Leonard was plastering. A plumber who was part of the team working with Fox testified to seeing this. This was a salient fact because a UFF figure boasted about knowing this, as well as about burying the guns used by the killers. Was he one of them? We do not know for certain, but I believe the police know his identity. I was told by a source that he was a dangerous individual who was a member of Ballybeen UFF.

On the puzzling issue of the same weapon apparently being used by the UVF to kill Jack Kielty and the UFF to kill Leonard Fox, HET investigators, and the RUC at the time, could have cleared this up by explaining that there was some crossover of weapons between loyalist groups. As one source put it to me, 'weapons were jealously guarded but some found their way to different units and different groups'. Another person I spoke to with detailed knowledge of the confusion surrounding the .357 Magnum offered a familiar loyalist narrative: 'The Jack Kielty murder was a UVF job but it came about because members of the UDA in the Shankill were told by a British agent in the UDA that Kielty was a source for a TV programme about loyalist racketeering and had fingered a member of the Watson family who died at the hands of the IRA. The UDA in the Shankill believing that this information was genuine, and wanting Kielty dead, passed it to the UVF. Delbert Watson was happy to kill Kielty but he insisted that the UDA/UFF supply the weapons, one of which was a .357 Magnum. Ballybeen UFF provided the guns and Watson promised to return them after he killed Kielty, which he did. That is how the gun that killed Kielty was later used in the Fox murder.'

Losing her father motivated Paula Fox to mount a campaign to demand answers to his murder and to bring the perpetrators to justice. As the years passed and she had three children of her own, she became even more determined to devote all her energy and resources into getting justice for him.

'I was mad,' she admits. 'I looked at my own kids and thought, *He should be here to enjoy them*. Time had passed and I could now talk to my brother, Leonard, about it. For fourteen years, he would not speak about our dad's death. He was traumatised. We both were. When our dad was shot, my brother ran to his side and tried to revive him, only to discover that he was gone.'

Leonard Jr, or Lennie as he is known to friends, has indeed rarely talked about the murder of his father but he helped me understand how his father could be so fatalistic as to ignore threats from loyalist paramilitaries: 'He was always saying, "If it is gonna happen to me, it's gonna happen and there's nothing I can do about it." I argued with him, trying to tell him that we were taking too many risks but he would say, "If they're gonna get me, they're gonna get me anyway and there's nothing I can do about it." We worked in so many places where Protestants lived and when the threat came from the UVF about Banbridge he was not worried because we had not worked there for a long time. There was no threat about Ballybeen and we had been there for six months or more. We were working in a quiet place on the edge of the estate.'

Paula remains convinced that RUC Special Branch issued an Out of Bounds (OOB) order to clear the Ballybeen estate of security force patrols on the day of the murder, making it easy for the killers to escape. She turned to leading human rights lawyers KRW Law, run by Kevin Winters, to guide her through the complicated process of demanding answers from the authorities. Like many other women featured in this book, she was relentless, using the media to highlight her concerns in an effort to shine a light on the reluctance of the security forces to respond to her questions about her father's murder.

In 2020, for example, her lawyers asked the Police Service of Northern Ireland (PSNI) to confirm if an OOB order was in place at the time of her father's murder. The response was that they could not disclose any information without a public order. It was a predictable response, which led her lawyer and his team to demand a judicial review on the basis that the PSNI was being unreasonable and acting unlawfully. This was a legal challenge that would set a precedent, but a PSNI legal representative described it as speculative, claiming that it was a fishing expedition by the law firm. Events have shown, both during the Troubles and especially after they ended, that getting answers to even basic queries from the State is like trying to extract blood from a stone. For example, I was denied information I requested about the weapons used to kill an IRA commander who was also an MI5 agent. My request was made almost thirty years after his death. Winters dismissed the fishing-expedition accusation, telling the media that a 'proportionate PSNI response would go a long way to confirming suspicions about collusion, or indeed helping to dispel them altogether'.

While this book is not about the legal cases brought by relatives of many of the victims of the Troubles, it is notable that many young women who lost their fathers, brothers or husbands to violence have demanded answers. As grown-ups, they have been persistent in their quest for truth, which has not been forthcoming from the security forces or the State. Given the official roadblocks they have faced from the British government and some of its institutions, they have had to seek legal advice to help them navigate a complex legal system in pursuit of judicial oversight. Like Paula Fox, many of them believe the answers they seek will alleviate some, if not all, of the pain they have lived with, as well as bringing closure for their loved ones.

Westminster wants to wrap up the mysteries of the past and put them in a dark cupboard alongside classified files on crimes committed by the State or agents of the State. There is a genuine fear in the corridors of power in London that if the Troubles issue is not settled by ending legal and other inquiries about unsolved murders, at some stage the dam will break and demands for accountability will increase exponentially. On the other hand, conflict resolution is not achieved with smart words or clever legislation. Truth is the only acceptable antidote. It requires opening secret files and compensating living victims for injustices; spending whatever public funds are necessary to see the process through.

On 17 May 2022 Kevin Winters upped the ante again, issuing

a writ of summons on behalf of plaintiff Leonard Fox Jr, who was witness to his father's murder in the High Court of Northern Ireland, Queen's Bench Division, seeking aggravated and exemplary damages. The defendants were named as the Ministry of Defence, the chief constable of Northern Ireland and the secretary of state for Northern Ireland. While noting that Leonard Jr was present at the scene of his father's murder, the writ alleged that: 'The persons who carried out the shooting were the Defendant(s), their servants, employees, and/or agents. The deceased suffered damage, loss, personal injuries, and death because of personal negligence, malfeasance in public office and trespass to the persons (assault and battery) of the Defendant(s), their servants, employees, and/or agents.'

The thrust of the reason for claiming damages was stated as the 'tortious conduct of the Defendants, its servants and /or agents'. The writ further pointed out that damages were being claimed pursuant to the 1998 Human Rights Act on the basis that the chief constable of Northern Ireland failed to carry out an adequate, effective, independent and prompt investigation in keeping with the requirement of Article 2 of the ECHR – European Court of Human Rights.

The writ hit all the issues surrounding the murder, especially the unanswered questions. It was an example of how women like Paula Fox will fight until justice prevails.

5

BRIDE OF 'TOP GUN'

TRACEY COULTER WAS SIXTEEN IN 1994 when she first locked eyes with Stevie 'Top Gun' McKeag, a well-built young man with an air of self-confidence and a big smile. He was eight years older than her and had a reputation as a notorious gunman; he would later be credited with the murders of at least twelve and possibly up to twenty Catholics, some of whom had republican family connections but many of whom did not.

McKeag had seen Tracey outside the UDA's new C Company HQ on the Shankill Road, waiting for her dad, Jackie Coulter, a tall, bespectacled UDA brigadier. Like the famous flautist James Galway, who was once a youth member of a flute band in Tiger Bay in north Belfast, Jackie learned to play the flute in a Protestant flute band. Jackie liked to remind people that Galway, who went on to become the lead flautist with the Berlin Philharmonic under the equally famous conductor Herbert von Karajan, was a Belfast lad like himself from a loyalist background. Jackie would often try to emulate Galway's rendition of John Denver's 'Annie's Song' because his favourite aunt was called Annie.

Jackie, born in 1954, was renowned in band circles for establishing the 'Bucky' McCullough flute band to honour his friend and UDA commander 'Bucky', who was murdered by the INLA. McCullough was set up to be killed by UDA leader James 'Pratt' Craig, who secretly did business with the IRA and INLA. Craig targeted McCullough for threatening to expose him for stealing funds intended for weapons purchases and the welfare of UDA prisoners.

Tracey Coulter, born in 1978, was the eldest of Jackie's three daughters and he was very protective of her, though he realised she was a free spirit. At her birth he had lifted her into the air to signify his joy, she was told. According to Tracey, she often 'acted out', making life difficult for her parents. She was not easily dissuaded from doing what she wanted to do and felt free to make her own choices. Nevertheless, she remained very close to her father.

Her parents and her teachers recognised her keen intelligence and her creative instincts. She had shown early promise as an actress-singer and was selected for a drama workshop at Belfast City Arts Theatre. Her father wanted more for her but at sixteen she left school to work in a care home. It was not lost on Jackie that Top Gun was attracted to his daughter and he did not approve. The gunman's fascination with Tracey was obvious in the way he could not take his eyes off her.

Jackie knew all about Top Gun's violent history. The younger man was one of a new breed of UDA C Company members, many of them in their mid-twenties. C Company was run by Johnny 'Mad Dog' Adair, who had once been a skinhead. Some in his ranks were neo-Nazis in their youth. This new breed became the spearhead of UDA violence emanating from west Belfast after the IRA assassinated UDA leader John McMichael and after James Pratt Craig's death at the hands of his own men. The deaths of those senior figures opened a void in the UDA's west Belfast leadership, making room for younger men with a much more gung-ho approach. Their goal was to take the fight to the Catholic community. Some of them were ideal tools for British intelligence, while others were already long-term Special Branch assets.

Tracey was an intelligent teenager but, as she now admits, she grew up in a closed society in a tribal war. Her family lived at the intersection between Catholics and Protestants in west Belfast – some called it the dividing line or 'the Peace Line'. In places, it was marked by a huge wall topped with barbed wire. In Tracey's neighbourhood there was a yellow road sign reading 'Closed' to indicate where the Protestant Shankill became the Catholic Falls area. In her recollection, every day introduced an element of conflict, especially when darkness fell. Catholic and Protestants would toss bricks and petrol bombs at each other over the wall. Her grandmother, whom she remembers was an inoffensive lady, would store empty milk bottles to be used to make petrol bombs.

One day, the unexpected happened. This is how Tracey recalls it: 'Us kids were at home finishing dinner and getting ready for bed when my brother ran down the stairs screaming that a man was in the bathroom. My daddy ran up the stairs and all we could hear was this banging and knocking. The next thing my daddy kicked a man down the stairs. The man grabbed me, probably thinking this would stop the beating. My dad pulled him away from me and asked him who the hell sent him to our house. It turned out the guy was drunk. He was a Catholic who got lost and climbed in through our bathroom window. Daddy felt sorry for him. He could have had him assassinated, but instead he walked him through our area to the Springfield Road where he lived. This was my daddy. He was a very kind man. He taught kids to play flute and basically parented them and kept them out of organisations because, God love him, he did not want that life for them or for my older brother.'

Tracey considered the incident 'really scary'. To understand how she viewed the world at that age, one must realise that she was living in a part of the city where a siege mentality had infected daily life. Catholics were on the other side of the wall from her home and they may as well have been aliens. She knew little about them because Northern Ireland had segregated education. She was ostensibly living in a Protestant ghetto and had no concept of what 'the other side looked like'. She imagined Catholics having the best houses and being well-dressed and better educated. She based these assumptions on what her twenty-four-year-old father told her.

'As a child, I remember thinking of Catholics dressed in ancient, Roman-style clothes. When there was a riot, which seemed to be every night, kids would stay in bed but the neighbourhood would be outside as a whole. I did not know that Catholics were normal human beings like ourselves. My daddy was a commander in a unit of C Company but for several years he had started doing welfare work within the UDA, driving families to visit prisoners in jail. He was strict with us girls and sent us to Sunday School at the Shankill Baptist Church. He was a very smart man, very intelligent. He would always say, "While the Prods are drinking, the Catholics are thinking. Their kids are more educated than we ever were." So, I did drama at Cairnmartin Secondary School and I was picked for the lead role in the musical *Grease*.

'My daddy was so proud of me and I was chosen to study drama at the Arts Theatre in Belfast. My mummy and daddy paid for it and it was a lot of money for them back then. I was the only Protestant in the theatre group. My school was so proud that I had been accepted into it that they paid back the money to my mummy and daddy.'

Tracey first interacted with Catholics when she and her brother were chosen to be part of an Irish-American Children's Fund project which sent Catholic and Protestant kids to live for six weeks with American families. Tracey enjoyed the experience and says that she 'fancied' a Catholic boy she met, but the reality was that they returned to their respective closed worlds; she to the Shankill and he to the Falls.

The event which would change her life and set it on a path she could never have imagined was meeting Stevie 'Top Gun' McKeag, but before that, a year earlier, a horrific episode had a major impact on her life; she still recalls it as traumatic to this day. On Saturday, 23 October 1993, Tracey's father left home to go to the old UDA HQ in rooms above Frizzell's fish shop on the Shankill Road for a weekly strategy meeting with C Company hardmen like Adair and McKeag. Even knowing the purpose of the rooms, the security forces never bugged them. The reason, explained to me by an RUC detective, was that there was no need to bug them because Special Branch had informers within the UDA leadership, especially in C Company. Anyway, British intelligence was supplying C Company, as they had once done for prominent loyalists like John McMichael and Billy Wright's Loyalist Volunteer Force (LVF), with intelligence on republicans the British wanted to eliminate.

The IRA learned from a source in the Shankill area about the purpose of the upstairs rooms and decided to blow up the building and kill the entire C Company leadership. The republicans had already failed three times to kill Adair, who had a habit of boasting about killing Catholics, and on this day, they expected him to be holding his weekly meeting. However, Adair was visiting a loyalist prisoner in the H-Blocks and the Saturday meeting ended earlier than normal. In fact, the upper rooms were empty by lunchtime as a three-man IRA bombing unit, in a Ford Escort car, drove out of the Catholic Ardoyne and down the Crumlin Road to the Shankill Road, where they parked in Berlin Street, close to Frizzell's. The car's driver was tasked with remaining with the car while his companions, Thomas Begley (23) and Sean Kelly (21), left with a powerful Semtex bomb. Begley was carrying the device with orders to leave it in the fish shop. It had a fuse set to let him and Kelly make good their escape before it exploded. The IRA bomb-maker constructed the bomb so that the blast would go upwards, destroying the building but not those on either side. This is exactly what happened, but the bomb exploded prematurely. The result was, as Lord Chief Justice Gibson later said, 'wanton slaughter'. Begley was killed, together with ten innocents, among them women and children. Another fifty were injured. Kelly, the second bomber, was dragged from the rubble and survived. The IRA getaway driver made it back to the Ardoyne.

When Tracey heard about the bombing, she expected the worst. Accompanied by her mother, they went in search of her father, fearing that he was among the dead. For over an hour, they stood near the bombed-out building, sure that he was buried in the rubble. To their amazement and joy, they later found him among the crowds of shocked onlookers on the Shankill Road. Like other members of C Company, he had left the building before the bomb was placed in the fish shop. The horror of the atrocity and the fact that she could have lost her father had a lasting impact on Tracey. In some ways, I suspect that the terrible event led to her and many others in the Shankill to believe that they needed the protection of the hardmen in C Company.

I have two sources who are convinced that Adair was tipped off by British intelligence to be nowhere near the fish shop on the day of the blast. His absence ensured that the meeting he normally chaired ended early and none of the members of his company, which was an effective British intelligence tool, was there when the bomb exploded. My sources point out that it would not have been unusual for British intelligence to have had prior warnings of IRA bomb attacks. In this instance, they might not have been able to prevent the bombing without exposing one of their IRA sources in the Ardoyne, where the bomb was assembled. There are many examples throughout the conflict of bombings that were permitted to take place to protect an important informer in the IRA or loyalist paramilitary ranks. C Company was a very important cog in a dirty war of state-sponsored killings. As such, my sources conclude that Adair and McKeag were people who needed to be protected; they also admit that had the bomb not exploded prematurely, fewer people, if any, would have died. However, I do not subscribe to this theory because it lacks substance due to an absence of meaningful source materials.

After Tracey left school at sixteen, she spent her spare time with Top Gun. She remained living at home until she was eighteen, at which time she moved in with him, much to the disapproval of her parents. A year later she gave birth to their daughter, Stephanie. Tracey quickly discovered that the love of her life was a man with major emotional issues, some of which she would later attribute to post-traumatic stress disorder (PTSD). He was the type of gunman who enjoyed the experience of killing Philomena Hanna, a Catholic mother who worked behind the counter in a chemist shop. He revelled in his moniker Top Gun and in the adulation he received from fellow UDA paramilitaries. Stories surfaced that he was given an annual Top Gun award at C Company functions, but Tracey denies this.

Her view of McKeag and Adair is that most people did not see their humanity. 'I know people see Johnny Adair and his people in a certain way,' she argued, 'but they were only human beings. Now me, with Stevie being a military commander, he was my first love – proper love. My daddy didn't like this and Stevie came up and spoke to him and asked could he pursue me and my daddy told him no. He wasn't happy with him, but I thought, *I love him*. I was so in love with him.'

According to Tracey, she felt strongly that she was an adult free to make her own choices, but it is hard not to feel that she was a teenager in an adult world she did not fully understand. There is nothing to suggest that she ever had any desire to engage in violence. Nevertheless, she knew that Top Gun did not get his moniker for singing in a choir and she did not disapprove of his military role, which she must have known involved killing. This seemingly confused aspect of her personality can be explained. Her father was a UDA brigadier, whom she insisted had left the military aspect of the UDA in his past in favour of doing charity work for the organisation. There is no credible evidence that he was a gunman and his desire to keep his son out of the organisation spoke to his belief that it was not an ideal organisation in which his kids should have a role. Nevertheless, he was a committed member of a paramilitary army with a violent history and attended C Company strategy meetings. Tracey, like many loyalists, viewed the UDA as a necessary weapon to defend her community against the IRA, in the same way many nationalists and republicans considered the Provisional IRA their defenders against the British Army, RUC and loyalist paramilitaries. Tracey, and many of her contemporaries, were certain the UDA was the bulwark against 'the other side'.

One of the failings in some analysis of the Troubles is a reluctance by observers to understand that views about paramilitary violence in both communities were not dissimilar. Republicanism had its own versions of Top Gun and Mad Dog throughout its history. There was one distinction between loyalist paramilitary groups and the IRA, however, and it was the absence in loyalism of a female 'army' like the IRA's Cumann na mBan. There was no parallel group in loyalist ranks. Tracey believes this derived from the fact that the IRA had a longer history of conflict. She also offers the theory that UDA leaders before Adair took over C Company in 1990 were not 'as smart and intelligent as him' and did not understand the need for a women's militia.

According to Tracey, in the Adair C Company era, women 'washed things, moved things and picked up men after operations'. These were some of the chores undertaken by the women's IRA ranks too, but in loyalism women had fewer roles. The mother of the Shankill Butcher's leader, Lenny Murphy, used to visit a local launderette on the Shankill to wash her son's bloody clothes after he tortured and slit his victims' throats.

Tracey considered the IRA smarter, in part because her father seemed to think so. 'When I think about this,' she told me, 'I go back to what my dad told me: that Protestants exploit their own people. They extort their workers. They take money from them. Catholics don't do that. Catholics get the better houses. When you start thinking outside the box, why extort people when they are building houses and they need the money? When it came to women, I had to learn very fast that Stevie was a military commander. I thought, *Wow, what's goin' on?* I wouldn't have known anything he played roles in, but I was not so stupid as not to know there were roles being played. When I eventually lived with him, our home was raided a lot and it was very stressful. We didn't have cameras back then, but we had an iron door behind the bedroom door. I was so gullible. I asked my daddy what was going on. He was worried that the IRA would come and shoot Stevie and I'm living there with him. I said, "Daddy, I always spread my hair over the pillow at night so if the IRA comes to shoot Stevie, God forgive me, I thought if the IRA sees my hair, they'll know it's me and not Stevie." My daddy looked at me, shook his head and said, "Did you just fucking say that, Tracey?" In hindsight, it was a stupid thing to say.'

Over the years, Tracey has never hidden her admiration for Adair who, like his underling McKeag, was a charismatic figure. He had a shaved head and was built like a small weightlifter. He liked to be photographed with his German shepherd, Rebel, and loved media attention. His C Company was responsible for at least forty murders. Top Gun adored and admired Mad Dog and was the most efficient of C Company's killers. The UDA rank and file knew it and people feared both men, while Top Gun feared no one. 'He had a swagger about him' is how a UDA figure described him to me. Even the UVF, which regarded itself as the real loyalist military force in west Belfast, gave him a wide berth. UVF leader Gusty Spence once told me, 'McKeag's a loose cannon, best avoided. He's a Polo mint short of nuts.'

Tracey admits that when she got involved with Top Gun she was 'naive' but was still 'the opposite of everything that went on', suggesting that she did not fully support C Company's killing campaign. While her relationship with one of C Company's most successful gunmen drew her deeper into that world, it was not enough for her to become an active part of it.

Jackie Coulter, Tracey's father, considered Mad Dog a good leader but disliked and had less respect for his daughter's lover. He would say to Tracey about Adair, 'This wee man's gonna be a good 'un.' This suggests that he approved C Company's killing sprees, as well as its criminal pursuits. In contrast, Coulter knew that the man sharing a bed with his daughter was violent and unpredictable. Others knew this too but were wary of confronting a hitman who had no qualms about killing anyone who crossed him. When he discovered that Top Gun was abusing his daughter, Coulter faced a dilemma.

Until I interviewed Tracey in 2024, she had not spoken publicly about her personal life with McKeag, who had been previously married with two children, as well as having a third child with another woman. In C Company circles, he was considered a womaniser. 'I never wanted to talk about our life together because I loved him,' she confessed. 'I did not want to trash his memory, but the truth must be told. I was nineteen when I got pregnant with my Stephanie. If I'm to be honest, I broke my wee mummy and daddy's hearts. Stevie really beat me bad and cheated on me as well. Things started to get bad, dangerous and scary. My daddy and Stevie's mutual friends were put in a bad position because they knew he was beating me bad.'

Throughout their time together, Top Gun was unpredictable. He drank a lot and was under a lot of emotional stress. His life as a prolific hitman was upended in June 1998 when, an hour after buying a motorcycle, he crashed it on the Shankill Road. He spent weeks in intensive care with a broken pelvis and other serious injuries. He was not released from hospital until three months later. By then, he was dependent on painkillers. Tracey nursed him back to health but his doctor warned him if he did not stop abusing painkillers, he would give him two years to live before he died of a cardiac arrest.

Once out of his wheelchair, Top Gun's violent behaviour towards Tracey resumed, as did his womanising. Worse still, he became addicted to cocaine, which he bought from UDA associates in east Belfast who were big in the drugs trade. The consequences of the cocktail of painkillers, cocaine and what Tracey deemed bouts of PTSD were so stressful that eventually she sought an exclusion order against him. 'He was still beating me badly,' admitted Tracey. 'I'm talkin' fractured cheek bones. My daddy's heart was broke. My daddy went to see Johnny Adair and it was then I got the exclusion order against Stevie. I had moved to a flat beside my parents. The police were no help. They said things to Stevie like, "I'll bet you never thought anyone would do that on you." This kind of stuff from the police made matters so much worse for me.'

The exclusion order was a move, she admits, not recommended in a loyalist area where people did not seek remedies from the law. For some, it was akin to 'snitching', but Tracey reckoned she had Stephanie to care for and had no desire to put her child at risk.

'Top Gun was very angry by what he regarded as a challenge to his authority,' she explained. He did not blame Tracey. Instead, he reserved his vitriol, anger and threats for her father. 'Jackie Coulter is mine,' he told Adair, in effect declaring his right to kill Tracey's father. Adair told him that was out of the question.

'My daddy was crying when he went to appeal to Johnny and he said to him, "I'm done. I can't even protect my daughter." The rest of the leadership knew that Stevie was still coming to my flat to beat me but they were putting it down to domestic abuse because they beat their wives too. I was so young and I was gonna be beaten to death because he beat me so badly. I was still going back to him and I now know it was due to fear. Johnny begged my daddy, "Please leave this with me."'

Mad Dog had spent a short time in jail and had just been released when Jackie Coulter went to plead with him. He explained to Coulter that his complaints about Tracey were minor compared to some of the stories coming to him about how Top Gun had been misbehaving while he was behind bars and McKeag was running C Company. The UVF in west Belfast had complained that Top Gun was threatening some of its men, something they would not tolerate. There were also accusations that Top Gun was misusing C Company funds to buy cocaine. Mad Dog promised an investigation into Top Gun's excesses and, according to Tracey, stood down his favourite killer, although the suspension proved temporary. Meanwhile, Top Gun could not hide his hatred for Coulter. At a subsequent C Company meeting, he pointed to Jackie and said again, 'That man belongs to me.'

Adair replied, 'I can't believe you are saying this.'

Jackie Coulter was scared. On the one hand, he had been supportive of Mad Dog's leadership and felt that he deserved his respect. On the other hand, he understood that Mad Dog needed Top Gun's murderous skills. As a result, Top Gun presented an unchallengeable threat to the whole Coulter clan. All Mad Dog was prepared to do was to stand down Top Gun to give him time to kick his drugs habit. This was not the solution Jackie Coulter had hoped for. At the very least he had wanted Top Gun stood down with a stipulation that if he harmed Jackie or Tracey there would be serious consequences. Hours after hearing Top Gun's latest remarks, Jackie phoned his daughter, advising her to take her baby to his house.

'My daddy came home after a few wee pints,' recalls Tracey, 'and he looked so disheartened. He said that Stevie was being stood down for three months to get off the drugs. He also said that Stevie was good a soldier and a good man but as a partner, he was not. I understood then how dedicated and loyal a person my daddy was. That is when I started giving a lot more respect to Johnny Adair as a person because, as hard as that was for him, because he loved Stevie and Stevie loved him back, he made the right decision to stand him down for three months.'

Tracey's father's admiration for Top Gun's murderous activities demonstrated that he agreed with C Company's killing of innocent people. It begs the question of whether Coulter's role in running a unit of Mad Dog's C Company was confined solely to charitable work. Tracey, however, insists that her dad was not part of the violence committed by his fellow UDA members. Nevertheless, she proudly professes that Mad Dog treated her father with respect. He remembered her father as the old guard when he was rising through the ranks. She was impressed that Mad Dog had seemingly sorted out this matter, protecting her father and her in the process.

'I could say that Johnny saved my life,' she pointed out to me.

Adair ran a murder campaign that claimed the lives of innocent Catholics and some known republicans. C Company was responsible for the murder of the Catholic solicitor Pat Finucane. When loyalist hitman Billy Wright, a friend of 'Mag Dog's', was shot dead inside the Maze Prison, Top Gun was dispatched by Adair to kill Catholics to avenge his death.

Tracey's life with Top Gun ended in January 2000 when they permanently split up. He was thirty years old; she was twenty-two. He had never been charged with any of the many murders he committed.

That was the year which Tracey would later admit defined her future. C Company and the UVF at this time were feuding over Mad Dog and Top Gun's stomping ground in the Lower Shankill. Tracey's memory will always be fixed on Saturday 21 August. She recalls the events of that day as though it were yesterday.

'My daddy and Bobby Mahood were good friends. Bobby owned a pub, which was like my daddy's second home. Bobby was old-school

UVF. That morning, my wee daddy left the house about a quarter past twelve to go to the garage to get some cigarettes. Then he took himself to the bookies because he would have backed two flies going up the wall! He liked his horses. I have a picture of him and Bobby at the races in Ayr the year before. Both he and my daddy were like brothers. When my daddy was coming out of the bookies, he saw Bobby coming out of the bank. So they got into Bobby's jeep. A gunman came and opened up on them. The first shot killed my wee daddy immediately, which I was glad for, because the bastard shot him another five times.' The gunman then shot Bobby Mahood, who died later in hospital. The killer's target was Jackie Coulter. Mahood was later understood to have been in the wrong place at the wrong time and paid the ultimate price for befriending Coulter.

Tracey still has her father's jacket with the six bullet holes in it and a docket from the bookmakers he visited with his thumbprint in blood on it. She remembers how she begged her father on the day of his death to let her go with him when he left home, but he refused. He had met Mahood by chance, because the latter always went to the bank on Mondays to deposit the weekend profits from his pub. Tracey reckons that she could well have been with them when they were killed. Her father's murder was part of the ongoing feud between C Company and the UVF; Jackie Coulter was an easy target because he did not take special security precautions. He dismissed Tracey's suggestion that he was 'being watched' by the UVF. He may have felt that his reputation of handling UDA welfare issues and his good relations with the UVF gave him immunity. However, his closeness to Adair and McKeag put him on a UVF hit list.

Tracey's warning was not a fanciful suspicion. She had noted the registration of a car behaving suspiciously near her home. After her father's death, she passed the registration number to police and the car in question was found burned out. It was believed to have been the car used by her father's killers but no one was charged with the double murder and like other women in this book, Tracey has spent the years since the tragedy seeking answers and justice for her father.

Several weeks after her father was murdered, Stevie 'Top Gun' McKeag's relatives found him dead in his home. When Tracey heard the news, she ran to the house they once shared and saw his body, in a navy body bag, being wheeled into the street on a trolley. His funeral, like that of Tracey's father, was a well-attended event. Both men have since been honoured with wall murals to their memory in the Shankill area. A mural with an image of Top Gun dominating it confirms that the cult of the gunman remains a feature of life in Protestant as well as Catholic communities.

After Top Gun's death, lurid stories surfaced, claiming that he was murdered by Adair. The stories were upsetting for Tracey, who was featured in many of them, with claims that she had been Mad Dog's lover. 'Nasty lies and rumours were circulated,' she says angrily. 'They were published online, in newspapers and books, saying that I was a kind of Barbie doll between Johnny and Stevie, and Johnny had him killed out of jealousy. People can lie like this but the coroner does not lie. It is just that simple. Stevie died of an overdose of cocaine and opioids and was the first person in Northern Ireland to die from this drug combination. He was not murdered.'

On this issue, she is correct. There was no evidence that Top Gun's death was suspicious. An inquest confirmed the coroner's finding of death from a drugs overdose. The claims of an affair between Mad Dog and Tracey provided juicy tabloid fodder, as did some of the wild stories about the manner of Top Gun's death, with another story being that he had been forcibly fed a drugs cocktail to kill him.

Imagining that the deaths of her father and Top Gun brought peace and stability to Tracey's life would be a mistake. She was so upset and angry about her father's murder that she began campaigning for answers, pointing an accusing finger at the UVF for killing him. She threatened to name at least one of his killers, placing her own life in jeopardy. Like so many women interviewed for this book, Tracey alleged that the reason why the police never solved her father's murder was because informers within the UVF who were linked to the killing were protected by the State. She named a UVF leader she believes is involved in the double murder of her father and Mahood but, for legal reasons, I cannot publish this individual's name. I do, however, know that the person in question was a British intelligence asset.

By 2009 Tracey had remarried and had four children, one a baby, when six members of the UVF, wearing balaclavas and armed with baseball bats and pickaxe handles, forced their way into her home while she and her children were in bed. Stephanie (12) and Sarah (2) woke up first as the intruders, screaming foul insults, trashed the house. This happened days after a newspaper published a report in which Tracey reminded people that she knew the identities of members of the UVF who had murdered her father and was prepared to name them. Her home was later firebombed.

Tracey made it clear publicly that the UVF was not her only target. She was angry and fearless when she demanded that the UDA, of which her father had once been a prominent member, end its role in selling drugs to kids like her daughter Stephanie, whose father had died from an overdose. Tracey admits that her campaigns against two of the most lethal paramilitary groups placed her life at risk. 'I wanted to expose those who were poisoning our kids. I had multiple threats and paint was thrown over me. I also had paint thrown at my front door and windows. My name was sprayed from the top of the Shankill till the bottom, saying I was a police informer,' she confessed, with a mixture of anger and sadness.

Tracey Coulter has paid a considerable price throughout her life, not just with the loss of loved ones and the abuse she suffered when living with Top Gun, but with the threats she received from loyalist organisations like the UDA, which she was brought up to respect. There are few women who would have mustered the courage to confront the paramilitaries in the way she has done, subjecting them to public ridicule. Her focus on the loyalist paramilitary role in the drugs trade was admirable.

In many respects, Tracey was a victim of a society under siege. Her union with Top Gun was questionable, but she was only sixteen when she met him and he was a hero in her community. Today, she seems to be closer to happiness and has a loving family. Nevertheless, she has not given up her fight to bring justice to her father's killers.

6

ADDICTED TO DEATH

MARCH 6, 1988, WAS A warm, sunny Sunday on the Rock of Gibraltar – entrance to the Mediterranean and forged, if the Greek writer Homer is to be believed, when Hercules reached out his powerful hands and separated two mountains. Contrary to popular culture, it is not an island but an isthmus on the tip of the Iberian peninsula. The Greeks believed that the massive cave structure under the Rock led to Hades and the Underworld.

The Treaty of Utrecht in 1713 bequeathed Gibraltar to Britain in perpetuity, something that has never sat well with Spain to this day. Britain and the Rock itself have remained in a steady if rather bizarre partnership. Gibraltar is a major British military installation and many regiments that served in Northern Ireland undertook tours of duty there. While it remains very British and brings pomp and ceremony to events, it is also representative of the people and cultures of the regions surrounding it. A trip by cable car to the top of the Rock provides views of Spain's Costa del Sol and the Atlas Mountains of Morocco.

As thirty-two-year-old Mairéad Farrell made her way on foot through the border crossing from Spain on that sunny Sunday in 1988, she and her companion, thirty-one-year-old blond-haired Daniel McCann, looked like any other young couple crossing the border from Spain for a tasty lunch and a tour of the underground caves. Mairéad, tall and slim, had a slight tan from spending time on the Spanish Mediterranean coast with Daniel and some other Belfast friends. They had arrived in Spain on a flight from Dublin to Malaga before driving to Torremolinos, a busy, popular tourist resort where they did the usual thing of lounging by the hotel pool, drinking rum and Coke.

Walking around the Rock, Daniel and Mairéad were unburdened with the usual tourist paraphernalia. She wore a light jacket, an open-neck blouse, a dark skirt and stockings. A locket hung from a gold chain around her neck and she held a small handbag in her left hand. Daniel had on a pair of white jeans and a white shirt. Mairéad must have gazed out over the views, and it is possible that the Atlas Mountains reminded her of the Mountains of Mourne in County Down, which, as the song says, 'sweep down to the sea'. She was surely attracted by smells of fresh coffee and cooked food coming from the many little restaurants for which the Rock was famous. The British Sunday lunch of roast beef, Yorkshire pudding, potatoes, vegetables and thick brown gravy was traditionally served in British-themed pubs, with a Union Jack proudly displayed behind the bar. Perhaps one of the most popular songs of the week, Whitney Houston's 'Where Do Broken Hearts Go', was blasting from café loudspeakers.

Like Whitney, Mairéad knew all about lost love. Both addicts, they had much in common. Whitney's drug of choice was cocaine; Mairéad's was romantic nationalism. For both though, their addictions contained the seeds of their downfall. Mairéad's gold locket held her past while, like Whitney, her future was no longer in her hands.

When you flirt with death as these young women did, you develop an acute sense of your own mortality. This was particularly true for Mairéad Farrell. She felt that she could, and probably should, have been shot dead years earlier, yet here she was on a gorgeous day, looking like she did not have a care in the world. She might have temporarily dispelled her dark premonition of dying young.

In the pop music business there is the '27 Club', whose members, famous performers such as Jimi Hendrix, Janis Joplin and Kurt Cobain, never made it beyond twenty-seven years of age. Somehow, Mairéad had passed that milestone, yet she was never able to shake off the heavy image of death hanging on her shoulder.

In psychology it is said that a particular event can trigger a dark premonition. Clinical psychologists call it 'crisis telepathy'. I suspect that Mairéad, having escaped death once and given her particular addiction – that she would have called commitment – was convinced her luck would run out sooner or later. But how was it possible for such a highly intelligent young woman like her to be so fatalistic? After all, she was a fierce campaigner for prisoners' rights and equal rights for women. The answer probably lay in her early years.

Born in 1957, Mairéad was a happy little girl who loved Irish music and dancing. Some of her contemporaries on the Falls Road, where she lived with her parents and five older siblings, considered her privileged because her family had a small grocery-hardware store. Decades later journalists would describe her upbringing as middle-class, but in truth she lived in a deprived neighbourhood, sharing the same poverty as others. This was the Northern Ireland of the early 1960s, when Catholics had all but given up hope of seeing a change in their economic and political fortunes.

The IRA's ill-fated border campaign had fizzled out. Some said that it ended the day it began. Irish republicanism, however, was not dead. It was alive and respected in Mairéad's family. Her grandfather, who lived in Leitrim in the Irish Republic, adored his granddaughter and he enjoyed sharing with her daring tales of his role in the War of Independence from 1919 to 1921, when he evaded capture by the Black and Tans. His stories, she later admitted, filtered into her growing attachment to the Irish republican cause. The oral history tradition, especially in Irish republican circles, was always a vital component in keeping the past alive. It was a tradition replete with an attachment to the cult of the gunman, as well as tales of 'martyrs' and heroes who fought and died battling the British to liberate Ireland.

At school, Mairéad studied the Irish language and was a very bright student. She also went on trips to Gaeltacht areas in Ireland where Irish was spoken. One of the defining features of Irish-language learning in Northern Ireland was that it became closely linked to Irish republicanism, a fact that upset many traditional Irish-speakers who were non-political.

By the 1960s Mairéad, like many of her generation, would have been conscious of the deteriorating political situation. A civil rights movement, led by young, educated Catholics like John Hume, Bernadette Devlin, Eamon McCann and Austin Currie, was at the core of large protest rallies, demanding voting rights with the slogan 'One Man, One Vote' and fairness in the allocation of jobs and housing. These demands, considered revolutionary by Northern Irish unionists, merely insisted on basic civil rights for Catholics that were enjoyed by people in other parts of the United Kingdom. Within the ranks of the civil rights movement were IRA men with a deep political intelligence and knowledge of history. Many of them felt that the time had come to replace the gun in Irish politics with a Marxist analysis of how Ireland should be governed.

At the age of twelve Mairéad entered the upmarket Ardmore Convent Grammar School for girls in Belfast, just as a bonfire of tribal bitterness was set alight. It was August 1969 and civil rights marchers were already being beaten and forced off the streets by the RUC and by the Unionist government's favourite paramilitary force, the B Specials, which had a massive armoury. It was staffed by Protestants and was regarded by unionists as the last defence against the rise of Irish nationalism. The B-Men, as they were known in Catholic districts, were generally anti-Catholic. That month, in a bid to quell major unrest and protect the Catholic population, especially in Belfast, the British government decided to bypass this regular security apparatus by sending British soldiers into Belfast and Derry.

As a young reporter I watched British soldiers marching up the Falls Road in west Belfast. I was somewhat amused by the way they remained in step, with bayonets fixed to their rifles. My colleague Jim Campbell recalled Catholic women embracing soldiers and serving them tea and biscuits. It struck him, as it did me, that these 'liberators' looked confused. They had no knowledge of the tribal geography of the city. This was a place unlike Manchester or Burnley. The British Labour government, with its sparse intelligence on Northern Ireland, believed it was doing the right thing, but for decades Westminster had ignored fundamental flaws in the State it had created out of partition. It failed to grasp the dangers of leaving in power a Unionist government, unable to reform itself, with responsibility for security. This was a recipe for disaster. Within a year, elements would be in place for the start of a long war, and young people like Mairéad would be drawn into it.

There were perhaps two events which propelled Mairéad towards the life of an IRA operative. By 1970 the British government was being led by Tory Prime Minister Edward Heath, one of the most arrogant and obnoxious men I have ever met. My view of him is shared by many of the British generals who served under him. In July 1970 he encouraged the British Army to launch a massive search operation in the Falls area. The operation would later become known as the Lower Falls Curfew. By then, the IRA had been split into two bodies: one known as the Official IRA and the other, a new body, the Provisionals, whose leaders included Seamus Twomey, Joe Cahill, a young barman called Gerry Adams and Martin McGuinness. They espoused the romantic nationalism that had defined Irish republicanism until the late 1950s, when many of its leaders who had fought the abortive border campaign left prison steeped in socialist literature. Their time inside reading the works of James Connolly, the socialist revolutionary executed after the 1916 Rising, convinced them that violence was counterproductive. Some of them had even developed a liking for Marxism. These were the men left in charge of the Official IRA when the organisation split into the two factions.

I reported on the Lower Falls Curfew, which began on 3 July 1970 and ended two days later. The Provisionals benefited from it by moving most of their weapons out of the Lower Falls before a British Army assault on the area began, thereby ensuring their guns were not part of the huge haul of weapons seized by the army after the curfew ended. Official IRA leaders later claimed that the Provisionals deliberately instigated a major riot to draw the army into the Lower Falls so that the Officials would be decimated. In truth, the army did not need an excuse to invade the Falls. The operation had all the hallmarks of tactics used in other British colonial 'emergencies'. Overwhelming force was deployed and the area was sealed off as thousands of canisters of CS gas were fired into narrow streets before a curfew was imposed. I managed to escape the area before it went into effect but some journalists were not so fortunate. Scottish soldiers, most from a Protestant tradition, ransacked and looted homes, defiling them and smashing religious objects. Several British generals later admitted that it was an ugly, crude operation.

It appeared that the British Army had by then defined the Catholic population as its enemy in the way most armies need an enemy. Armies are not built for policing strategies, but this fact had been lost on Heath and his Cabinet in 10 Downing Street. The effect was immediate. Young men flocked to the ranks of the Provisionals, who had done a fine job painting the Official IRA as an organisation that had failed to protect the Catholics of Belfast in 1969 when Protestant mobs, watched over by police and B Specials, burned streets of Catholic homes. With its Lower Falls Curfew strategy, the British Army handed the Provisionals a major recruiting tool.

The curfew had a big impact on Mairéad Farrell. The Falls was her area and her people were brutalised but it would take one more major event to drive her into the ranks of the Provisionals. This would be internment without trial, introduced in August 1971. Thousands of Catholics, young and old, as well as trade union leaders and political activists with no Irish republican links, were dragged from their beds in the early morning and taken to detention centres. Some were selected for special interrogation techniques involving white noise and other crude procedures. With this policy, Heath was indicating that he believed there was a military solution to the political problems of Northern Ireland, although he did not have the backing of many of his generals. They detested him and felt that it was wrong to use the army to solve a political crisis. Heath was highly influenced by the advice of two people with extreme views in his Cabinet, namely Sir Dick White, head of intelligence, and Attorney General Quintin Hogg. The latter even suggested to Heath that it was legal for British soldiers to shoot protesters on the streets of Belfast because they were enemies of the Crown. White hid from the British Army's top brass the fact that a section of British intelligence had prepared a barracks in Belfast for the secret interrogation of selected internees.

After internment was introduced, fourteen-year-old Mairéad Farrell took to the streets with other girls, banging bin lids on pavements to warn of British Army incursions into her area. She threw stones and petrol bombs at army personnel carriers and, according to some reports, she was fearless, like many young people I observed at the time. Some of them were so much a part of the rioting that they appeared immune to the army's CS gas. Before long Mairéad transformed from rioter to junior IRA student-in-training. She became part of the junior wing of the Provisionals known as the Fianna and was required to take an oath, which specified the following:

> Commitment to the Republican Movement is the firm belief that its struggle both military and political is morally justified, that war is morally justified and that the Army is the direct representative of the 1918 Dáil Éireann Parliament, and that as such they are the legal and lawful government of the Irish Republic, which has the moral right to pass laws for, and to claim jurisdiction over the territory, air space, mineral resources, means of production, distribution and exchange and all of its people regardless of creed or loyalty.

Mairéad was trained in various techniques for hiding explosives and weapons on her person and how to evade the scrutiny of British Army patrols. She learned how to collect weapons from dumps and deliver them to IRA gunmen. Her trainers insisted on her membership remaining a secret; she could not divulge it, even to her family. She was to avoid at all costs drawing attention to herself. She would have been told to read the opening section of the IRA's *Green Book* of rules, dealing with security: 'Don't talk in public places: you don't tell your family, friends, girlfriends or workmates that you are a member of the I.R.A. Don't express views about military matters, in other words you say nothing …'

Mairéad was a quick learner and within several years she became a trusted operative who could disassemble weapons and reassemble them blindfolded. Gone was the young girl throwing stones at British soldiers. To this day, mystery remains about who recruited her. Rumour has it that it was Bobby Storey, a larger-than-life figure in the history of the Provisional IRA. He was affectionately named 'Big Bobby' by his friends because of his 6ft 4in frame. Those who crossed him did not regard him so affectionately. He was a critical figure in helping Adams and McGuinness win major debates within the IRA when those two leaders decided to negotiate with the British government and support the Good Friday Agreement. While some thought that Storey was just a 'hard head', as one policeman described him, he became a pivotal figure in IRA intelligence, deceptively so. Thousands of IRA members, men and women, dressed in black IRA garb, attended his paramilitary funeral in Belfast in June 2020.

I was intrigued by the fact that Storey, whose family was from the Bone area of Oldpark, was born in 1956, just a year earlier than Mairéad. By his own admission he joined the IRA in 1972, aged sixteen, a year after she was recruited, so he cannot have been her recruiter. Aged seventeen in 1973, he became the youngest internee. I have spoken to sources I trust and none link Storey to Mairéad at any point in her life. What makes this issue so intriguing is that someone started a bogus rumour that when the British government returned Mairéad's possessions to her family after her death, they included a locket on a gold chain purportedly with Storey's hair in it. My sources dismissed this as British disinformation.

I believe that Mairéad was initially recruited by a female member of the women's wing of the IRA, Cumann na mBan. Many commentators over the years have failed to grasp the fact that Cumann na mBan was an influential body at the outset of the Troubles. Its decision in 1970 to embrace the new Provisional IRA was critical to that group's sudden growth, and it was Gerry Adams who was instrumental in persuading its leaders to abandon the Official IRA in favour of the Provisionals. Cumann na mBan had its own leadership structure, but it was still somewhat marginalised within an IRA led by men, mainly because it was not permitted to undertake military operations. Instead, it was relied on to provide couriers and sometimes to conduct surveillance. In some respects, its role mirrored that of women in Catholic Ireland, who were expected to be obedient, childbearing housewives who also did the housework. Mairéad Farrell once remarked that women were not only marginalised within Irish Catholicism but in every sector of life. She was careful not to include Cumann na mBan but, according to her friends, she also meant the Cumann.

The Provisional IRA leadership, from its formation in January 1970, embraced the women's movement because it needed female operatives, many of whom were clever and reliable. The late IRA intelligence chief Brendan Hughes once told me that female IRA members were trustworthy and better at keeping secrets. It was not easy for the British to break them under interrogation or to compromise them. They did many of the important jobs their male counterparts could not, like moving weapons and taking written reports through security checkpoints. What he did not say was that women operatives could be just as committed and ruthless as the men. Mairéad Farrell and the Price sisters were a new breed of IRA females. The Price sisters, particularly Dolours, broke the mould by insisting that girls were just as capable as men of killing soldiers and should be allowed into the ranks of the IRA proper as active shooters and bombers.

Until 1976 Mairéad Farrell worked quietly and effectively in the shadows, but in the life that she led there was always the risk her luck would run out. She was now nineteen years old and by IRA standards was sufficiently experienced to carry out a major operation. Her chance came with the blowing up of the Conway Hotel at Dunmurry on the outskirts of Belfast. It was a location which was often used by British off-duty soldiers. The plan was to plant three bombs in the hotel after subduing security staff. Timers on the bombs would be set by one of her team members in such a manner as to allow the IRA unit to make a safe exit. There was to be no loss of life among hotel staff, many of whom were Catholics.

When it came time for the bombing team to choose their weapons, Mairéad chose a .45 Colt for its stopping power. It was a powerful weapon for a slight girl like her. She could have chosen a compact Vzor .45 Czech pistol, chambered with .25 ammunition, but she was keen to make an impression. Mairéad was teamed with operatives she knew well. One of them was her lover, Sean McDermott; another his friend Kieran Doherty, who would later die on hunger strike in the Maze Prison. Both were lads born in 1955, making them one year older than Mairéad. They were tall and attractive. Doherty was a fine Gaelic footballer and cyclist. The British Army knew him well, having shot him in 1972 when he exchanged gunfire with soldiers. Mairéad had fallen in love with McDermott when they met at an IRA training camp, but they kept their affair a secret from family and friends as required by IRA internal security protocols.

The fact that this trio was so young was testimony to the way their lives were shaped by the conflict. They started off as rioters and progressed to the serious business of terrorism. No one in 10 Downing Street or the upper echelons of the British military in the early 1970s was asking if British policies and strategies were radicalising the young. The Heath government was convinced the answer to the strife in Northern Ireland would be found if the British Army dealt firmly with 'enemies of the British Crown'. This ignored the elephant in the room – namely that a massive, perfectly legal paramilitary body, the Protestant, loyalist UDA, was committing grisly murders in the back alleys of Belfast and in loyalist drinking clubs. In other words, the British had a one-sided view of the conflict.

'Freeze!' is a command one might not readily associate with a young woman, but Mairéad Farrell shouted it as she pointed her .45 Colt at the security staff in the Conway Hotel. It sounded like something she might have heard in a Hollywood movie, delivered by a cop who had caught a criminal about to commit a crime – a media trope, as the police generally say, 'Show me your hands.'

Mairéad knew that the staff were not armed and when they saw her .45, they chose to comply. McDermott and Doherty went off to plant and prime the bombs in other parts of the hotel while she waited calmly in the lobby. She must have cut a strange figure wearing a balaclava, slacks and platform heels. The heels were not IRA-issue but they might have been part of her plan to look like a guest as she walked from the trio's stolen van to the hotel. By the time she got to the entrance, she had donned the balaclava.

She loved those platform shoes. Called 'disco shoes', they were all the rage, funky even, in the 1970s. Mairéad loved everything disco, especially disco dancing. It was easy to imagine her as a tall, slim disco-dancing queen in platform shoes and flared jeans. Was this what attracted Sean McDermott to her? It may well be and on that April day, she might have thought she looked good in a balaclava, with a .45 Colt in her hand, like an Irish version of Bonnie Parker. After all, her friends often remarked that she had an offbeat sense of humour, which could have explained her choice of outfit when she went on her bombing run.

She could not have known when she left home that the operation had already been compromised, since the IRA's Belfast Brigade had British spies in every level of its ranks. McDermott and Doherty had just planted their devices and set the timers when they heard police sirens and knew they had been rumbled. It was dangerous to try to get back to their van so it was a case of 'every man for himself'. McDermott shouted to Mairéad to make a run for it and the three took off into the hotel grounds. Mairéad sprinted away from her companions but quickly found that her shoes prevented her from running fast. Forced to hide in bushes, she was caught within an hour and did not put up a fight.

What happened next would trouble her for the rest of her life. She expected to be shot dead by the policeman who found her hiding place, but he showed no desire to do so once she surrendered peacefully. She would later say that had it been a different time and had the British Army found her, she would have been shot dead. This was the first time she had stared down the barrel of a gun expecting to meet death and it had a profound effect on her psyche. It triggered a growing premonition that she would die young.

McDermott and Doherty managed to escape the hotel grounds before the police caught sight of them. Needing to get back to west Belfast, they went to a house with a car parked outside it. They rang the bell, unaware that the man who opened the door and said hello was a police reservist. He backed into his house when confronted by McDermott pointing a pistol at him. When asked if the car outside was his, the reservist nodded and Doherty demanded the keys. The reservist explained that the keys were upstairs in his bedroom, so McDermott ushered him upstairs with the pistol still trained on him. The reservist pointed to a cupboard drawer beside his bed and McDermott told him to open it and fetch the car keys. The reservist opened the drawer but it was not keys he withdrew from it. It was his powerful RUC-issue Ruger Magnum revolver. He fired one round, which struck McDermott in the chest, although the IRA man managed to return fire, hitting the reservist in the ankle.

McDermott was fatally wounded but still alive. The shooting upstairs had given Doherty time to make his escape, but he was caught a short time later. In the meantime, McDermott succumbed to his wounds as three bombs exploded, devastating the Conway Hotel.

In custody, Mairéad Farrell initially expressed some regret for her actions but then quickly went silent, in keeping with IRA policy. She would not speak again until she appeared before a single judge and declared that she did not recognise the authority of a British court. She had told her solicitor, Paddy McCrory, as much when he first visited her after her arrest. He realised that she was a committed republican when she uttered the traditional republican mantra that British courts had no authority in Ireland and she would not recognise them. As such, she would not be entering any plea to the charges that she expected to face. He was somewhat taken aback by her political determination given her youth.

Before her solicitor's visit, Mairéad had received news that McDermott, the young man she loved, had been shot dead. She broke down emotionally but soon adopted a steely façade. She was facing fourteen years in prison for possessing a gun and explosives and for belonging to the IRA. Stoic was how some described her mood when she arrived in the women's prison in Armagh to serve her sentence. She quickly imposed her personality and authority on her IRA inmates, who respected her knowledge and her command of the Irish language. Despite her youth, she was appointed the IRA's commanding officer of Armagh prison.

***

If Farrell thought she was tough as she settled into prison life, it turned out that she now had a tougher adversary in Downing Street – the new prime minister, Margaret Thatcher. In May 1982 Thatcher would order the sinking of an old Argentinian battleship, the *General Belgrano*, in the South Atlantic, with the loss of 322 lives; arguably, her aim was to prove her ruthlessness to Argentina. The battleship posed no serious threat to the British fleet in the South Atlantic during the Falklands War. In 1979, when her close friend, Airey Neave, the Shadow Secretary of State for Northern Ireland, was blown up in his car while driving into the Palace of Westminster, Thatcher demanded that those responsible be brought to justice. The killers were identified as members of the

INLA, a breakaway group from the Official IRA. They had used a clever device called a mercury-tilt-switch bomb, which they placed under his car. It was the first time that such a bomb had been used in the British Isles and it indicated that the INLA had a scary level of sophistication. Within a year of Neave's death, Ronnie Bunting Jr, one of the group's leaders who was suspected of having sanctioned the murder, was assassinated in his home in west Belfast, along with a colleague, Noel Lyttle. The double murder, carried out with ruthless efficiency, had the support of British Military Intelligence.

The killing of fifty-one-year-old Miriam Daly, a mother and Queen's University lecturer, in June 1980 was also in revenge for the death of Neave. Daly was a political theoretician within the INLA's Irish Republican Socialist Party (IRSP). She knew Bunting personally and was a fierce defender of the rights of republican prisoners. She was living in the Andersonstown area when killers arrived at her home. She knew she was being watched, as she had a new reinforced front door, but on this fateful day she had left it open briefly. The killers remained with her for hours, probably hoping that her husband would arrive from Dublin so they could kill him too. At some point they decided that he was not coming back in time to suit their schedule, so they shot Miriam six times with a silenced gun. Her nine-year-old daughter returned home from school to find her mother in a pool of blood on the kitchen floor. It was clear that the killers had had enough time to interrogate their victim before shooting her. Although the UDA claimed the murder, this killing required the involvement of an organisation with the ability to carry out surveillance in a predominantly republican area. The only body with this skill and sophistication was British Military Intelligence. This was Thatcher's revenge. She had demanded swift justice for those who murdered Neave and this was her way of sending a message to her enemies.

Mairéad Farrell was in prison when Thatcher launched a policy to criminalise her main enemy, the Provisional IRA, especially within the prison population. After internment in 1971, IRA prisoners were accorded 'special category status', permitting them to wear their own clothes and to run the prisons with all the trappings of a paramilitary army. They drilled, held political education classes and plotted escapes while also helping to shape the war outside the prison walls. Thatcher decided to end this status and treat an IRA prisoner like any other in the UK. She insisted that they must do prison work and wear prison clothes. In this way, they would soon be perceived as ordinary criminals and not freedom fighters or revolutionaries.

While this decision would eventually lead to the hunger strike in the men's Maze Prison that claimed ten lives, it was preceded by what was called the 'dirty protest'. This involved Maze prisoners refusing to slop out their cells and wearing blankets instead of prison clothes. It soon took on a more extreme form when prisoners smeared excrement on cell walls and urinated on the floors.

As the officer in command of IRA women in Armagh Prison, Farrell objected to strip-searches and denial of toilet facilities as a form of prison punishment. She also objected to regular beatings of IRA female inmates and encouraged them to refuse to work or slop out the cells. This gave the male prison staff the incentive to administer more severe beatings. Women were locked in cells with no toilet facilities and the spy holes in doors were taped over. In response, Mairéad launched a dirty protest. Realising that this required tough mental determination, she encouraged those she chose to join her with the following words: 'They cannot defeat us because they do not own our minds. Our minds are our most powerful weapon.'

The stench in the women's cells was indescribable and many women became ill. It is hard to imagine what kind of mental toughness was required for these women to do what they did. They were told to urinate on the floors of their cells and to smear the walls with excrement and menstrual fluids. Some women had maggots on their bodies and their teeth rotted.

After the end of the dirty protest, Mairéad launched a hunger strike with two other women to show solidarity for the hunger strike in the Maze, which began when prisoner Bobby Sands refused food. However, the media and the Provo leaders did not pay much attention to Farrell's hunger strike, which almost cost her her life. Fortunately, the Armagh Prison hunger strike ended a day after the one in the Maze was called off following the deaths of ten men.

When Mairéad Farrell walked out of Armagh Prison in October 1986, she was twenty-nine years old. It was a new world outside. Gone was the era of platform heels and flared jeans. Ray-Ban sunglasses, denim, stone-washed jackets, cropped tank tops and leather jackets with shoulder pads were in fashion. In the October *Vogue*, a letter from Paris appeared stating that the 1968 generation 'tries to reconcile lurid cocktails, faded jeans, Molière, Marx, and the end of ideology'.

Mairéad was determined to change her life and compensate for the time lost in prison. She enrolled in political science and economics courses at Queen's University. She bought some new clothes and went dancing. In Belfast discos, people were dancing to the Communards' 'Don't Leave Me This Way' or to 'We Don't Have to Take Our Clothes Off' sung by Jermaine Stewart. Her close friends were excited about her enjoying life again. Their collective view was that 'she had done her bit for the republican cause and it was time to do something for herself'.

Her commitment to change, however, proved to be short-lived once she began spending time in Provisional Sinn Féin headquarters on the Falls Road, giving interviews about her time in prison. It was common for IRA activists to transfer to Sinn Féin after leaving prison as, being so well known to British intelligence agencies, they were of little use in active IRA operations. But within a short time, Mairéad was drawn back into the IRA; she had remained a member, even though, with her prison stint, and especially her hunger strike, she would have been free to walk away and lead a normal life or work exclusively for Sinn Féin. Someone persuaded her to return to active service and whoever he was, he had no concern for her well-being. She was a prominent IRA figure with her photo in files held by every British security agency. She would be instantly recognised passing through security checkpoints at airports or borders.

***

On that March Sunday in 1988, as she strolled through Gibraltar with Daniel McCann, it was less than two years since her hunger strike. Was it on her mind that her last major operation had been compromised, costing the life of her lover and almost ending hers? The new Gibraltar operation had been approved by the IRA's Belfast Brigade after it consulted the Army Council in Dublin. Martin McGuinness must have known about it, as would the Belfast Brigade's intelligence chief, Bobby Storey. There was also scope for British assets within the senior ranks of the IRA in Belfast to learn about it. Sending well-known operatives like Mairéad to Spain on flights out of Dublin was sure to alert security agencies that the IRA was planning something big.

The Gibraltar operation remains puzzling because of its obvious flaws, primarily the use of prominent IRA operatives. Mairéad's two companions on that day in Gibraltar – McCann and Sean Savage – were experienced gunmen, with Savage also being a trusted bomb-maker. He knew how to wire Semtex, set timers and detonate bombs by remote control. He knew all about mercury-tilt-switch bombs and had used one a month earlier to blow up UDA Brigadier John McMichael in the driveway of his home. The late IRA intelligence chief Brendan Hughes once explained to me that it was unwise to use known IRA members for special jobs. British intelligence agencies would regularly issue alerts when prominent IRA people did not appear on their radar for days or weeks. An alert would then be relayed to multiple intelligence outlets to be on the lookout for them because they might be planning something big. Was such an alert issued in January or February 1988 for the trio now in Gibraltar and their two associates still in Torremolinos? We may never know, but one thing is certain: MI5 found out about this planned operation and the way it was supposed to unfold. It was compromised in Belfast in autumn 1987.

The 6 March visit to the Rock by Farrell and McCann was a dummy run to see if Savage could park a car he had driven over the border that day from Spain in one of several public spaces at the side of the governor's residence. The car did not contain explosives. They were hidden in a separate car Farrell had parked in an underground garage back in Torremolinos. It would be driven to the Rock if Mairéad and her companions, after their reconnaissance trip, could demonstrate that they could drive a car into Gibraltar and park it without drawing scrutiny. The target of the attack was to be the Military Guard and members of the band of the 1st Battalion, Royal Anglian Regiment. They performed every Sunday, watched by local families and tourists, in front of the governor's residence. There were some public parking spaces nearby, between two high stone walls, so the potential for mass casualties was obvious. If a powerful Semtex bomb exploded, not only would it create an intense, massive blast due to the compressed space, but it would spread shrapnel in all directions.

Mairéad believed that the operation was justified, even though it was sure to result in mass casualties, including the slaughter of women and children. Her ideology dominated her consciousness and humanity, despite a year earlier telling friends that she disagreed with the IRA bombing of a Remembrance Day ceremony in Enniskillen, which killed twelve and injured sixty-three. What changed her outlook or had anything changed? Had the prison experience left her psychologically damaged over time? Had it made her tougher and cynical or was this the old Mairéad Farrell, totally committed to a cause in which 'collateral' damage was acceptable? Was she on a vengeance trip for the death of her lover?

Margaret Thatcher knew that Mairéad and her two companions were in Gibraltar. She had been briefed for weeks as British and Spanish intelligence agencies tracked Farrell and her companions from the time they arrived on the Costa del Sol. Spanish intelligence filmed Mairéad parking the rental car – the one with the Semtex in it – in an underground garage in Torremolinos. They had eyes on this vehicle in case someone moved it, but it never left the garage and neither did the explosives. This confirms the theory that British intelligence knew that the car driven into Gibraltar by Sean Savage had no bomb on board.

For decades, the British authorities have told so many lies about the Gibraltar operation that it is difficult to unravel the truth, but the bottom line is that they knew from their own sources in Belfast how the operation would unfold and that there was no bomb on the Rock that day. In other words, they allowed Farrell, McCann (who had been an officer commanding the Belfast Brigade during his IRA career) and Savage onto the Rock because they had something special in store for them.

Early on that March morning, Thatcher was going through her customary routine in 10 Downing Street, laying out the Sunday newspapers on her desk. She liked browsing the tabloids first, especially *The Sun*, which was read by her most loyal followers. Its front-page headline was 'Easter Coach Outcry'. Apparently, clubs, coach companies and pubs were concerned about some new Department of Transport regulations limiting coach travel. *The Observer* had a big feature on the death of Fleet Street. The author of the article told a wonderful story about media magnate Rupert Murdoch, who entered a room in his *Sun* newspaper premises to find its executives drinking from large brandy glasses. An indignant Murdoch later remarked that they were drinking his Scotch from 'goldfish bowls'. Thatcher's husband, who loved a tipple, would have enjoyed the story. Her eyes may also have settled on a *Times* article warning that inflation had risen to 18.4 per cent; a revelation that threatened her premiership.

Later that morning, military and intelligence figures arrived at No. 10 to brief Thatcher in an upstairs room known as GEN42. No one knew how it acquired its name, just that it was where secrets about Northern Ireland were discussed. A direct line to Whitehall and a satellite link to Special Air Service (SAS) HQ in Hereford kept everyone aware in real time about events in Gibraltar, with minute-by-minute reports on the surveillance of the IRA trio. The British military operation had been given the name 'Operation Flavius'. Thatcher's 'boys', as she liked to refer to soldiers of the SAS, were in Gibraltar to eliminate targets, not to arrest them. This was to be a repeat of the killings she ordered after Airey Neave's murder.

We do not know what Mairéad Farrell's plan was once Savage proved he could park his car beside the governor's residence and leave it there for several hours without arousing suspicion. Would she have gone back to Torremolinos and returned to the Rock the following Sunday with the other car containing the powerful Semtex explosives or would the two IRA operatives in Torremolinos have been tasked with delivering the bomb to the Rock? But on that Sunday, after Savage parked the rental car and walked away from it, the trio began strolling casually along Winston Churchill Avenue with McCann and Farrell some distance from Savage. Perhaps, they planned to go for lunch or visit the underground caves, but whatever their plan, it did not come to fruition because this was the moment three armed SAS soldiers sprang into action. Farrell spotted two of them leaping over a fence near a petrol station and running towards her and McCann. She instinctively raised her hands in the air and so too did McCann. He even tried to shield her with his body, realising that these armed strangers were professionals and meant business. I wonder whether Mairéad Farrell expected to be arrested as she raised her hands, as had happened outside the Conway Hotel. It was not to be. This time, she was shot three times in the face and neck from three feet or less away. While she was lying on the ground, she was shot a few times in her back. McCann was shot twice in the chest and head and three times in the back as he fell. Both were then shot again at very close range.

Savage saw the shooting and took off running with another SAS soldier in pursuit. He shot Savage in the back, bringing him to the ground, and then shot him eighteen times at close range. It was overkill; a pathologist later wrote that Savage was 'riddled'. The killing of the three was observed by reliable witnesses. While the SAS shooters claimed that the trio looked like they were reaching for weapons, the evidence of the witnesses proved this to be a lie. It was a triple execution.

British papers were quick to offer false narratives provided by British intelligence disinformation specialists, who had already prepared the groundwork for what they would tell the media. Bogus stories were fed to the tabloids about a bomb in Gibraltar in a car parked by Savage and that the trio had the capability to detonate it remotely, which led to the SAS being forced to take them out. However, it seems clear to me that Farrell and her companions were allowed to enter Gibraltar without a bomb that morning so they could be liquidated. This was Thatcher's revenge. She was sending a personal message to the IRA leadership.

After Armagh Prison, Mairéad Farrell had spent much of her time in the spotlight. She was highly intelligent and many journalists sought interviews with her. She presented herself as a smiling, articulate young woman. She never avoided awkward questions because she felt that she represented other IRA women like herself. 'Everyone tells me I am a feminist. All I know is that I am just as good as others, especially men,' she once said.

When asked about her past, she did not exude bitterness like some of her generation in the IRA ranks. However, as her solicitor, Paddy McGrory, once observed, she was mentally tough and a deeply committed Irish republican. Although she was intelligent, she was also gullible. She trusted her male IRA bosses, who considered her expendable when they sent her to Gibraltar. They had never cared much about her role in the dirty protest or the hunger strike that almost cost her her life in Armagh Prison. According to her, the men who ran the IRA thought women were only good for certain roles, not for running the show. She did not seem to grasp that her last operation was foolhardy. Unlike many of her male counterparts who were given 'cushy' roles in Sinn Féin after serving prison time, she was put back on the front lines, exposed to MI5 and MI6 as well as Spanish intelligence. She was a well-known member of the IRA and so too were McCann and Savage. The three were prominent figures on British intelligence watch lists.

There have been many conspiracy theories about who might have compromised Mairéad and her companions. In the opinion of a senior IRA source I trusted, the decision to send those three to Gibraltar was taken at a high level in the Northern Command, but the 'top lads' in Dublin knew about it too. Even if one, or more than one, British asset in the Belfast Brigade had got wind of the operation and leaked it, there had to be someone, or more than one person, in authority in the IRA's Northern Command who gave approval for three high-value IRA operatives to be offered up as 'sacrificial lambs' because 'no one in their right mind' would allow figures like Farrell, McCann and Savage to travel to Gibraltar in these circumstances unless the plan was to 'eliminate' them.

After their deaths, Martin McGuinness, as officer commanding the Northern Command, was told by the IRA's Army Council to hold a court of inquiry to establish the cause of the Gibraltar failure. In a move which raises questions about McGuinness' judgement, he asked Frederick Scappaticci to sit on the inquiry board. This was akin to asking the fox to run the hen house. 'Scapp' was the biggest British spy in IRA ranks. He was infamous for running the IRA's Internal Security Unit (ISU), also known as 'The Nuttin' Squad' and may have been involved in the killing of and in ordering the deaths of many people suspected, often wrongly, of betraying the IRA. Based in Belfast, he had been apprised of all the planned features of the Gibraltar operation. The fact that he knew about it meant that British intelligence, particularly the Force Research Unit (FRU), which ran him as an asset, knew what was planned for Gibraltar and who would be taking part. The IRA court of inquiry conveniently attributed blame for the Gibraltar debacle to Daniel McCann. It concluded that he had 'loose lips'.

In the eyes of some senior IRA figures who were close associates of the man they called 'Big Dan' McCann, the inquiry was a whitewash. They later concluded that McGuinness, like Scapp, was a British spy. 'The Court of Inquiry was a ploy to keep the lid on it because McGuinness and Scapp knew that some of us suspected treachery,' said one of my sources. 'It was not lost on those of us who fought alongside Big Dan that he would never have blabbed about such an important operation. He was tight. The bottom line is that this Gibraltar crew of Dan, Mairéad and Sean was sold out – sacrificed if you like.'

While there was much faux emotion expressed in the top echelons of the IRA over the loss of Mairéad Farrell, because it suited Sinn Féin to promote her as a woman who gave her life for the cause, nobody cared enough to explain who ran the Gibraltar operation or why three well-known IRA officers were sent to Spain or how the whole operation was compromised. According to one source, 'a few among us wondered if the operation was sold out by those involved in secret peace talks in London to prove to the Brits that our side was serious about ending the conflict. No better way to do it than offer up an operation. I don't subscribe to that, but I am sure the op was dead in the water the moment it was conceived. It was overseen by dirty people from the start. It was a suicide mission is what it was.'

It was naive of Farrell and her companions to think that they could escape the eyes of the international intelligence world by flying into Spain and entering a British military site like Gibraltar. She was, on the one hand, foolish and, on the other, a young woman who was determined to leave her mark on history even if it killed her. Dying for 'the cause' was the last act of a romantic nationalist. The IRA trio was executed in the most clinical fashion. It had all the hallmarks of a political assassination.

Mairéad Farrell, like many Catholic teenagers of her generation, was drawn into the ranks of the IRA by people with a long attachment to romantic nationalism. She was determined to change the political status quo by any means necessary. Political activism was not enough for her. She wanted to act even if it meant joining a misogynistic military organisation, one that proved it did not respect her right to live. Her addiction to armed conflict was so all-consuming that it put her on a path to self-destruction that claimed her life. She placed her destiny in the hands of IRA leaders who cared little for her safety, provided she served their cause. It was an organisation riddled with spies who compromised the Gibraltar operation from the outset. Nevertheless, she was sent on a suicide mission by her bosses.

In an article for *The New York Times*, John J. O'Connor offered this reflection on her life: 'To the people of the Falls, she was a patriot. To the British she was a terrorist. To her family, she was a victim of Irish history.'

7

LOSS OF A YOUNG SOLDIER HUSBAND

CAROL NICE FINISHED HER NURSING studies in October 1988 and took a job in a London hospital. At the start of the new year she and her girlfriends began planning a long holiday to France and Spain. She would soon be twenty-three and it was time to let her hair down. Anyway, her relationship with a soldier was over and she was a free spirit.

After Easter, as spring lifted its wintry cloak off central London, she and her friends felt that it was the right time to put the finishing touches to their forthcoming European trip. They would not be typical tourists but more like backpackers who would happily seek part-time jobs to earn pocket money in tourist spots along the Mediterranean. One evening in early April, they gathered in The Friend at Hand pub in Russell Square to plan their trip. Its regulars were nurses like themselves, as well as soldiers and policemen who worked shifts and went there to relax and enjoy the bar food. It had old stripped wooden floors and a jukebox. At some point, Carol left her friends and made her way to the jukebox. She imagines that she selected the song 'The Only Way Is Up' sung by Yazz. She was about to return to her friends when she glanced at a young man lounging against the jukebox.

'He was gorgeous,' she recalls.

They smiled at each other and he introduced himself as Simon Ware. Minutes later, he confessed that his eyes had been on her for some time. He told her that he was a soldier in the 1st Battalion, Coldstream Guards. Carol smiled and explained that her ex had been in that battalion.

Simon laughed. 'I saw you with him several times,' he said, 'but I decided to bide my time because he was a roamer.'

By 'roamer' he meant a man with a roving eye for other women. Simon admitted that he thought if he waited long enough, Carol would leave the 'roamer' and he would have an opportunity to approach her. That evening, he had finally decided to make his move.

Carol liked his honesty. She forgot about her friends at the bar and spent the rest of the night talking to Simon. She learned that he was from north London and was an Arsenal Football Club supporter. He was also an avid fisherman and had been selected for the army's fishing team. At twenty-two, he was two years younger than her but he seemed mature for his age. His younger brother, Darren, was also a soldier, serving with the Royal Green Jackets Regiment. Simon had good relationships with his parents, who were divorced, but sadly his father had recently passed away. Nevertheless, he remained close to his mother. He was not one of the big, burly soldiers one might associate with a member of the Parachute Regiment. He was 5ft 9in tall and slim and there was a softness to his personality which Carol found endearing. He was, he insisted, a committed infantry soldier and had reached the rank of lance corporal in one of the most elite regiments in the British Army.

Simon and Carol bonded quickly when it transpired that he was from the same area of north London as her family. He talked about the cemetery in Enfield where his dad was buried and the school he had attended. Carol was familiar with Enfield. When she was a child, she often accompanied her mother on trips to its centre to buy clothes and school uniforms. All these personal details and memories of familiar places gave them something to talk about and brought them closer. Still, she had other things on her mind, like her European trip, and was reluctant to get wrapped up in another relationship. Nevertheless, Simon captured her imagination because he was different to other young men she had met. In particular, he was considerate and had a sense of humour. He also had a lovely smile and deep brown eyes.

Days after meeting him, she left for Europe with her friends, remaining there until the end of the summer, when she came back to London and took a full-time nursing job. Simon had kept in touch with her and, not long after she was home, they started a relationship. By the end of the year, they were engaged. As busy professionals, they needed the whole of 1990 to plan their wedding. Carol had a settled career in London and they both agreed that, after the wedding, they would move into the army's married quarters at Balham in south London. The army, however, had other plans for Simon. At the end of 1990, a Military Order was issued to send the 1st Battalion, Coldstream Guards to Germany. With their marriage on the horizon, this news was not well received by Carol, but Simon assured her that he had a solution.

'I had been a staff nurse for a year,' explains Carol, 'and suddenly I was offered a better job in general practice. When news came in December 1990 that Simon was being moved to Germany, I told him that I did not want to go – not that I did not want to be with him but I had just begun a new job. Simon understood and right away transferred to the 2nd Battalion. His former buddies in the 1st Battalion left for Germany and were soon after deployed to fight in the First Gulf War.'

Simon's transfer to the 2nd Battalion let him remain in London and continue planning their nuptials. He made the change right away but little did he know that his decision would have unforeseen consequences. Nevertheless, it was ideal at the time because Carol had just started her general practice job and was employed in a doctor's surgery. She could begin to develop her career, which would have been impossible had she been obliged to move with him to a military barracks in Germany. Now she could earn enough money to help her and Simon build a life together. Although they were young professionals, they were not particularly well-paid in 1990s' Britain. Career advancement would more than help pay the bills once they were married. They might eventually be able to save for a house of their own.

After the switch of battalions, Simon was unexpectedly informed that the 2nd Battalion was being deployed to Northern Ireland. If he had not made the transfer, he would have fought in Iraq – a war from which all his former colleagues returned safely. Despite all their planning, Carol and Simon learned that even the best-laid plans can go astray.

'Our wedding was set for April,' says Carol, 'but Simon was told that he would be going to Northern Ireland two days after it. So we were married on Saturday 9 April, and he went back to barracks on Monday 11 April and arrived in Northern Ireland on 12 April. It was all so fast, like in the blink of an eye.'

However, the wedding was a success on a bright spring day. Carol and Simon's favourite song, 'Never Tear Us Apart' by INXS, was played for them to dance to.

Simon had explained to Carol that his deployment to Northern Ireland would not be his first tour of duty to the war zone. He had been there before and had no fears about going back. He and his fellow soldiers were unusually casual when Northern Ireland was mentioned.

According to Carol, this was how they addressed any inner fears they might have had.

'They were very philosophical,' she says. 'They all knew the risks. They all knew they might not come back. They were even blasé about the fact each of them had to write a will. They also had to sort out their finances and things like that; particularly those that were married. We had just got married, but Simon had sorted out his will before we married. He did it as soon as he learned he was going to Northern Ireland. He was advised to do that because he was about to be a married man. He and his fellow Guardsmen were all a bit like "It's what it is" mentality. I guess, in the back of your mind, you know something could happen, but you push it away because you think it's not going to happen to you. Simon and his friends would joke and make light of it, saying, "Well, if I come back in a box, at least I have my will sorted." Us nurses shared that kind of dark humour in our profession. We might laugh at some of the weird stuff that happens, but you cannot get through your day sometimes unless you can laugh at something. It is a coping mechanism. Simon had done a tour before in Northern Ireland so he thought, *Okay, I've done a tour before, so it's fine, and I'll be fine.* He was sort of reassuring when he told me, "I've been there before and they make you do these things because it's a protocol kind of thing and it'll be all right." I tried not to think about it much, and I worked full-time to occupy myself.'

It was an era when there were no smartphones and laptops so Carol only heard from Simon via landline calls from his barracks in Northern Ireland. It was difficult for him to schedule calls because of the uncertain nature of his duties. Other soldiers' wives faced the same issue so when they gathered in each other's homes in married quarters for meals, they came with long extension cables into which their phones were plugged, hoping their husbands would call from a payphone in their barracks. Simon also wrote letters, saying how much he missed her and was looking forward to seeing her.

Carol was busy buying new furniture, bedding and curtains, determined to make their military quarters homely and stylish, knowing that Simon would be due for some R&R time in London. Sure enough, he arrived home for a week in May and Carol took time off work.

'We visited friends and relatives but we also had the opportunity to stay at home because we had only been able to spend two nights together in our married quarters before he left for Northern Ireland,' she says.

Decades later, Carol still vividly remembers the week they spent together: 'When he came back, I had furnished the place. It was a completely different home from the one he left. Sometimes, I'd be a bit irritated because he was a little messy. He would squeeze toothpaste from the middle of the tube and all that sort of stuff. I used to tidy up after him, but we never argued. You get so used to being on your own. All of us soldiers' wives helped each other with the electrics and chores. We would get a manual and say, "Let's see how this or that works." While Simon was home on leave, we did not have a lot of money. He was a soldier who was not paid well and I was a nurse, not paid particularly well either, so we did not have spare cash to go out and eat nice meals. We would meet friends for a pint at the Richmond in Shepherd's Bush, which was a traditional pub at the time, and go home with a take-out curry and a bottle of wine. We enjoyed being together. His brother was on leave too and we saw him.'

The way Carol talks about the few days Simon spent with her is reminiscent of other young couples with so much potential yet with limited resources, like so many of their generation.

On 17 August 1991, a mere three-and-a-half months since her marriage, Carol was up early to join other wives on a day trip to France, organised by the regimental families officer. They were taken by coach to Dover and by ferry to Calais, where they visited duty-free shops and cafés. On this same day, Simon was up much earlier for duty in the County Armagh countryside. A damp mist was lifting off the land, rising slowly into the air as he led a foot patrol through Tullyogallaghan townland, near Newtownhamilton. He may not have talked to Carol about the dangers facing the British Army in Armagh, but all soldiers drafted to the area knew that it was one of the most dangerous parts of Northern Ireland. It had the largest contingent of British troops compared to areas with a similar population. There were 3,000 troops supported by police in a county with a population of 23,000. Mostly rural, and close to the border, the area was the stomping ground of the IRA's South Armagh Brigade.

In respect of the IRA throughout Ireland, the South Armagh Brigade was a law unto itself. It had a tightly knit structure of people from families who knew each other over generations. British intelligence found it almost impossible to penetrate its ranks. Between 1970 and 1997 the brigade killed 123 soldiers and forty-seven policemen. Ninety civilians were killed and ten members of the South Armagh Brigade itself. Its snipers were lethal and it also brought down five army helicopters. Most significantly, its technicians had perfected the use of landmines. The first of these demonstrated its lethal ability in 1973 on a country road in Tullyogallaghan. It killed Norris Harrison and Terence Brown, members of the Parachute Regiment.

Now, on this early morning in August 1991, Simon Richard Damien Ware was the third man in a single line of a four-man foot patrol. Their route took them through the Cold Brae Forest in the townland of Carrickrovaddy. It was a beautiful woodland, known for its wildflowers, birds and animals. At exactly 7.30 a.m., Simon was walking along a narrow track when a bomb hidden in banked undergrowth exploded next to him. He died instantly.

Seven hours later, as Carol and other soldiers' wives boarded the ferry at Calais for the journey back to London, some of them noticed that the regimental families officer had left their group and not returned. When he came back, after a considerable time away, one of the wives asked him what was happening. He explained that he had been worried that their coach driver might have 'downed' a few drinks too many. He had checked on him and he was okay. What they did not know was that the officer had received the news that Simon had been killed hours earlier in Northern Ireland. The army 'Brass' in London had decided that breaking this news to Carol was not ideal while she was just about to board a ferry, hours from the British capital, hence the need for a bogus story about the coach driver.

After the wives left the ferry and boarded the coach, the families officer motioned to one of Carol's friends to leave with him. Minutes later, another wife, a nurse who had worked with Carol, was also asked to exit the coach. Finally, the officer summoned Carol.

'I was thinking, *Oh my God, what's happening? Maybe I have too much duty free; too many cigarettes and too much booze. I have done something wrong. I am going to be arrested or whatever.* Suddenly, I saw this man in a suit walking towards me with two female police officers, or WPCs as we called them in those days. They led me to a toilet block where there was a sort of family room. The man in the suit introduced himself as the regimental adjutant. It was not the nicest place but there was nowhere else to go. We were, after all, in a ferry port. The poor guy, who could not have been much older than Simon, had a horrible job to do. I can remember his words: "I am sorry to have to tell you but your husband was killed by a landmine this morning." The poor guy was so upset, he just crumbled and sat down on the floor, while I was screaming and crying hysterically. I was taken to my brother's home in Hertford because my parents were not alive at that time. News of a military death in Northern Ireland had been on the news but army protocol was that the name of the deceased could not be made public until a wife was informed.'

Simon's brother, Darren, who was on a two-year tour of Northern Ireland, was brought home after he received the sad news, but after Simon's funeral he chose to return there even though he could have requested a new posting.

'I think Darren wanted to go back for his brother, to carry on the fight as it were,' suggests Carol.

She acknowledges that she was so busy organising Simon's funeral she did not have too much time to grieve or to dwell on her loss. She praises the regimental families officer and the regiment for coming to her aid. According to her, their support was excellent and invaluable because they helped her a lot with the funeral arrangements. She was asked if she wanted Simon to be cremated or given a traditional burial. She opted for the latter.

'I knew Simon would have wanted to be buried in Enfield with his dad, who was Catholic, and there was a family grave. I also knew back in those days the Catholic Church disapproved of cremation. Simon and Darren were Catholics because their father converted to Catholicism years before. Simon was not very religious, but his burial had to be a traditional one.'

Carol remembers that this period in her life was a 'bit of a blur' as she returned to her married quarters with a range of matters to address.

'You're kind of, "What do I do now?" but you don't know what to do,' she says. 'You are twenty-four and you never thought you would be a widow, so where do you go? But that is where you are so lucky with the army. They kind of take everything out of your hands. They say, "Here are your finances and this is how it works." You get a pension and compensation etcetera. It was all a bit of a whirlwind, and you think, *I don't want any of this*. You just want your husband back. Nothing can compensate you for his loss, yet it helped me to some degree to plan for my future. But it is irrelevant really. In time, you think, *I am not really interested in a pension or what compensation I am going to get.* Nothing ever makes up for the loved one you lost. You cannot think what you might do next in your life. I never thought I would be living without Simon.'

One of the issues which Carol found 'challenging' was when the army asked her what inscription she planned for Simon's headstone. She said that she wanted one to include the words 'Killed by the IRA', but she was told that this was not permitted because it was a political statement. It puzzled her, as it would likely puzzle any right-thinking person. She was told she could only have the phrase 'Killed in Action'. She remembers this part of the funeral arrangements because it made her very angry.

'I just wanted people to know how he was killed,' she insists.

Before the funeral, the army asked Simon's brother if Carol would like to view her husband's remains. He replied that his sister-in-law was a nurse and was therefore clever enough to know that there was nothing to view.

'I freaked out. I knew exactly how Simon was killed. I knew that there was not much to see,' she says. 'It all comes down to you being unable to say goodbye.'

She points to the fact that, since she was never able to say goodbye to Simon because he was in a sealed coffin, this lay at the core of the loss she felt then and in the years since.

'No matter what happens in your life, the loss is with you all the time,' she says. 'It is there on every Remembrance Day and every year on his birthday.'

Carol is one of the most honest women I interviewed. She never sidestepped any of my questions about her life. She admitted that Simon's death had a resounding impact on her life going forward, especially when she tried to form personal relationships with other men, although she equally acknowledges that relationships are a 'two-way street'. For example, years after Simon was killed, she remarried, but the marriage collapsed. Carol believes that her second husband could not cope with the reality that Simon was still in her heart. How could he not be since he had been the love of her life, cruelly snatched from her? She revealed that when trying to rebuild her life after Simon's death, she discovered that men could not understand her depth of loss and grief. She was not alone. Many soldiers' wives who lost husbands, or girls who lost boyfriends, to the war in Ireland had similar experiences. Carol felt that her second husband saw himself as secondary in her affections. Nevertheless, she is happy with the fact she has a loving daughter from the failed union.

'I have a daughter from that marriage, and now a grandchild, for which I am grateful, and my daughter has always been very supportive. My husband felt that he was a lesser person than Simon in my affections. While he was initially understanding, he believed that our marriage was clouded a little bit by the fact that I had lost someone I loved more than him. It was a terrible thing for him to say. That was not the only problem in our marriage,' she insisted, 'but it did not help.'

Like many of the women I interviewed for this book, Carol was not offered any kind of psychological support. Society had no awareness of the emotional suffering and pain these women had to endure. There was no medical expertise or any institution ready to listen to the women's fears and their guilt at being survivors. They were left to find their own mechanisms to address societal attitudes, their anguish, uncertainties and depression. It is surprising that so many of them found the inner strength and motivation to go on with their everyday lives and in many instances, to fight for justice for their lost loved ones. They founded support groups to help each other navigate the bureaucracy of institutions and the complexities of the law.

Nowadays, Carol has met someone she believes understands her. She reckons that it may be partly due to the fact that she is much better at explaining herself and her past to others. She has, she says, found ways to talk about her trauma. 'I have got to the stage with people when I can say: "This is my past, and it is something I cannot change, or forget."'

For example, she no longer worries about having photos of Simon or artwork reminding her of him displayed in her home. In her hallway there is a framed citation signed by the late Queen Elizabeth, honouring him for giving his life for 'Queen and Country'.

Carol is quick to point out that though Simon was murdered in Ireland, she does not blame the people of Northern Ireland or Ireland. 'I kept all the amazing cards and letters I received from Irish people telling me how sad they were at what happened to Simon. I have no issue with the people of Ireland, but I am still angry with the IRA.'

She is also upset that there has been no justice for those who murdered her late husband. The bombers were never caught.

Something else which upsets her is the use of the term 'the Troubles'. 'It trivialises the past, making it seem almost irrelevant. It was a war. When people say, "He was killed in the Troubles," well, fine if that's what you want to call them, but as far as we, the family and the soldiers, were concerned, it was a war and it will always be a war.'

8

THE FIERCE CAMPAIGNER FOR JUSTICE

IN 1992 EIGHTEEN-YEAR-OLD PETER MCBRIDE was a petty criminal living with his mother in the New Lodge Road area of north Belfast, a Catholic enclave under the control of the Provisional IRA. It was a part of the city marked by communal violence, gun battles between the British Army and the IRA and some of the most brutal sectarian murders of the Troubles.

Peter was Jean McBride's only son, whom she liked to say was her pride and joy. She realised he was no angel, but there was little she could do to rein in his criminality. She gave birth to him when she was in her early twenties and readily identified with his youthful exuberance, thinking that he was a typical teen of his generation even though he had already fathered two little girls. His crowning achievement in her eyes was that, in contrast to many of his contemporaries, he had not joined the IRA or the INLA. She was opposed to violence for political ends and was fond of saying, 'All mothers grieve, no matter if they are Catholic, Protestant or the mothers of soldiers.'

Small, with cropped blonde hair and large, dark spectacles, Jean was considered a loving mother, if a little too tolerant of Peter's waywardness. In a tightly knit Catholic community like the New Lodge, most considered Peter 'harmless'. He was a distinctive local personality easily recognised by his dyed hair, which had gone through several colour changes. Lately, it was spikey and bright blond. He liked to wear jeans, distinctive red runners and a fleece jacket.

Peter had no steady job, yet he was always on the move, doing 'business', mostly outside of the New Lodge. Jean had warned him that he risked being 'kneecapped' by the local IRA if he was caught dealing drugs or stealing from homes or businesses in his New Lodge 'patch'. The punishments meted out to petty criminals and drug dealers included beatings and bullets fired into the back of each kneecap to cause as much damage as possible. Victims of kneecapping were often left permanently disabled, though doctors and surgeons in Northern Ireland had dealt with thousands of young and old men subjected to this brutal procedure and had devised techniques to repair some of the bone and ligament damage.

Loyalist paramilitaries also reverted to kneecapping, occasionally resulting in bizarre events. There was a case in the Shankill area of a UDA member found guilty by his bosses of committing petty crimes. When he was told that he would be kneecapped, he was concerned that the trousers of his newly purchased suit would be permanently damaged. As a concession, UDA chief James 'Pratt' Craig allowed him to roll the trousers up above his knees before he was shot.

The other danger facing petty criminals was that they became well-known to the British Army. For example, in the New Lodge area, when a new army battalion moved into the district, it was briefed not just about the IRA and its sympathisers but also about the identities of drug dealers and petty criminals. Army intelligence officers knew that criminals were particularly vulnerable to recruitment, a fact the IRA also understood well. The army often arrested drug dealers or thieves and threatened to expose them to the IRA and its kneecapping punishment if they did not agree to become informants. This meant that Peter McBride's name was in military files. Patrolling soldiers were instructed to detain drug dealers and shoplifters briefly and engage them in conversation in ways that made them feel comfortable.

Usually, young petty criminals like Peter did not observe the norms of Belfast, in which sectarian boundaries defined where people walked, shopped and travelled. While Catholics and Protestants rarely mixed socially, the social and political barriers separating them were ignored by the criminal fraternity. Criminality was a kind of brotherhood in which sectarianism played no part because it had no monetary value. In some areas of the city, like west Belfast, criminals tried to buy protection from the IRA by bartering information about others, especially about police and army routines. I investigated one case after criminals broke into a car in the city centre. It belonged to two British undercover officers who were having an affair. They were in bed in a Europa Hotel suite when their car was burgled. It contained files of classified documents relating to surveillance of IRA suspects. The criminals gave those to the IRA in exchange for a guarantee that they would not be targeted by kneecapping squads. This intervention led to a criminal gang being singled out by British Military Intelligence for assassination.

Jean McBride was not bothered that her son had Protestant friends from the Shankill and other dangerous parts of the city because she believed that he and his buddies were not serious criminals or terrorists. They were teens, crazy about partying. Many were goths, punks, ravers and indie heads, all of them obsessed with music, dance and the joys of the new party drug, ecstasy. At the start of September 1992, Peter and a few fellow ravers were talking about The Prodigy's world tour and the staging of a gig at the Maysfield Leisure Centre in Belfast. According to people in the scene at the time the city was 'buzzing' about it, despite the political violence. Theirs was a world of which most of Peter's New Lodge Road contemporaries knew little. It was a life that gave him some thrills in a violent city.

Jean knew little about the raves but was convinced that they fed into Peter's love of music and brought together kids from both religions. One of the striking features of such events was that they spanned the religious divide in a tribal society.

Peter may have been peddling ecstasy at all-night raves in Belfast and other parts of Northern Ireland as he was not short of money and often did not return home for a day or two. He did not confide much about his extracurricular activities to his mother, knowing she would not have grasped the significance of the scene he inhabited. However, she liked to boast that he had friends 'from all over the place'. 'He is a nice wee lad, well-liked by everybody. He is a petty criminal but that is a far cry from a member of the Irish Republican Army with a bomb, isn't it?' she insisted on telling anyone willing to listen.

It is interesting how Jean rationalised her acceptance of Peter as a petty criminal. I suspect that she saw him as a burglar who trafficked in stolen property and never suspected that he could be selling drugs. In a society in which some of his contemporaries were in the terror business, Jean considered her son's crimes 'the lesser of two evils'. Perhaps she was right, since he was not a major drug dealer. Knowing how she felt about his waywardness, Peter exploited her leniency.

Like many people in troubled districts, New Lodge residents had their radios or their televisions tuned to the police–army radio feeds. It was almost a tradition and a way of monitoring what was happening in their neighbourhood and in nearby districts like the loyalist Tiger's Bay. It was also a mechanism for some people to inform the local IRA or its sympathisers that an army–police raid was in progress. It was in effect a local news service and people liked to feel that they knew exactly what was happening around them and share it with neighbours. In other societies it would have been akin to discussing the weather.

THE FIERCE CAMPAIGNER FOR JUSTICE 111

On the early evening of 4 September 1992, Jean was expecting Peter for dinner. She had her TV tuned to army radio traffic while she waited for him. Suddenly, she heard a loud burst of gunfire; perhaps six or seven shots, she thought. They were close by. She was trying to process this when the army radio announced that a civilian had been shot. She glanced out her bedroom window just as a security guard in a building opposite ran to her house.

'Your Peter's been shot,' he shouted.

She ran outside and saw an area taped off at the top of her street. She ran towards it as an elderly woman yelled, 'Jean, your wee son is lying down there.'

Jean saw police gathered round a body and ran towards them, but a soldier tried to stop her progress. 'Com 'ere,' she said, gripping his uniform, 'my son's lying down that entry and nobody's gonna stop me seeing him. Now get outta my way!'

The soldier, realising that he was dealing with a very determined mother, backed off as Jean ran to her son. Bending down, she took his hand in hers and looked into his eyes, usually bright blue. Now, they were glassy, opaque and she knew for certain that he was dead. From my experience of seeing people who have been killed, and autopsy photos, his skin would have lost its elasticity and his hand might have been clenched, which often happens if someone has been holding something when they die suddenly. Peter was holding a plastic bag containing a T-shirt when he was shot.

One cannot grasp the horror and pain Jean felt as she looked into her son's lifeless eyes. She never expected her boy to suffer a violent death. What had he done to deserve this kind of execution? Two high-velocity bullets from self-loading 7.62 rifles had entered his back. He was not killed by the IRA as she had first feared when she heard that he had been shot. Instead, his killers were two members of a British Army foot patrol of the 1st Battalion of the Scots Guards Regiment.

The army patrol had stopped Peter as he entered the New Lodge and body-searched him. They looked inside the plastic bag he was carrying and discovered that it contained a T-shirt. He posed no threat and was free to go. He began running towards home and was approximately seventy metres from the patrol when two soldiers, James Fisher (24) and Mark Wright (19), fired five times at him. The first round struck him in the back, sending him crashing onto the bonnet of a parked car. A second round entered his back as he slid off the bonnet. The likelihood is that he was dead before impact with the ground. According to the two soldiers, when they saw Peter running from them, they feared that he had a bomb. They were pursuing him when they opened fire. In this instance, they claimed that he probably had a coffee-jar bomb of a type known to be used by the IRA, even though the patrol had already searched him and discovered he was clean.

Since Peter was seventy metres from the two Scots Guards when they opened fire, they had enough time to aim to make their shots count. They carelessly fired five rounds in a highly populated area, not caring who else they might kill. The time taken to zero in on and kill Peter was clear evidence of premeditated intent. They had decided to shoot a young man who posed no threat to them or to anyone in the vicinity. After he was searched and cleared to go about his business, they had tracked his progress through their high-powered rifle sights.

Over the years, covering army shootings, I found that the statements made by Fisher and Wright were very much in keeping with the way some soldiers justified murder. They would insist, no matter the circumstances, that the victim was at fault and posed an existential threat to them or to others or the victim was killed in crossfire. In this case, they came up with the absurd claim that he was carrying a coffee-jar bomb.

What really motivated them to kill Peter?

The British Army held the opinion, shaped by its post-colonial treatment of Catholics during the Lower Falls Curfew on 3–5 July 1970 that the Catholic population was its enemy. This distorted mindset filtered down through the ranks and by 1992 it was a fixed conviction that all people in nationalist/republican areas posed a threat. The two Guardsmen who shot Peter McBride were infected with that prejudicial virus. They felt comfortable opening fire, probably aware, though maybe not consciously so, that soldiers were rarely charged with murder or found guilty for shooting Catholics.

No one should argue that the army did not suffer or that the life of an ordinary soldier was not very stressful, but the army and the military establishment failed to impose proper discipline among military ranks. Some regiments had a reputation for behaving badly and they included Scots regiments and the Parachute Regiment. One might ask, why Scots regiments? I believe that the presence of young men in Scots regiments from divided religious communities in Scotland was a factor. In cities like Glasgow, enmity between Catholics and Protestants mirrored the religious divide and bitterness in Belfast. The destruction of religious items in the searches of Catholic homes during the Lower Falls Curfew was the work of a Scots regiment. The Parachute Regiment was a gung-ho outfit, which needed an enemy. Their killing of innocents in Belfast and Derry has been well documented. On another level, the British Army, like most armies, was not built for policing. Therefore, it was given an impossible task when it was sent to Northern Ireland in August 1969 to do just that. It also faced a serious problem when the British government left unionists in charge of security in 1969. It was perhaps inevitable that the army, in needing an enemy, found one in July 1972 in the Lower Falls. Many of the army generals from the period have since admitted that much of the blame for the deteriorating political climate in the early 1970s, leading to a long war, should be levelled at the men who sat in No. 10, such as Harold Wilson and Edward Heath.

Another factor, with its origins in the early 1970s, was that many in the British military, especially those running their own dirty war, felt that they were above the law because they were the law. A friend of mine, Eugene Devlin, who later became a successful New York bar owner, was one of several young men who were shot by Military Reaction/Reconnaissance Force (MRF) undercover troops in 1972 while travelling by car. Eugene was paid a few hundred pounds in compensation and no one was brought to justice. Much too often when an innocent person was shot, all soldiers had to do was tell the courts that the victim fired at them or was about to plant a bomb or was killed in crossfire by the IRA. There were too many people in the administration of justice in the early Troubles period who were from a unionist background and their prejudices were evident in dispensing judgments from the bench. This does not excuse the IRA, which often put its own people in danger by firing at the army in urban areas, knowing this would generate a response likely to kill innocent civilians.

Scots Guardsmen Fisher and Wright were young men, but they had been in the army for two years and were fully fledged, well-trained soldiers. Those who claimed that they were too young to be in a conflict zone ignored the fact that the British Army could boast, with decades of evidence, that it had the best-trained soldiers in the world. Before Peter's shooting, Fisher had been in the Scots Guards 1st Battalion for ten months and Wright for seven. Their tour of duty in Northern Ireland was their first and they had been patrolling the streets for four months. The courts would later hear the army give this defence for their actions:

> The general security situation was tense and particularly so in the New Lodge area where the unit had suffered recent casualties

including a fatality. At the team briefing on 4th September, they had been advised that the situation was high risk and that there was an expectation that those associated with terrorist groups would be likely to be carrying personal weapons. Furthermore, the threat of coffee-jar bombs at the time of the offence was very real: soldiers had been maimed and, on occasion, killed by this weapon. The coffee-jar bomb was a device which was very easy to conceal until the moment of throwing. While this dangerous and volatile situation might have rightly led to heightened awareness, there was no evidence of individual or collective premeditation to commit a criminal offence.

After Fisher and Wright shot Peter McBride, they were whisked off to their base at Girdwood Barracks. For ten hours, RUC detectives were denied access to them. The reason for this was simple. It was a familiar military delaying tactic and it was possible because the RUC had no authority to enter a military base without the permission of the base commander. Several detectives told me that trying to investigate the military, who considered themselves the law, was almost impossible. Co-operation was rarely forthcoming.

Twenty-four hours after Peter was shot, Wright and Fisher were charged with murder and remanded in custody, but three years would pass before they arrived in court. They appeared not in a regular court but in a Diplock Court before Lord Justice William Basil Kelly, a former unionist attorney general. The Diplock Courts were courts with judges sitting alone without a jury. They were established to end the threat of jury-tampering by the paramilitaries on both sides. The fact that the two Guardsmen appeared before such a court appeared to confirm that their crime was political murder. Lord Justice Kelly was refined and erudite. He was always impeccably dressed, like a gentleman ready to enter a private London club. He was involved in the first IRA supergrass trial during which he wore a bulletproof vest while on the Bench and handed down 4,000 years of sentences. For a period, he was even protected by soldiers of the SAS. He also delivered some bizarre judgments. For example, in February 1992 he sentenced the notorious UDA assassination chief and British spy Brian Nelson to a mere ten years in prison even though he was linked to scores of political murders. It was obvious that Justice Kelly had been amenable to pressure from British Military Intelligence to be lenient on their asset.

If the British Army thought that Justice Kelly would be a pushover, easily persuaded that Fisher and Wright were just two young men in a stressful environment, they were in for a shock. He told the two Guardsmen that they were liars. They could have apprehended Peter McBride, even shot him in the legs, but to kill him after searching him and finding he possessed nothing to threaten them was ridiculous. He dismissed their claim that Peter was an IRA sympathiser, pointing out that there was no evidence to support this. In finding them both guilty of murder, he accused them of being 'untruthful and evasive' and sentenced them to life imprisonment in February 1995.

Jean McBride, her husband, Peter Sr, and their daughter, Kelly, were pleased with the outcome, believing that the trial and judgment brought them an element of closure, but their legal battle for justice was far from over and it would lead to a mother and daughter becoming, with the aid of one of the best legal firms in Northern Ireland, the Finucane Centre, a formidable campaigning duo.

It did not take long for the tabloid press in Britain, especially the *Daily Mail*, to launch a campaign for the release of Fisher and Wright, who were among only three soldiers to be sentenced to life for murder during the Troubles. Jean McBride was disturbed by ever-increasing calls for the soldiers to be set free so they could return to army life. False claims were made in the *Daily Mail* linking Peter to the IRA.

Jean responded by seeking a meeting with Tony Blair's Minister of State for the Armed Forces, Scots Labour politician John Reid. Jean may not have been aware that Reid, as minister, had lobbied for the release of the two Scots Guards. Efforts to get a meeting with him came to nothing, though he met groups campaigning for the soldiers' release. Jean insisted on meeting the Labour Secretary of State for Northern Ireland, Mo Mowlam, convinced that Labour leader Tony Blair and Mowlam would never bend to pressure to release her son's killers.

Jean's belief in Blair and the Labour Party leadership was misplaced, and her hopes were dashed when Mowlam phoned her to say that the two soldiers would be released to return to the ranks of the Scots Guards. Jean was devastated but not defeated. The prospect of Fisher and Wright back patrolling the streets of Northern Ireland was too much for her to bear. With Peter Madden, a solicitor with the Finucane Centre, she met Taoiseach Bertie Ahern. He assured her that he would personally petition Blair to have Fisher and Wright dismissed from the army.

Jean was still not satisfied. She wanted to take her son's case further by meeting Tony Blair herself, but he was never available. She demanded to see the new Minister of State for the Armed Forces, Doug Henderson, not knowing that he had been on the Army Board that authorised the return of Fisher and Wright to life in uniform. Jean lost her cool in a meeting with Henderson when she realised he had no interest in her case. He was in effect arguing that the tense atmosphere at the time of the shooting justified Peter's killing. She could not listen to him any longer so she got up and stormed out of the room. She knew that Henderson and the other members of the Army Board, mostly military figures, were convinced that the two soldiers had served long enough sentences. She was terribly upset when she read what the Board said in its judgment:

> It took account of the following: ... the security situation in the area of the incident at that time was tense and the Guardsmen's unit had suffered a recent fatal casualty, and the Guardsmen had shown contrition for their action, which they had admitted was an error of judgement which they very much regret; they had paid the price for their action with a lengthy prison sentence during which time their behaviour had been exemplary; their continued loyalty to the Army and their previously unblemished military records; and finally their wish to continue serving their country. The Board concluded that these factors did amount to exceptional circumstances justifying the retention of the two Guardsmen in the army.

The injustice in this philosophy made Jean more determined than ever to fight for a reversal of this decision. Perhaps she understood that remaining neutral and silent was a bad strategy. The forces ranged against her were powerful but that seemed to give her strength. (Activist, writer and Holocaust survivor Elie Wiesel once said that silence encourages the tormentor, not the tormented.)

Jean asked her lawyers at the Finucane Centre what she should do next. They recommended an appeal to the Northern Ireland High Court for a judge to review the Army Board's decision. This move proved beneficial when Lord Justice Kerr ruled that the Board was duty-bound to reconsider the case. He referenced Lord Justice Kelly's imposition of life sentences. Like Kelly, he said that there were no exceptional circumstances which would have obliged him to take a more lenient position.

Jean and Kelly flew to London to hand in a letter to 10 Downing Street, addressed to Tony Blair, calling on him to act. The letter in question was lost. Within a year, a new Army Board disagreed with Justice Kerr's ruling and reinstated Fisher and Wright in the ranks of the British Army. This did not cause any let-up in Jean's crusade for justice. She remained the tireless campaigner she had always been, reading newspapers, listening to media reports and, with the help of her daughter, her husband and the Finucane Centre, canvassing politicians. When asked if she was going to give up, she had this response for the media: 'This campaign will go on each day and every day that they remain serving soldiers. I have said it before and I repeat it on Peter's anniversary, I will haunt Tony Blair until he does the decent thing and then, only then, can my family find peace.'

On 1 December 2000, the day that Jean McBride called an International Action Day for Peter McBride, a Christmas card arrived in the mail at the offices of her legal team. The envelope was from the United Nations Protection Force. Inside was an official British Army card from 'All Ranks, 1st Battalion Scots Guards, Nanyuki, Kenya', the same regiment Fisher and Wright were reinstated to serve in. It was a sick joke. Her legal team lodged the following complaint with the United Nations:

> We can only be grateful that whoever sent this didn't have an address for the McBride family. It's been a desperate time for them. An Army Board, including a senior government Minister, concludes that the murder of their son was a less serious offence than smoking dope and then the tabloid press, spearheaded by the *Daily Mail*, runs headlines referring to 'courageous soldiers, jailed for doing their duty'. Put in this context it's hardly surprising that a gloating and offensive card is sent signed on behalf of the 1st Battalion, Scots Guards. It's pitiful.

Jean was terribly upset when she learned about the Christmas card. She felt that she had been 'kicked to the ground by those who had done so much to hurt her family'. Coincidentally, on the day the card arrived, she received a massive bunch of flowers from a man in Japan who had read about her campaign.

Labour Member of Parliament (MP) Kevin McNamara considered the card a 'sick and callous act of intimidation'. According to him, it demonstrated the folly of letting the two soldiers back into the military. He demanded an investigation by the Ministry of Defence, but the issue was shelved in Whitehall and no action was taken, nor was any mention made publicly of the fact that the British Army was considering Wright for promotion.

In 2003, after Wright was promoted to lance corporal, Jean lost hope and felt that her trust in Tony Blair's government had been misplaced. Blair, when asked about Wright's promotion, said that it was an 'internal employment issue'. This confirmed that he had no desire to have his fingerprints on the issue. It was a classic example of passing the buck. Jean and her family were hurt by his coldness and indifference, but they did not let his words slow them down. They remained busy trying to get the message out. Jean McBride said, 'I have one message for this government. I will fight to have Fisher and Wright dismissed while I have breath in my body.'

When she learned that Fisher and Wright were on active service in Germany, she expressed incredulity. Her comments were picked up by European news outlets and bore fruit. The German government responded by complaining to the British and a Scots Guards Regimental Band performance in Italy was called off. The Irish government made its indignation known about the Army Board's behaviour in letters to 10 Downing Street, but its efforts were ignored.

In Britain there was a big effort under way, supported by the *Daily Mail* and by some public figures, to defend the Board's decision and to denigrate Peter McBride. Among those at the forefront of the campaign was Ludovic Kennedy, a prominent author and television journalist who had served in the British Navy in the Second World

War. Jean told friends that she felt that she was battling not just the British government but the British media as well. She was outraged when Kennedy called for Fisher and Wright to be compensated for their time in prison. It was a ludicrous demand made by a public figure who once had a stellar reputation. Kennedy had been made a lord by Prime Minister John Major, although Margaret Thatcher had tossed aside a recommendation from a Tory clique in Scotland to make him a knight. Thatcher did not like media types and was not fond of Kennedy, whose intervention in the Peter McBride scandal was reflective of a man who had no journalistic integrity. According to Kennedy, the army had evidence that Peter McBride was an IRA asset and that he may have been in the process of attacking the patrol with a coffee-jar bomb. He even speculated that the IRA had spirited away the bomb after Peter was shot. To further this lie, he denounced the witness evidence at the trial of Fisher and Wright. It was clear that he was being briefed by the army.

Jean and her daughter continued their mission, calling for boycotts of events and appearances by public figures linked to the British government and the military. Kelly stood as a candidate in a by-election in Brentford, England, knowing that she would not be elected but certain that it would help get across her mother's message, which boiled down to 'kick these two murderers of my son out of the army'.

When a second judicial review found that the Board was within its rights to reinstate the soldiers in their regiment, former IRA leader Martin McGuinness, by then the deputy first minister in Northern Ireland's power-sharing Assembly, wrote to Tony Blair using words which left the British prime minister in no doubt about his outrage over the Army Board's decision-making: 'It is astonishing that the British Army would want to have convicted murderers and liars in its ranks.' However, McGuinness' views on the matter were unlikely to have been given much weight, considering his personal role in terrorism.

Having explored so many avenues to spread the word about her son, Jean McBride wrote an open letter to the Queen, hoping another mother would understand her pain. She hoped that the Queen, as commander-in-chief of the British forces, might clarify why two soldiers who killed her eighteen-year-old son, Peter, were released and allowed to resume their military careers. The letter arrived in Buckingham Palace as the Queen was getting ready to visit Northern Ireland to mark her Golden Jubilee celebrations.

This is how Jean explained her motive for writing the letter: 'I have nothing against the Queen. I don't wish to put any marks on her visit but it's a chance for me to let her know that these two soldiers are still in the army, serving under her command.' She never received a reply, though her letter was published as a full-page advert in *The Irish News*.

Jean was an honest, non-sectarian woman. At no point in her campaign did she, Kelly or her husband, Peter Sr, express bitterness towards the British government or the British Army. Her criticism was directed at those who defended the two soldiers convicted of murdering her son. She was well served by her legal team, who guided her through a legal morass and helped her make her case to the world. When she died in September 2012, she was in her late sixties. There is a photo of her sitting in her home, holding a gold picture frame containing an image of the head of a crucified Christ alongside a photo of her son. The picture frame is in one hand and a pair of Peter's gold-coloured runners in the other. She has a quizzical look on her face, as if to say, 'I know my Peter was no saint, but he was my boy and he did not deserve to die.'

Jean McBride never gave up her fight for justice for her murdered son, although she was let down by successive British governments, Tory and Labour. She only wanted to bring accountability to his killers because he was the victim of their reckless behaviour. She also wanted to give hope to mothers and relatives of other victims who perished in the conflict. She was relentless in her battle against bureaucracy, the courts and, above all, the British military establishment. Like most female victims who lost loved ones on both sides of the religious divide, including British military families, she sought closure. Jean was not the only mother seeking justice for her son but her fearlessness, courage and determination made her a symbol for all mothers, sisters, wives and girlfriends who lost loved ones during the Troubles.

9

JUDGES' DAUGHTERS REMEMBER

APRIL 8, 1984 WAS THE fifth Sunday of Lent, two weeks before Easter in the Catholic liturgical calendar. It was a cool day and early morning fog had cleared over Belfast, leaving a little drizzle in its wake. By midmorning, the weather was spring-like. In seven days, palms would be distributed in churches to mark Jesus' entry into Jerusalem on a donkey and the start of Holy Week.

Judge Tom Travers lived in the Malone area of South Belfast. He was a regular at Sunday Mass with his family, sometimes in St Brigid's Church at Deravolgie Avenue near their home. However, being a Catholic judge was no defence against the Provisional IRA, which was on a crusade to kill as many members of the judiciary as it could, even if they were Catholic and liberal.

In 1972 the IRA stalked Resident Magistrate William Staunton, also a Catholic. I remember him from the time he was a barrister in the Belfast courts. He was a kind and thoughtful man and he was helpful when a young reporter like me sought his advice about criminal cases. The IRA in the Falls area knew William Staunton's morning schedule. On 24 January 1973 his car was followed as he was driving his teenage daughter, Sally-Ann, and her friends to St Dominic's Convent School on the Falls Road. As he slowed down outside the school, two assassins on a motorbike drew alongside and the pillion passenger shot him. He was rushed to the Royal Victoria Hospital across the road where he died from his wounds. He was the first member of the legal profession to die in that fashion but unfortunately, he would not be the last. The IRA leaders who ordered the killing were unconcerned about the horror the young girls in his car experienced. They did not just kill him; they killed innocence. He was the girls' protector, driving them to school in one of the city's most dangerous areas. The murder etched into their young minds would leave them with a horror that they would carry into adulthood.

Tom Travers was a devoted family man who knew William Staunton. Like him, he assumed that he was a potential IRA target, even though he had not been handling major cases arising from the conflict. As a judge, he had a reputation for being fair to all who came before him, showing no favour to any side, especially in cases of a political nature, but the IRA had its own measure of fairness. Travers was careful about his security, wondering whether attending the same church too often would create a pattern which would attract the attention of those who wished to do him harm. He was aware that another Catholic member of the judiciary, Judge William Doyle, had been murdered on 16 January 1973, after the IRA detected a predictable pattern in his behaviour. Doyle had been offered a twenty-four-hour protection detail but turned it down. Married with two children, he was shot after leaving midday Mass at St Brigid's, the same church Travers would attend from time to time. Since he was a regular church-goer, Doyle was an easy target for assassins. On 16 January he was sitting in his green Mercedes outside the church. Beside him was an elderly female churchgoer to whom he had promised a lift. They were waiting for his daughter Elizabeth to leave the church when two men suddenly tapped on the driver-side window. The moment Doyle rolled down the window, both men fired five times, killing him and seriously injuring his passenger. Shockingly, fifteen minutes earlier, while Doyle was receiving Communion, his killers were also at the altar receiving the Sacrament.

On hearing the gunshots, Elizabeth ran from the church and saw two men sprinting past her. They stopped briefly to hand their guns to a girl walking a dog. It was a classic IRA-style execution, using two gunmen and a female operative waiting nearby to take possession of the guns and return them to an arms dump. It meant that the gunmen, if stopped by police, would not be armed and hardly anyone would suspect a girl with a dog to be carrying weapons. Had Elizabeth Doyle been in the car on this fateful day, the killers would have shot her too, to prevent her becoming a witness.

The murders of his two fellow judges were no doubt on Tom Travers' mind a year later when it came time to go to Mass. He even wondered if he should attend Mass in St Brigid's or go to another church. A week earlier, he had gone to Mass in a different church, unaware that IRA assassins had been at St Brigid's waiting for him. Like Judge Doyle, he had refused twenty-four-hour police protection.

Travers' professional life at this time was rather uneventful, except for a judgment he had delivered weeks earlier when he remanded two suspects in custody for the murder of William McConnell, an assistant prisoner governor. A detective giving evidence against the two had described how they and a young female held two pensioners hostage in their home across the street from McConnell's house. The next morning, as McConnell was checking under his car for boobytraps, something he did every morning, the two male suspects ran across the street and shot him dead. They made off in the pensioners' car, driven by their female companion, who was not identified. The detective assured Judge Travers that he could link the suspects to the McConnell murder, so Travers rejected a defence plea to toss the evidence against the accused and remanded them in custody for trial for another judge to decide their fate. This may have been enough to seal Judge Travers' fate. Although the IRA already had him on a list to be assassinated, it seems likely that his decision in the McConnell murder case accelerated the IRA's decision to kill him. He was just another Catholic judge whom the IRA had decided was in the enemy's corner.

Tom Travers loved his wife and children, but he was especially fond of his oldest daughter, Mary, a twenty-two-year-old schoolteacher. On 8 April, the day he had doubts about going to Mass in St Brigid's, he put aside his concerns when he learned that she would be at the church because of work she was doing with her pupils. As Tom, his wife, Joan, and Mary were leaving the church after Mass, two killers opened fire. It was clear from the moment the first shot was fired that the IRA had given its assassins orders to wipe out the entire family. Had Tom's son and his other daughter, fourteen-year-old Ann, been with him, they too would have been targeted.

Mary was shot in the back, propelling her into her mother, sending both to the pavement. A second gunman shot Judge Travers six times. The gunman who shot Mary walked up to where she was lying across her mother. He pointed his gun at Joan's head and pulled the trigger twice but the gun jammed. Then both gunmen, who were wearing disguises, ran off.

Ann was at home, a short distance from the church, and heard the gunfire. Moments later, her brother rushed into their house, shouting that Mary and their father had been shot. Ann hurried with him to the scene to find Mary being loaded into an ambulance and their mother screaming for medics to help her husband, who was barely conscious.

Searching the neighbourhood a short time later, police came across nineteen-year-old Mary McArdle walking her dog. She was dressed like she belonged in the middle-class Malone district but something about her demeanour made them uneasy. They remembered how the killers of Judge Doyle were seen handing their guns to a girl with a dog. McArdle was nervous when questioned about her address and what she was doing in that part of the city. She was searched and two guns and a wig were found strapped to her thighs, concealed inside thick surgical stockings. Her job had been to remove the guns from the murder scene and transfer them to an IRA arms dump. One of the guns was a powerful police revolver, a Ruger .357 Magnum. It had been lost by a policeman during riots in the Catholic Andersonstown area of the city. Subsequent forensic testing confirmed that it had been used to kill Judge Doyle, William McConnell and Mary Travers, as well as members of the security forces.

Tom Travers made a miraculous recovery from his six bullet wounds. Had he been shot with the .357 Magnum, it is doubtful that he would have lived. When police showed him photos of known IRA gunmen, he picked out Joe 'The Hawk' Haughey, a tough, overweight, disreputable figure celebrated in the IRA's ranks. He was a well-known gunman and enforcer who was disciplined by the IRA at one stage for stealing the organisation's funds. He was banished from its ranks but welcomed back into the fold when he agreed to pay back the money he stole and after he killed several people, one being Queen's University lecturer Edgar Graham. He carried out that murder with another ruthless IRA figure, Frederick Scappaticci. Like Scappaticci, Haughey was a British military agent and was adept at deflecting any scrutiny of himself by members of the IRA who hunted moles in the organisation. He bolstered his image as a committed member of the IRA by killing people for them. 'The Hawk' was also deeply involved in racketeering and did business with the UDA in the Shankill and with James 'Pratt' Craig.

Travers' powerful eyewitness evidence would seal a conviction in most jurisdictions, especially coming from a witness who was a sitting judge, but 'The Hawk' had excellent legal support. Judge Travers had suffered an awful trauma, brushing shoulders with death and seeing the murder of his daughter. The experience took an immense emotional toll on him. During Haughey's trial, Travers' account of the fateful day was subjected to withering scrutiny and relentless cross-examination, which questioned the accuracy of his memory. Haughey's defence counsel was Desmond Boal, who was famous for his terrier-like interrogation of witnesses. Boal was one of those curious figures of the Troubles who represented terrorists on both sides. At times in the witness box, Judge Travers teared up under Boal's unrelenting scrutiny but never recanted his testimony about his shooter being 'The Hawk'. Nevertheless, Haughey was found not guilty by Judge Donald Bruce Murray, sitting alone without a jury. Apparently, Haughey had not left any forensic evidence on his gun and it seems Judge Murray was not persuaded by Judge Travers' eyewitness testimony. By any standards, it was a bizarre ruling by a fellow judge. Murray was later appointed a High Court judge, given a knighthood, made Justice of the Court of Appeal in London and appointed a member of the Privy Council advising the Queen. While Mary Travers' killer was not brought to justice, Mary McArdle, the girl walking the dog, did not fare so well. She was sentenced to life imprisonment.

The IRA predictably applauded the shooting of Tom Travers but claimed that the bullet which killed his daughter was one of the bullets which had gone through him and struck her. The IRA's attempt to deflect from the horror was obvious and was quickly exposed as a cynical piece of propaganda since its plan had been to wipe out the entire family.

Fourteen-year-old Ann Travers did not witness the actual shooting of her father and sister, but she was in the ambulance with Mary and saw her father lying bloodied on the pavement. Ann's initial shock and dismay was replaced by deep feelings of sadness and pain. She had to deal not only with her sister's death but with the pain and suffering her parents endured, especially her father, who understandably took on guilt for having his beloved daughter with him on the day of the attack. Ann could never unsee what she had witnessed. She adored and admired Mary, who had treated her to a restaurant meal when she received her first pay cheque. Ann's hero had died in an instant, leaving deep sorrow in her wake. She was not alone in her suffering. Many girls and women witnessed loved ones murdered and had to identify their bodies in cold mortuaries or funeral homes. Some gave evidence in courts where justice did not always prevail.

One disturbing element in the lives of the many women I spoke to was their frustration with the inability of the policing and judicial system to bring killers to justice or at the very least to name them. For Ann, growing up did not erase her memories of Mary's murder. Sometimes commemorations or perhaps a piece of music triggered feelings of sadness and loss. Survivors admit that they cannot control the world of the subconscious or alter images of the ugliness of past events. Those who suffer traumatic episodes often have nightmares and are prone to spells of depression.

When Ann Travers was asked how she coped with her loss, she rightly pointed out, 'I don't know how any of us really gets over it.' Grief became an element of her life which she could not dismiss. Those you lose are 'always there with you' she would say. She understood that the healthy way to deal with her grief was to get on with life and she did this by marrying and having five children. Nevertheless, like other victims of tragedy, she was a realist. There would always be those hidden triggers to return her to the day it all happened, no matter how hard she tried to ensure that only treasured memories defined the past.

Tom Travers suffered emotionally and physically; something his children had to share and observe. It was the same for their mother, who lay with Mary in her arms, bleeding and dying. Tom Travers' words in a letter to *The Irish Times* best illustrate how he really felt:

> May I say that on the day my lovely daughter was murdered her killer tried to murder my darling wife also. At that time Mary lay dying on her mum's breast, her gentle heart pouring its pure blood on to a dusty street in Belfast. The murderer's gun, which was pointed at my wife's head, misfired twice. Another gunman shot me six times. As he prepared to fire the first shot, I saw the look of hatred on his face, a face I will never forget.

It is shocking, on reading his words, to realise that his memory of a face he would never forget was insufficient to guarantee Haughey's conviction. Haughey would later die of pneumonia and he was never denounced by IRA leaders in Belfast who knew that he was an MI5/Special Branch asset, just as they knew that the paedophile and Markets area IRA commander 'Ruby' Davison and the torturer and murderer Scappaticci were also State agents. The fact that Haughey was a State agent leads me to wonder if the lack of forensic evidence on the gun he used to shoot Tom Travers was 'disappeared' to ensure his freedom so he could continue operating. It is not unreasonable to consider the possibility that Judge Murray, in dismissing Judge Travers' eyewitness testimony, acted on the advice of 'men in suits' from London.

As Ann Travers tried to forge a better future, an event occurred which provided an unexpected trigger, upsetting her and her family. Mary McArdle, the girl who had hidden the guns on her body, was released after serving fourteen years in prison. Her freedom was guaranteed, as it was for so many other terrorists, by the terms of the Good Friday Agreement. McArdle was welcomed back into the ranks of Sinn Féin and in 2011 she was made a special adviser to Sinn Féin's Culture Minister in the new Northern Ireland Assembly. Like the 'beauty queen' bomber, Martina Anderson, and many other former IRA operatives who served time for terrorist offences, she ended up in a good job. Her appointment, however, sparked controversy. When asked about the murder of Mary Travers, McArdle replied that it was a 'tragic mistake'. Ann was outraged, making her anger known in a local BBC interview:

> Mistake? Mistake? My sister was murdered. There were two gunmen, one standing over my dad shooting him and one who shot my sister in the back and attempted to murder my mother but the bullets jammed in the gun. The fact that she [McArdle] calls my sister's murder a mistake, well, that day two gunmen went with two guns, so if they were just planning to kill my dad, why did they go out with two guns? They knew my dad wasn't armed. After 27 years I would have thought I would be able to speak about my sister's murder factually and without grief but when I heard of Mary McArdle's appointment last Thursday it did something to me which I just have not been able to contain the grief it brought back. Rather than Mary McArdle and Sinn Féin saying her death was a mistake, what they should be saying is Mary Travers' murder is an embarrassment which has come back to haunt them.

Ann confronted the controversy head on, forcing Sinn Féin to transfer McArdle out of her new post. Ann also began devoting her time to survivors, working with excellent organisations like the South East Fermanagh Foundation (SEFF), set up to address the needs of victims as well as represent their interests and draw attention to their individual and respective experiences.

Ann's brother, Tom, who was also in the ambulance when they took Mary to hospital, later emigrated to Australia. Nevertheless, he felt compelled to speak out when news about the McArdle appointment reached him. He shared his thoughts with the *Belfast Telegraph*:

> In 2011 we are told to put the past behind us and move on. I go home every year to visit my family and notice the murals to the hunger strikers are lovingly maintained. My sister Mary did not starve herself to death. She was murdered by those who now claim to be the 'peacemakers'. Mary has no mural. However, her memory is as alive to me now as it was 27 years ago when I travelled with her bloodied body in the ambulance. It is the same for the other victims of the Troubles.

McArdle served fourteen years for Mary Travers' murder, but murder squad detectives believed that she was also involved in other IRA operations. Her name was on notepaper in the pocket of one of the men who killed Assistant Prison Governor McConnell. She was a Cumann na mBan operative and assisted several IRA units by providing them with weapons and returning those weapons to a dump after killings. She also conducted surveillance on potential targets. She and 'The Hawk' refused to divulge the name of the gunman who had shot Mary Travers, sending a bullet into her spine which ended her life. However, this gunman was known to the authorities. I have always been puzzled as to why he was never brought to justice, but sometimes in this dirty war decisions were made in the shadows not to pursue some of the killers because they were also in the pay of the State.

Friends of Judge Travers felt that he was betrayed by some of his colleagues. He reportedly told those close to him that he had not been offered the support he expected and that some in his profession did not believe his testimony about Haughey being the shooter. Those who attended Haughey's trial felt that Travers held his own under Desmond Boal's relentless questioning of his memory of the shooting.

Boal once asked the RUC Chief Constable to investigate me after he read what I wrote in *The Dirty War* about a solicitor who often hired him to represent members of the UVF. I revealed that this solicitor was a 'bag man' who received cash from the terrorist organisation for legal representation. I made it clear that this information was confirmed in a Special Branch surveillance report about the solicitor. Even though I did not name the solicitor in the book, Boal knew to whom I was referring. He wanted me charged with possession of classified information to unlock my sources. A senior police officer was dispatched to my home to ask me how I had come into possession of a highly classified Special Branch file. I offered the policeman a glass of Bushmills whiskey and told him we could talk about anything but this matter. I never heard any more about the issue.

Judge Travers told his family and friends that Desmond Boal was 'a man who would do anything for a briefcase of cash'. This comment appeared to confirm that Travers believed Boal was specifically chosen to defend a British intelligence asset and was well rewarded to do so. Even with his murky past, Boal was a formidable lawyer whose flamboyant courtroom skills were respected and admired by everyone in the legal profession. When he died in April 2015, his family received a condolence note from the Travers family. It was not, as some media outlets reported, sent by Joan Travers, who was ill at the time, but by her daughter, Ann.

***

While all IRA killings of judges, and in some cases family members, were despicable, one of the murders stood out as particularly shocking and shameful. It was the murder of another Catholic judge, Rory Conaghan, the father of two girls, Dee (9) and Mary (17), who was in her last year of school.

This photo of sixteen-year-old Bernie O'Hanlon was taken in 1974, weeks before a loyalist bomb in Dublin's Talbot Street scarred her for life.

Paula Fox with her father, Leonard, a former IRA operative who was murdered by the UDA on 24 September 1992.

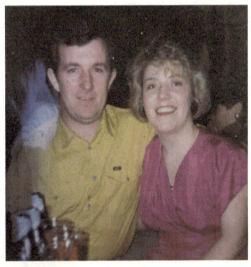

Tracey Coulter and her late husband, Stevie 'Top Gun' McKeag, a prolific UDA assassin. He died of a drugs overdose on 24 September 2000, weeks after Tracey's father, Jackie Coulter, a UDA brigadier, was murdered by the UVF.

Rosemary Nelson, a mother and well-known solicitor, was blown up in her car on 15 March 1999. (Courtesy of Pacemaker)

Mairead Farrell was thirty-two when she was shot dead on the streets of Gibraltar on 6 March 1988. (Courtesy of Pacemaker)

Carol and her husband, Simon Ware, enjoying married bliss on 9 April 1991. Three months later Simon was blown up while leading a patrol in South Armagh.

Tracy Doak was a highly respected member of the RUC when, on 20 May 1985, she and three of her colleagues were blown up by an IRA bomb.

The late Jean McBride, a relentless campaigner for justice for her son, Peter, shot dead by soldiers on 4 September 1992. She is seen here with a photo of him and a pair of his favourite shoes.

Martina Anderson, sometimes referred to as the 'beauty queen' bomber, joined the IRA in Derry in her late teens. She was an elusive figure until she and an IRA bomb team were caught in an MI5 sting operation in Glasgow in 1985. (Photo by David Iliff. License: CC BY-SA 3.0)

The late Vera McVeigh with her favourite photo of her eighteen-year-old son, Columba, who was abducted, murdered and secretly buried by the IRA. His remains have never been found. (*Irish News*)

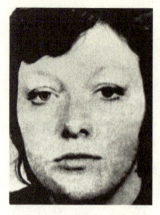

The late Dolours Price. She and her sister, Marian, were student activists who joined the PIRA and became part of 'The Unknowns'. (Courtesy of Images4Media)

Caroline Moreland (34), a mother of three murdered by the IRA in 1994. She was blackmailed into working for British intelligence, and questions remain about the identity of a lover who may have been a senior IRA figure likely to know why she was murdered weeks before the IRA ended its campaign of violence. (Courtesy of Pacemaker)

Bernadette McAliskey and her daughter, Róisín, carrying the coffin of Dominic McGlinchey, former INLA chief. Bernadette described him at the 'finest republican of all' when delivering a graveside oration. (Courtesy of PA Images/Alamy Stock Photo)

For the Conaghan sisters, the morning of 16 September 1974 was a typical weekday. They shared a family breakfast before going upstairs to their bedrooms to dress for school. By 8.30 a.m. Mary was in her room and Dee had gone downstairs. Suddenly, Mary heard what she thought was a bomb going off. She ran downstairs screaming, 'Watch your eyes,' believing the major risk to her family would be flying shrapnel. Her response was emblematic of the reaction of a young girl who lived in a violent city. When she reached the hallway, she saw her father lying on the floor and Dee standing over him.

Judge Conaghan had heard the doorbell ringing and thought Mary must have already left for school but was returning because she had forgotten something. He opened the front door with Dee by his side. They were confronted by a man dressed in a standard General Post Office jacket with a badge on his lapel bearing the number 288. Over his shoulder was a postbag.

'Is this Mr McGonigal's house?' he asked.

Before Conaghan could reply, the bogus postman drew a gun from the bag, shot the judge at point-blank range and ran off. A neighbour who saw him later described the gunman as aged eighteen, 5ft 5in in height, with bushy hair. Dee, on the other hand, thought that he was twenty-eight or twenty-nine, 5ft 6in, with a small beard. He was not wearing a wig, she later said, because she could see his hairline and his black curly hair rising upwards. She also noticed his big round eyes and large front teeth, which she said were in good condition.

Decades later, in an interview with *Irish Times* journalist Róisín Ingle, Mary recalled, 'As the gun came out, my father shouted at the top of his voice, "I've been done; call a priest!"' Judge Conaghan must have realised in that terrible moment that he was facing certain death.

Conaghan's wife, Gabrielle, had been in the kitchen with his sister when the gunman opened fire. She hit an alarm, which activated a siren in the local police station, and ran to the hallway. She saw her husband lying on the floor and realised that he was still breathing. Nevertheless, his condition suggested that he was dying, so she whispered a prayer in his ear before rushing to ask her neighbour to summon a priest from nearby St Brigid's to give her husband the Last Rites.

While Gabrielle ran to the neighbour's, Mary held her father in her arms, pleading with him not to die. Meanwhile, Dee, who had witnessed her father being gunned down, was standing nearby in shock. As the last breath left their father's body, the two girls covered their father with sheets and waited for help to arrive. Police and ambulance services were on their way.

Hours later the IRA issued a statement; they claimed that they had killed both Judge Rory Conaghan and Resident Magistrate Martin McBirney on the same morning in Belfast because they were agents of a corrupt judicial system. Both men were considered liberal, honourable and fair by friends and legal colleagues. Perhaps the person who wrote the IRA statement did not realise that it was Judge Conaghan who jailed the Rev. Ian Paisley and his associate Major Ronald Bunting on 25 March 1969 for leading a counter-demonstration against a lawful civil rights march in Armagh in December 1968. Paisley was angry because he had to spend time as a common criminal in Belfast's Crumlin Road Gaol. He was released weeks before his sentence was completed because of a general amnesty for those guilty of political crimes. What the public did not know was that Paisley had written a personal letter to the Northern Ireland Prime Minister, James Chichester-Clarke, threatening a 'conflagration' if he was not released. Chichester-Clarke knew that Paisley did not make idle threats, so he introduced the amnesty to free him.

Despite a claim by the IRA's press office in Dublin, late on the day of Judge Conaghan's death, that the IRA had warned him several times that his life was in danger if he continued working as a judge, Gabrielle told investigators this was a lie. Her husband had never mentioned threats from the Provisional IRA. Instead, it was retaliation from loyalist paramilitaries and Paisleyites that the family had feared. In the aftermath of his jailing of Paisley, Mary remembers that she and her parents were genuinely scared of reprisals from Paisleyite thugs because Paisley was a powerful figure whose words terrified those who opposed him.

The IRA leaders who condemned Judge Conaghan to die in front of his young daughter did not know, or did not care, about his fairness or that he, like the other Catholic judges they were murdering, was a man of conscience and integrity. For example, before his death and much to the displeasure of the British government and unionist leaders, he awarded damages to sixteen Catholic men who had been arrested during the 1971 internment swoop and were subjected to unusual and degrading treatment under interrogation. Rory Conaghan judged everyone equally under the law, showing no favour to any grouping or individual. What the IRA did not understand was that men like Judge Conaghan believed the judicial system required reform, which could be better achieved by working within it.

The IRA condemned Conaghan's daughters to live with the horror of witnessing the brutal death of their father. Some of the women I contacted when writing this book had similar experiences but found it too painful to recount their stories for me because revisiting the past would have opened raw wounds, bringing back terrible memories. Mary Conaghan, who later became a bereavement counsellor, acknowledged to *The Irish Times* that the pain never vanishes: 'It may all be in the past for the perpetrators, but this is our present. Our feelings never go away. I want to speak for my father, to honour his memory. He was a good man. A man who lived for the rule of law and for justice, and a man who could have contributed so much more to Northern Ireland had his life not been cut short at the age of 54.'

The experience of watching her father's murder left Dee very traumatised. She later admitted that she 'switched off everything in life'. I found her comments, made years later to the *Belfast News Letter*, a powerfully sad testimony of a personal tragedy: 'The only part of me that was kept alive was through drama and when we moved to Derry, I went to see a woman who would do drama all day with me – poems, character sketches, and it was such a lifeline for me. It kind of saved me.'

After finding drama such a transformative element when trying to reclaim her life after her father's murder, Dee would go on to form the Stage Beyond theatre company to cater for the young and disabled who lacked opportunities in the arts, especially in drama, in Northern Ireland. The company has become a great success and has gone from strength to strength. Mary and Dee, like Ann Travers and many other victims, have dedicated their lives to helping others deal with personal trauma. It is, I believe, one of the resoundingly positive characteristics of the way many victims, men and women, have addressed their pain.

No one was brought to justice for the murder of Judge Conaghan and this troubled his wife, Gabrielle, who died aged eighty-three in 2009. It continues to upset his daughters. It is an issue which troubles me too, because Special Branch knew most of the senior IRA active service operatives in 1974 and had agents within the IRA's Northern Command, especially within the Belfast Brigade. It struck me, when examining some of the major unresolved murders in the 1970s and 1980s, that intelligence on killers and their crimes did not always mean they would be pursued or prosecuted, especially if they were Special Branch/MI5 or Military Intelligence assets. One security source suggested to me that Judge Conaghan's decision to award damages to those sixteen Catholic men 'would not have gone down well in certain quarters', meaning with the security forces, but that does not support a theory that the security forces had him killed. An unanswered question is whether Special Branch knew the identity of the bogus postman who murdered Judge Conaghan and his two associates (because IRA hit squads operated with two male shooters and a female to dispose of their weapon) and, if so, why was no one held accountable? Victims are entitled to answers and there are organisations who have those answers in their files.

In 1998 the RUC carried out a review of the intelligence it received in 1975, the year after Judge Conaghan was murdered, and concluded that there should be no further action due to a lack of new information. So what information was available to police investigators in 1975? According to the HET, the security authorities had no prior intelligence that Judge Conaghan was about to be killed, so the police could not have prevented the crime. Such a declaration by HET must be matched against the fact that its personnel lacked access to the most sensitive Special Branch/British military and MI5 files covering early 1970s' violence. HET detectives assigned to Judge Conaghan's murder also stated that between September and December 1974, seventeen members of the Provisional IRA were arrested and questioned about the murders of Conaghan and Magistrate Martin McBirney. Police believed there were five suspects who were tied to the murder of Conaghan. By 1975 two of the five were interned, a third was 'living outside' Northern Ireland and there was 'no record' of what happened with the other two. The man 'living outside' Northern Ireland was, according to RUC files, 'not specifically' involved in the killing.

In 1975 the RUC received additional intelligence, identifying eleven suspects involved in the murders of Judge Conaghan and Magistrate McBirney. It appears that in total, twenty-six suspects were questioned about the murders. Nine were released without charge; nine were charged with terrorist offences. This was a time when huge arrest sweeps were conducted in which suspects were held for days and interrogated with the investigative focus on terrorism generally and not necessarily on a particular murder. It was a haphazard process. None of those arrested in this instance were charged with the murder of Judge Conaghan. In fact, only one IRA operative, Edward Maguire, was charged with murder and it was the murder of McBirney. An eyewitness picked him out of a line-up. He had been doing construction work in a house close to McBirney's home and, days before the murder, had asked a neighbour if the magistrate still lived at the address. On 26 April 1977 Maguire received a thirty-year life sentence. He denied that he was involved in the murder.

HET staff told the Conaghan family that the murders of Judge Conaghan and Magistrate McBirney were sanctioned at a very high level of the Provisional IRA command structure. This was, of course, true but not entirely revelatory. The murders of judges, some of them Catholics, were part of a major, co-ordinated plan involving several IRA active service units under the immediate command of the Belfast Brigade. The murders were all carried out with precision, indicating surveillance and planning. They had the approval of the IRA's Army Council and its Northern Command, led by Martin McGuinness. They were also approved by the Sinn Féin leadership.

Judge Conaghan was a man who knew that his work carried serious risks. Mary says he insisted he would never give in to terrorism. She admits that he could be hard-headed but this, for him, was a matter of principle. He was a liberal who tried to be impartial, just like Magistrate McBirney. Judge Conaghan expected his critics to understand that he was a principled judge, even when he became involved with Diplock courts, highly politicised trials used to handle terrorist cases where a judge sat without a jury. He had several run-ins with the British government and was not timid about speaking his mind when he felt that the judicial system was being over-politicised and, therefore, compromised. Those who were close to him admired his willingness to take on powerful people, even figures within his own

Catholic Church. From the Bench, he ruled against a Catholic Church decision to withhold the Sacrament of Confirmation from Catholic children who were taught in Protestant rather than Catholic schools.

When he was asked about his lack of security, he replied that his plan was always, if possible, to remain in 'a State of Grace'. It meant having God in his soul and being free from mortal sin. He went to Mass and Confession regularly and was considered by friends an 'intelligent, moderate Catholic' who was not averse to criticising his Church when he felt that it was failing his society. His call for a priest to give him the Last Rites as he was dying was the plea of a man who was determined to be in a State of Grace when meeting his Maker.

After the murders of Judge Conaghan and Magistrate McBirney, the government ruled that it was mandatory for judges and magistrates to have twenty-four-hour security details.

10

MARKED FOR DEATH

A CUP OF TEA AND a slice of toast with a copy of *The Irish News* open at the obituary pages was how my Grandmother Clarke began her day. Catholics throughout Northern Ireland relied on the paper to inform them of the death of a friend or distant relative. It was a time when people did not have mobile phones or access to social media. When I worked in *The Irish News* from 1968 to 1973 as a rookie reporter, the death notices helped sell the paper.

With the advent of the Troubles, nothing much changed, but *The Irish News* was fully committed to reporting in detail the growing violence throughout Northern Ireland. I spent many days and nights in the middle of violent confrontations between the British Army and rioters, and many lonely mornings visiting back alleys where the bodies of victims of sectarian killers were dumped. Those alleys were known locally as entries: dark, dismal places sandwiched between the backyards of tiny terraced homes. Stray cats roamed the tops of the entry walls, leaving the ground to skinny, half-fed dogs, mice and rats. As a child, I was warned by my mother to stay out of entries and this was before killers decided that they were ideal places to dispose of the brutalised bodies of their victims.

Like my grandmother, Rosemary Nelson liked to start her day with a newspaper and a cup of tea or coffee. On the morning of 15 March 1999 her husband, Paul, left for work in a taxi and she was home alone. Her teenage sons, Gavin (13) and Christopher (11), were on school trips to Europe and her youngest, nine-year-old Sarah, was already on her way to school with classmates. It was one of those cold mornings and Rosemary was a little under the weather as she reached for a box of tissues. Paul told her that he would ring her later to check if she felt better, but it was already 9.30 a.m. and she had no plans to leave for work right away even though she was a busy solicitor. Hot coffee and an aspirin would do the trick, she thought. Anyway, she had to read *The Irish News*. Paul had said there were two stories about her in it, one of them about the way she drew comparisons between the attitudes of some members of the RUC and racist policemen in Britain.

Some of us are naturally fearless, but those who are fearless in a society at war are special human beings. While fearlessness can be an attribute, it can also be a dangerous liability if it brings a person into proximity with those who will kill for a cause or revenge. When fearlessness derives from a commitment to pursue justice, it is found in very special individuals. Rosemary Nelson, *née* Magee, was such a person. She lived within the law, respected it and acquired powerful enemies when she was laser-focused on defending her clients. At forty, she was a success story with a thriving law practice in her home town, Lurgan. Most of her clients were from the Catholic nationalist and republican communities in the area nicknamed 'the Murder Triangle', comprising Lurgan, Craigavon and Portadown, all bitterly divided towns in which sectarianism was rampant.

Rosemary Nelson was an instantly recognisable personality because she never shirked from responding to journalists' questions when she handled high-profile cases. Of medium height, with blonde hair, spectacles and a girlish smile, she looked more like an academic than a busy lawyer. She was in constant demand because she was ready to take on the most difficult cases, often related to the actions of members of the RUC, the British Army and the British government. There was little about the law which she did not grasp, especially when it concerned the human rights of the individual. Many of her friends in the legal profession would not have swapped their lives for hers, but after running her practice for ten years, she was a fixture in the daily legal life of Lurgan.

I have met only a few people like her over the years. Some were detectives, others were priests who gave the Last Rites to men about to be executed by the IRA, and then there were medics who ran into danger to transport the injured and dying to local hospitals through streets littered with the detritus of conflict. All of them had one thing in common, namely overarching respect for human life and for their professions.

On that Monday morning in 1999, Rosemary Nelson retired to her bedroom and dressed as elegantly as she always did, her midlength hair combed to perfection. She had not slept well for several nights because there had been considerable British military activity in the vicinity of her home during the weekend. She was accustomed to helicopters flying overhead, but it was particularly disquieting when they were over her house after midnight or when they landed in fields behind it, as she had seen happen on one occasion. Local police files would later show proof of excessive levels of military and RUC activity in her neighbourhood over a period of weeks at this time, for which there has never been a proper official explanation.

Rosemary was unaware that specialist surveillance teams run by MI5/Special Branch and the British military had been carrying out an extensive surveillance operation between 10 and 14 March. For those running such operations, it was crucial to ensure that they were not compromised by ordinary army or police patrols straying into the area when it was under close surveillance. To make sure this did not happen, a blanket OOB instruction was issued to local police and soldiers to keep the area 'pristine'. In other words, they were to stay away.

This special operation had ended on the afternoon of Sunday 14 March. It is, therefore, surprising that the OOB order remained in force, which meant that there was no normal surveillance of the Nelson property and no military or police security in the vicinity of her home on Monday 15 March. For the sake of argument, if the goal of a person or persons in the State security apparatus was to leave her vulnerable, this lack of protection achieved its goal. What is not surprising, given what we now know, is that all documents related to the surveillance operation and its OOB protocols have since vanished. More than likely they were shredded, a common practice in Northern Ireland's dirty war. However, several documents were known to confirm that during the operation, Rosemary's silver BMW was parked in her driveway. This tends to imply that there was some secret surveillance of her house.

I spoke to a security source about the events of that weekend and he offered the following explanation: 'A police/mil op in progress was likely in place to trap a high-value IRA target known to transit the area. An OOB would have kept the area sterile to make sure the target believed he was not being observed and to allow for his arrest or his elimination by a specialist team. This is problematic because Rosemary Nelson was a number-one loyalist terror target because of her work as a Roman Catholic lawyer, so it would be unthinkable to leave her exposed without any security. It would have been incompetence at the very least.'

What would have surprised many was that Nelson had already been, for several years, the target of British intelligence and that she was the victim of surveillance of various kinds, including the placing of bugs in her phones and her office. This was known to Special Branch and MI5 and presumably to the occupant in 10 Downing Street, Tony Blair. A valid question is whether he or Secretary of State for Northern Ireland Mo Mowlam provided MI5 with the authority to bug Rosemary's office and phones. Since it was a classified decision, we will never know the range of options MI5 and RUC Special Branch were given to investigate the lawyer. Mowlam was considered a champion of social justice, so this would, one suspects, have been a tough decision for her, unless Special Branch, which briefed MI5 about Rosemary, provided Mowlam with explosive material to justify its three-year surveillance of her.

Why did Special Branch have Rosemary under surveillance for so long and did MI5 tell Mowlam about this or the fact that the Branch had bugged her office? I doubt Mowlam was presented with all the facts. MI5 received RUC Special Branch reports about Rosemary and knew that she was a surveillance target. There was, however, no legally justifiable reason for such scrutiny of her life, personal or professional. And no one in the RUC or MI5 asked what the Branch was up to or why it felt free to tap her phones. I was told by a former Branch officer that she was not the only Catholic lawyer being 'watched'.

I believe, from my enquiries, that MI5 told Mowlam it had evidence that Rosemary was having an extramarital affair with her IRA client, Colin Duffy, who was a high-value security-force target, and that she had rented him one of her properties in Lurgan. This information, and a host of bogus, salacious claims about Rosemary's character, were presented to Mowlam. It still begs the question: what legal right did Special Branch have to watch her for so long? For example, they never produced evidence to support their surveillance of her, and neither did the Criminal Investigation Department (CID), the RUC detective branch or MI5.

We may never know if Rosemary was aware of the years of secret surveillance of her or whether she felt that it was inevitable she would be on Special Branch's radar because of some of those she represented. The prospect was probably not foremost in her thoughts as she finished putting on her make-up that chilly March morning. She was still feeling a bit under the weather when Nuala McCann, her personal assistant and close friend, arrived, as she did most mornings. When she sat at the kitchen table for a cup of tea, Rosemary laughed about her newspaper photo before praising the coverage of how she had delivered stinging criticism of the RUC during a meeting with Prime Minister Tony Blair and Catholic residents of Garvaghy Road in Portadown.

It was 12.30 p.m. when Rosemary and Nuala decided to drive to work. Nuala left first, expecting Rosemary to overtake her in her zippy BMW. Instead, at the bottom of a hill where Rosemary would normally make a turn, a mercury-tilt-switch bomb detonated when Rosemary braked. The device had been planted beneath the driver's side of the car, sending the blast upwards through the driver's seat. Nuala rushed back and found Rosemary's car a crumpled heap in a hedgerow, filled with black smoke, and her friend barely alive. Rosemary had been pushed backwards in her seat by the explosion. Nuala ran to a nearby house to contact emergency services and when she got back to the car, a nurse who lived nearby was tending to Rosemary. A local doctor soon arrived on the scene and made every effort to stabilise the injured lawyer. It took a considerable time for the fire service to arrive to cut her from her car and rush her to hospital, where she died mid-afternoon.

Disturbing reports later surfaced about police and soldiers making fun of Rosemary as she was being cut from the wreck. They knew that this was the lawyer some senior RUC officers referred to as an 'immoral woman' because she had called them out for behaviour unacceptable in a modern police force. She had previously been physically assaulted by police officers and had been subjected to verbal abuse by others. During a street protest, one policeman had hit her with his baton. She had also been receiving threatening calls and letters directed at her and at her family. She filed an official complaint with the Independent Commission for Police Complaints, describing systemic abuse by policemen, but the commission did not handle her complaint impartially or offer her security.

Members of the security forces were aware of a loyalist leaflet circulating in the Murder Triangle towns naming Rosemary as a former IRA bomber. She often received anonymous, threatening notes like the one which warned her, 'We have you in our sights, you republican bastard. We will teach you a lesson, RIP.' She deeply resented claims that she was involved in paramilitary activities.

Even though the RUC knew that she was a terrorist target, they denied her adequate protection. She was left vulnerable to her killers, who had detailed knowledge of her movements and must have known that security had been withdrawn from the area surrounding her home and its vicinity, making it easy for them to booby-trap the car in her driveway. But how did this mother of three become such a thorn in the side of loyalist paramilitaries, the RUC and British intelligence?

Rosemary Nelson was not always a terrorist target. When she first set up her practice, down the block from Lurgan police station, she proved to be a very capable advocate for women dealing with domestic violence issues. She was also an expert at handling conveyancing matters. Police in Lurgan referred women to her and some even asked her for legal advice. She quickly built up a reputation as the go-to solicitor because of her success rate for pleading cases in court. She was not only thorough, she was a hard worker who gave many of her clients more of her time than was customary. It was perhaps inevitable that, sooner or later, her legal successes would draw her into cases related to the Troubles.

Soon, she was being asked to represent republicans when they were arrested and interrogated in Lurgan police station or in Gough Barracks in Armagh. It did not sit well with the RUC or its Special

Branch that men they deemed to be a threat to the State were getting expert legal advice from Nelson. Her successes in court also angered MI5 and the FRU, which ran a dirty war in the shadows. As a lawyer, she was frustrated by RUC interference with her work. For example, they would deny her access to clients and not allow her to be present when her clients were being processed. According to her, the RUC was unable to separate her from the alleged crimes of her clients.

After receiving so many threats she could have decided to stop representing republicans, but she was a committed lawyer and if people sought her help and she felt that they deserved it, she would not hesitate to represent them. Some officers among the RUC top brass referred to her as 'that republican bitch', others as 'the whore'. These men were instrumental in creating a dangerous narrative about her throughout the police force, which also found its way into loyalist paramilitary ranks.

Her relationship with one client, Colin Duffy, dragged her into the limelight and made her a pariah in security and loyalist circles. Duffy was a prominent Provisional who almost died in 1990 when he was twenty-two years old. He was leaving Lurgan police station with two other republicans after signing bail documents when the three were ambushed. One of the trio, Sam Marshall, was killed, and Duffy was wounded, though not seriously. The attack was mounted by members of the UVF led by its notorious gunman Robin 'The Jackal' Jackson. He was linked to rogue elements of the security forces, especially in the UDR, as well as to Special Branch and the FRU. By all accounts, the ambush in which Duffy was shot was made possible because of collusion between the security forces and loyalist terrorists.

In 1995 Duffy was locked up for the murder of John Lyness, a member of the UDR, but Rosemary Nelson got him off on a technicality. In 1997 he was again charged with murdering two policemen and she persuaded the judge to drop the charges due to a lack of credible evidence. The Duffy cases cemented her reputation in the eyes of her enemies as a tool of the IRA, but this was not unusual, especially in loyalist circles. There were whispering campaigns by members of the police and army about lawyers when they successfully defended republicans. When Nelson arrived at police stations to speak to clients, members of the police and military tried to intimidate her, telling her clients to pass threats from them to her.

Nelson's relationship with Duffy was a complicated one. I believe that as a lawyer she overstepped the professional line in her dealings with him by renting him one of her properties in Lurgan. It was a foolhardy thing to do. If he needed housing, she must have known from her legal training that she could seek an emergency review on his behalf from the Northern Ireland Housing Executive. By becoming a landlord to a well-known republican, she behaved unethically. At the very least, as a conflict of interest, it bolstered suspicion in security agencies that she was compromised. It further provided her enemies with the opportunity to spread salacious gossip about her and Duffy; gossip that leaked into the RUC ranks, as well as among loyalist and republican prisoners.

The Duffy legal saga was not the only one to bring down the wrath of loyalists upon Rosemary Nelson. The residents of Garvaghy Road, a Catholic enclave in Portadown that was part of the route of sectarian Orange parades every July, asked her to represent them in trying to persuade the authorities to re-route the parade. The parades issue was a tribal one, which became a major focus of anger on both sides of the religious divide. Catholics had no say about Orange Order parade routes, where bands played anti-Catholic tunes and marchers sang vile anti-Catholic songs while passing through their streets. The Orange Order and the Unionist government, which ran Northern Ireland for fifty years, regarded the parades as a symbol of Protestant triumphalism and marches through Catholic districts firmly made this point. Times, however, were changing and Catholics were no longer prepared to have such naked bigotry imposed on them. Their view was that the Orange Order had every right to march to celebrate King William's victory in the Battle of the Boyne but it should do so in its own districts or on public thoroughfares that did not traverse Catholic districts. The proposal upset unionists, especially those who called themselves loyalists, including members of paramilitary groups like the UVF, UDA and LVF.

The bitterness was particularly apparent in Portadown, where Orangemen gathered annually in Drumcree churchyard before marching with their bands and followers along the Catholic Garvaghy Road, whose residents now had a fearless advocate in Rosemary Nelson. In unionist circles, she became the face of their opposition.

Another shocking legal case occurred that further immersed Nelson in controversy and upset loyalists as well as the RUC, from its top brass to street-level constables. On the night of 27 April 1997 Robert Hamill (25) was walking through Market Street in Portadown with friends, their destination a Catholic social club, when they were attacked by a large group of men described as loyalists. The incident was observed by some policemen who stood idly by while Robert was beaten and kicked unconscious. He died twelve days later in hospital. A short time before the fatal assault, a man warned the police that Robert and his companions, including two girls, would be coming by shortly and alerted them to the presence of a gang of loyalist thugs gathered nearby. Robert's beating, which lasted about ten minutes, was savage, yet the police failed to intervene. A young man with Robert was also set upon and knocked unconscious, but he recovered hours later in hospital. The RUC later issued a statement claiming that there had been a riot between rival gangs. This was a lie designed to deflect from the failure of policemen at the scene to intervene.

After a public outcry, six young men were arrested but only one was charged with his role in Robert's death. The other five were released. The person charged with murder was subsequently cleared and given a four-year sentence for 'affray'. The Hamill family turned to Rosemary Nelson to represent them, a move which antagonised loyalists. In a legal pleading, Rosemary drew parallels between Robert's murder and that of black teenager Stephen Lawrence in London in 1993. He was killed by a group of young white men while waiting for a bus. There was clear evidence of police racism in the handling of the London case when no charges were initially brought against the perpetrators. In 1998 Sir William MacPherson, who headed a public inquiry into the Lawrence murder, pronounced the London Metropolitan Police Force 'incompetent and institutionally racist' and many people seemed to agree with him.

Rosemary directed the same accusation at the RUC, not just because of its handling of the Robert Hamill murder but for its core behaviour towards her, her clients and other lawyers. On the day she died, one of the articles on the *Irish News* front page published a critique by her of institutionalised bias within the RUC.

A week after her death, on 23 March 1999, the US House of Representatives of the 106th Congress, in its first session of the year, condemned the brutal murder of Rosemary Nelson and urged the protection of defence lawyers in Northern Ireland. A bipartisan resolution called on the British government to launch an independent inquiry into her murder. The resolution described her as 'a champion of due process rights and a conscientious and courageous attorney'. It added: 'She became an international advocate for the rule of law and the right of the accused to comprehensive defence and an impartial hearing. For this she was often the subject of harassment and intimidation. For her service to her clients, she paid the ultimate price with her life – the victim of a car bomb.' It further stated that, in the last decade of her life, she knew the risks she faced.

There have been several investigations into Nelson's death over the years, but the question of who killed her remains unanswered. Billy Wright, a notorious loyalist hitman, was one of her enemies. Rumours circulated about his involvement in advocating her assassination. She once described a disturbing encounter with him to friends. He had stopped alongside her in a police station and whispered in her ear that she was 'not long for this earth'.

Tall and rangy, with a shaved head and occasional thin moustache, Wright was an inflammatory UVF figure whose stomping ground was the Murder Triangle, especially Lurgan and Portadown. In the autumn of 1996 I interviewed him when writing my book *God and the Gun* and found him deceptively articulate, co-operative and soft-spoken. His reputation as a brutal killer was legendary in loyalist and republican circles and so too was his penchant for professing weird evangelical principles about walking with God and the Devil.

Rosemary Nelson sensed Wright's darkness when they first met face to face. He bent down and whispered in her ear that she had better watch herself and her children because he knew where they lived. This troubled her and she referred this threat to the RUC, but they ignored it even though the upper echelons of the security agencies knew that Wright did not make threats he could not act on.

Wright was no longer of concern to her when he appeared in court in January 1997, charged with threatening to kill a female witness in an assault case against one of his associates. He was later found guilty and sent to Maghaberry Prison where he realised that his life was under threat from republicans. The peace process was gaining momentum and the British government was thrilled that he was behind bars because he was a powerful voice in opposition to peace talks. British intelligence feared his potential to upend the peace process if he were on the loose. After a month in Maghaberry, he requested a transfer to the highly secure Maze Prison where he expected to be safe from IRA retaliation. He arrived on 26 April and was dead before the end of the year, murdered by members of the INLA.

This loyalist bogeyman who had threatened Rosemary Nelson's life was dead, but a purported prison diary of his revealed that she had been on his mind. However, the diary has been withheld from the media and questions remain about its authenticity. So, those who argue that Billy Wright masterminded the assassination of Rosemary Nelson before he died have little information on which to base this claim, though it is conceivable that he could have told his murder squads in the Murder Triangle to kill her. Her murder was claimed by the Red Hand Defenders, a cover name used by loyalist paramilitary groups, especially Wright's LVF, when they did not wish to openly declare their responsibility for shootings or bombings.

Wright's animosity towards Rosemary Nelson could have encouraged his followers to proceed with a plan to assassinate her if they knew it had been something he had planned to do when he was freed. The UVF and UDA denied involvement and reliable sources within those groups appear to confirm this, leaving Wright's LVF hitmen as the perpetrators. Many of them, like Wright, were tools of British intelligence. This, however, was a well-planned assassination, suggesting an element of collusion between terrorists and some British intelligence agency.

The RUC have since admitted on the record that there was no evidence that Rosemary Nelson was immoral, but the Special Branch file on her has conveniently vanished. It is easy to get trapped in a morass of gossip and unfounded allegations, but they do not alter the basic question of who murdered her and why her killers have never been brought to justice.

Nelson's assassination was planned to perfection by experts. After her murder, an LVF bomb-maker from east Belfast, Thomas 'Tucker' Ewing, was named by Special Branch as 'the Rosemary Nelson bomb-maker'. Ewing subsequently died of AIDS. It is known that he met members of Wright's LVF in Lurgan weeks before Nelson was murdered, but the truth is that Ewing and the other members of the LVF at this time lacked the skill to make a mercury-tilt-switch bomb, though it is possible that he was given the device and instructed on how to install and arm it. This leaves us with the question of who built the bomb.

According to credible rumours, one of the LVF suspects linked to Rosemary Nelson's murder was Frankie Curry, a loyalist terrorist with a long history of killing and bombing. He liked to boast that he had killed at least twenty people and would sometimes name his victims when drinking with associates. He was an unstable individual who shared friendships with some of the most notorious loyalist killers, such as the UVF's Lenny Murphy, leader of the Shankill Butchers, John White, a vicious hitman, and Billy Wright. Curry spent time in the ranks of the UVF, UDA, Red Hand Commandos and the LVF. His propensity for changing allegiances was due to his tendency to acquire enemies because of his violent, unpredictable temperament, his heavy use of drugs and his drug-running, a form of criminality rampant in the loyalist paramilitary world. Like many loyalist hitmen, he was a Special Branch asset, listed in the files of the Branch's E3 sector. Curry was known to offer information to Special Branch about loyalist associates, especially those he considered enemies. As a quid pro quo, Special Branch did not interfere with his terrorist activities.

At the time of the planning of Rosemary Nelson's killing, Curry was offering his bomb-making skills to all comers in the loyalist paramilitary world but, as with Ewing, he lacked the skills to make the kind of bomb that killed her. Nevertheless, he did have LVF associates capable of planting the bomb under her car using a magnetic plate. At the time of her murder, Curry was in prison for a minor offence, but as we know from the case of Billy Wright, sending messages from prison in the form of notes or phone calls was easy. Two LVF operatives whom Special Branch privately alleged planted the device that killed Nelson were in contact with Curry before he went into prison and while he was inside. He was released two days after she was murdered and met a violent fate that same day, shot through the back of the head in broad daylight when walking through the Shankill. His death was attributed to a loyalist feud over drugs and his killing of another loyalist.

From all the evidence, there is little doubt that Rosemary Nelson's murder was part of the dirty war. Known loyalist terrorists were recorded on police files as being in the vicinity of her home in the weeks leading up to her death but no action was taken by the RUC to arrest and question them. The files related to this have vanished. This was unconscionable behaviour by the RUC, though the blame lies more with Special Branch, which ran assets within the LVF and refused to provide them for interviews when requested by investigating detectives. Even before this, however, the State had failed to protect her rights as a citizen and a courageous lawyer dedicated to her job. She advocated for her clients, respecting the rule of law and the rights of the individual.

Rosemary Nelson became a victim of the system and paid a terrible price for promoting principles essential to a functioning democracy. Her own words speak to her integrity: 'I believe that my role as a lawyer in defending my clients is vital. The test of a new society in Northern Ireland will be the extent to which it can recognise and respect that role, and enable me to discharge it without improper interference. I look forward to that day.'

11

THE 'BEAUTY QUEEN' BOMBER

ON 26 FEBRUARY 1962 THE IRA called off its disastrous six-year border campaign, which had begun with a flourish under the code-name 'Operation Harvest' and ended in failure. Six weeks later, on 16 April, Martina Anderson was born in the Bogside area of Derry.

Few could have predicted that this pretty baby would embrace a new IRA by the time she was eighteen years old. Nothing much was happening in politics on the day she was born. One of the main items on radio was that responsibility for Belfast Zoo was being transferred from the city's transport department to its parks and cemeteries department. The Belfast city 'Fathers' assured the public that a department which tended to cemeteries had the skills to stop the decline of Belfast Zoo. Perhaps they had a premonition that the zoo's polar bear would die falling through ice on its enclosure pond, as happened years later.

Housing the polar bear in a safer enclosure was, however, not as big an issue as housing allocation throughout Northern Ireland. Working-class Protestants were as deprived as their Catholic counterparts but they were brainwashed by 'big-house' unionists into believing that they were better off, like a chosen people almost. Perhaps if everyone had visited the zoo to observe the polar bear, they might have agreed on their shared economic suffering. This bear was later stuffed with a smile on his face. This is not an urban legend. I saw him in a glass case in the Ulster Museum.

In Derry's Bogside, as in the Lower Falls in Belfast where I was born, space was at a premium. Large families lived in small houses, two-up two-downs with an outdoor toilet. Unemployment was high and depression was considered an integral part of the cost of living. In the Bogside, young Martina was one of a family of ten: seven girls and three boys. Her parents were a mixed-marriage couple, with her father Protestant by birth. Martina bloomed into an attractive teenager and many friends suggested that she should become a model. Before long she got some modelling work and, consequently, tabloid newspapers would later call her a 'beauty queen', which was hardly an adequate description for someone who did what she did.

It was not the prospect of becoming a famous model but the politics of her community that was the driving force in Martina's life. She was almost ten when Bloody Sunday happened and it had a profound impact on her, as it did on many girls and boys of her generation. One can see nowadays how violent events in societies across the globe deeply impact the young, sometimes leading them into the ranks of organisations run by men with long historical memories who are either seeking revenge or have wider political objectives.

The British Paratroopers in the Bogside on Bloody Sunday, 30 January 1972, provided a recruiting tool for the Provisional IRA because kids of Martina's age knew many of the people who lost their lives on that day and some felt the loss personally. As a young reporter, I saw broken and tortured bodies and it had a profound effect on me as a person and as a writer. I felt hurt and angry seeing the brutalised body of a mentally challenged victim.

When death happens to someone we know, it invades our subconscious, leaving us with pain and confusion. Martina Anderson and many of her contemporaries were also left with a residue of sadness and anger, as these deaths were entirely unnecessary. Those feelings would motivate some of them to join the IRA.

By her teens, Anderson had been associating for some time with known republicans. On reaching seventeen, she joined the IRA's ranks with several of her friends and was put under the control of a local Derry IRA commander. She received training in weapons and explosives in camps in Donegal. At eighteen, she was considered old enough to blow up a furniture store in her own city. She was now part of an IRA strategy to destroy the economy of Derry, a city rife with unemployment. The IRA's argument for blowing up shops, hotels and public buildings, in which people held down much-needed jobs, was a fatuous one. It said this was to cause damage to the British economy but the reality was that it was counterproductive. The British economy was also the Northern Irish economy. Nevertheless, sustained bombing of commercial properties suited the IRA because it had plenty of explosives and blowing up such targets did not require much effort. It realised that it could not face down the British Army so instead it punished the population, making Northern Ireland ungovernable and poorer. This is one of the aspects of the conflict which has not been fully explored. Who in the IRA leadership, aside from Brendan Hughes, devised this bombing policy, which led to the slaughter of innocents on Bloody Friday in 1972, and what kind of political thesis at Belfast Brigade level underpinned it? Some brigade leaders, still alive, have the answers to why bombing became a shorthand for the IRA's long war campaign. It is doubtful that it was a well-framed military strategy. Perhaps it was one of pure convenience? Hughes later spoke of Bloody Friday as a miscalculation that he regretted.

Martina Anderson was arrested leaving the furniture store in which she had placed a bomb. She was subsequently charged with possessing a pistol and causing an explosion, and was sent to Armagh women's prison to await trial. Since it was her first offence and as she was from a respectable family, she was released on bail after two months, with instructions to appear in court later to answer the charges against her. Once free, she reported to her IRA bosses, in particular the Derry commander Martin McGuinness, who was also a member of the IRA's Army Council. He had no intention of letting her appear in court, knowing that she would be imprisoned for up to ten years and more importantly that he would lose her as an operative. McGuinness understood the value in having young, attractive females in the IRA's ranks. They were well trained, not well known outside of their own communities and were good at wearing disguises when operating in Ireland and abroad. Anderson was ordered to go into hiding in Donegal. As a result, she would be off Special Branch's radar and could further her skills in bomb-making and surveillance techniques.

While in training camps in Donegal, Anderson met experienced IRA men who had been involved in military engagements within and beyond Ireland. It is interesting that IRA leaders at the time were concerned about personal relationships between men and women working together, while living in the same safe houses; such relationships were deemed off-limits yet many females secretly formed relationships with the men they met while training and those with whom they operated. The British Army's undercover units in Northern Ireland faced the same issue.

Martina Anderson would form a secret relationship with a young man she first met in Donegal, which only came to light years after the two had been involved in some very serious crimes. After she fled Derry, she vanished from Special Branch's radar and was not seen again until she was apprehended fourteen years later, on 24 June 1985,

THE 'BEAUTY QUEEN' BOMBER

in a flat in Glasgow. She has never revealed where she was for those missing years, and Sinn Féin has instructed her not to offer details about her past, but sometimes a person's associates say a great deal about their life and in Anderson's case, they offer a window into her years in the shadows.

In the Glasgow flat where she was arrested, she was not alone but with an IRA unit composed of four men and two women. Police found a 'bomb calendar' listing ten English seaside resorts earmarked for attack. The Reubens Hotel on Buckingham Palace Road, London, was on the list, with indications that it had already received their attention. The following day Scotland Yard's explosives experts discovered a bomb in Room 112 of that hotel. It was timed to explode within weeks.

The Yard's counterterrorism chiefs concluded that this IRA unit was planning to place bombs in hotels in all the calendar-listed seaside towns, including Bournemouth, Dover, Southampton and Blackpool, as well as in London, with the devices timed to explode on consecutive days over a fortnight to generate mayhem. There were pistols and rifles in the flat too, confirming that assassinations of public figures were planned. Police found a magazine profile of a senior SAS officer whom authorities believed was about to be targeted. Martina Anderson had a pistol in her handbag and a false passport under the name Mary Webster.

This was one of the deadliest IRA units discovered in Britain. It was led by Patrick Magee, a highly experienced bomber. It transpired that the unit had two rented flats in Britain, the other being on Hackney Road in London's East End, where explosives were later found hidden under floorboards. The Glasgow flat, at 236 Langside Road, was one of eight at that address. The unit's flat had a small upper room, which had been converted into a mini bomb-making factory. Magee had rented both properties, putting down two months' rent on each. When signing for the one in Glasgow under the cover name Alan Cooper, he was accompanied by Ella O'Dwyer, a twenty-four-year-old Tipperary university graduate.

IRA operatives often worked in couples. They wore wigs and dyed their hair to move smoothly around Britain undercover. They used aliases when registering in hotels – a tactic preferred by Magee. The other IRA members using the Glasgow flat were Donal Craig, Gerard 'Blute' McDonnell and Peter Sherry, who was known to be good with guns. His IRA moniker was 'the Armalite Kid'. Normally the unit would have had five members but Sherry was added because the IRA wanted an experienced gunman to carry out planned assassinations.

This unit would never have been unmasked had it not been for Ian Phoenix, a senior RUC undercover detective in Belfast. He discovered that Sherry had arranged to travel on a coal boat from Belfast to Ayr on Scotland's west coast. Phoenix knew from experience that when a deadly IRA operative was on the move, especially en route to Britain, something big was going down. Since Sherry was not a known bomber, Phoenix concluded that he was being sent to Britain to shoot a high-profile individual. He informed Strathclyde police and a surveillance operation was mounted. It included some of Phoenix's best undercover specialists.

Sherry was followed when he got off the boat in Ayr, and after he boarded two trains to Carlisle, where he booked into a hotel, Phoenix informed Special Branch, MI5 and Scotland Yard. The next day many experienced surveillance 'watchers' were on Sherry's trail. They got a break when he met Magee and the duo hopped on a train to Glasgow. Even though Phoenix had no photos to confirm Magee's identity, he concluded that he had to be an important terrorist. His suspicion was confirmed when Magee demonstrated counter-surveillance tactics by taking Sherry on a bus ride, then walking in one direction before retracing their steps to see if they were being followed. Phoenix was tempted to seize the two suspects there and then but calmer minds prevailed.

After stopping at a café, Magee and Sherry appeared relaxed and went for a stroll, which ended when they entered 236 Langside Road where the other members of the unit were waiting. Phoenix did not know which of the eight flats in the building Sherry and his companion planned to visit or if there might be other IRA operatives there. MI5 decided to act fast and go after the two men without delay. A team of armed, plain-clothes detectives was assembled. The plan was for two armed officers to knock on the door of each flat. When the target flat was identified, every armed officer would move to that position.

The arrest plan was launched at 7.40 p.m. when Magee, who had installed extra locks on the door of the unit's flat, was in the kitchen with Anderson and O'Dwyer enjoying a dinner of steak, Brussels sprouts and boiled potatoes. When there was a knock on the door, believing it was the landlord collecting rent, Magee left the kitchen and opened the door. Before he could react, two undercover officers seized him, pulled him out of the flat and slammed him to the ground, leaving space for other officers to rush in. McDonnell, armed with a pistol, left the kitchen but was brought down and disarmed. The whole raid happened at such speed that Anderson, O'Dwyer and Sherry were still at the kitchen table eating when they found themselves staring down the barrels of police pistols.

Chief Inspector Ian Phoenix, who would later perish in a helicopter crash that killed twenty-nine of the most senior counterterrorist figures in Britain, had just wrapped up the IRA's main bombing team, and Martina Anderson was a vital part of it. While Scotland Yard was sure that she had operated with most of the major IRA bombers in Britain and Europe before her arrest, she and O'Dwyer refused to talk under interrogation.

One must look closely at the way bombers like Magee and his female companions functioned before 1985 to understand the IRA world in which Anderson was a major player. Nine months before

Magee was unmasked in Glasgow, he was involved in one of the most spectacular bombings of the Troubles, in Brighton, an English seaside resort seventy miles from London. On that occasion, he had something very big in mind. He was planning to blow up the whole British Tory government and especially the woman leading it, Margaret Thatcher, who was hated by the IRA as well as by British miners battling police on the streets of British cities in 1984. Magee had operated in Britain for years, moving in and out of English and Scottish cities, interspersed with visits to Dublin to meet senior IRA planners who ran what some of them called the England Department. He could pass himself off as an Englishman and often dressed like a university professor.

In late summer of 1984 he assumed the name Roy Walsh, the name of an IRA bomber from Belfast who was imprisoned in England. By any measure, it was a strange choice for someone so security-conscious to use the name of a bomber already in police files. In fact, it was an example of Magee's self-confidence and supreme arrogance. He liked to boast that he was untouchable, the IRA's version of the Scarlet Pimpernel. To some extent, he was a shadowy figure and a lot still remains unknown about him and about the young IRA women who were his accomplices.

Martina Anderson was a seasoned operative, having been in Britain for years according to Scotland Yard's counterterrorism experts. When she was arrested in Glasgow she had maps of London and the London underground in her handbag. To this day, retired Scotland Yard experts believe that she was an 'important cog' in IRA operations in Britain, and possibly Europe, in the years 1982 to 1985. We do not know this for certain because IRA operatives of the period in Britain and Europe have not offered up their secrets, especially with regard to the identities of young female operatives. What we do know is that Magee always worked with a female to give him better cover, masquerading as boyfriend and girlfriend or husband and wife. Females were also ideal for carrying out surveillance on targets.

Magee's big target in the summer of 1984 had been the Grand Hotel in Brighton, where the Tory Party was due to hold its annual party conference in the second week of October. Magee and an unknown female partner spent time in Brighton in July and August, visiting the hotel and assessing where best to plant a bomb which would collapse the building. Then, on 15 September 1984, Magee, dressed like a respectable businessman, approached the front desk in the Grand and asked for a room with a sea view. He was allocated Room 629. He registered as Roy Walsh, gave a bogus London address and paid cash for three nights; enough time for the bomb to be delivered to him and for him to set the timer, wrap it in cellophane and plastic and conceal it.

It is not known who visited Magee at the hotel or who he met while in Brighton. Some investigators later speculated that the explosives, wrapping and timer were transferred to him by a young woman he was reportedly seen with in the city.

Within forty-eight hours of his stay in the Grand Hotel, Magee had primed his bomb and concealed it in the bathroom of his suite. He signed out of the Grand on the third day of his stay and returned to his safe house in Hackney in London. At 2.45 a.m. on 12 October, almost a month after Magee strode casually out of the Grand, his bomb exploded. As he had anticipated, the explosion, in a confined place, had a powerful punch and brought down not only the roof but a large brick Victorian chimney atop it, which sank through the floors below. Margaret Thatcher, famously a night owl, was awake and writing her speech for the next day when the device went off. It was pure luck that she and her husband, Denis, were not injured, thanks in part to the fact that the Grand was a sturdy old Victorian structure. Her bathroom was badly damaged but not the rest of her suite. She got dressed right away and confidently led Denis out of the suite where her security detail was waiting to whisk her off to a local police station. The blast killed five of her party entourage and injured over thirty, leaving some severely disabled.

Nine months later Magee was arrested in the Glasgow flat while planning another outrage on a grander scale. According to Scotland Yard, he was identified as the Brighton bomber months after the explosion at the Grand Hotel because he left his fingerprint on a card when he was registering as Roy Walsh. This enabled MI5 to follow him for months, leading to his arrest in Glasgow. I have never believed this Yard claim. There were no photos on file of Magee when Phoenix and his RUC specialists saw him with Sherry in Glasgow. Had Magee been known to MI5 as the man who almost killed Margaret Thatcher, Phoenix, as one of the leading counterterrorism experts in Europe, would have recognised him. I believe that the MI5 claim was an effort by security authorities at the highest levels to cover for their failures in Brighton. It also leads one to question the other claim that they identified him by a fingerprint. If this was so, why did they spend months trawling through files and consulting snitches to find out the identity of the Roy Walsh from Room 629 in the Grand Hotel?

Months after Magee's arrest, an Old Bailey judge described him as 'a man of exceptional cruelty' and handed him eight life sentences, recommending that he serve no less than thirty-five years. The Home Secretary later decided that Magee merited a longer sentence and changed it to life.

Martina Anderson and the others caught in Glasgow received lengthy sentences for conspiring to cause explosions. Anderson and O'Dwyer were sent to Brixton Prison after their arrest and were then moved to Durham Prison following their conviction. They were considered Category A prisoners, a status defining them as high risk. Anderson later reflected on more than a week's intense interrogation after her arrest, describing it as a stressful time but nothing like the year that followed when she and O'Dwyer were regularly subjected to strip-searches in Durham.

After eight years as Category A status prisoners, the two women were transferred to Maghaberry Prison in Northern Ireland. They never made headlines in prison. O'Dwyer gained a doctorate from the University of Ulster while she was serving her sentence. She often referred to having two families – her republican family and her natural family. An honours English graduate from University College Dublin, she later attributed her journey into the IRA as a response to the hunger strikes and the death of Bobby Sands. She was articulate and always willing to explain her political leanings but I found it strange that she never mentioned the fact that she got married while in Durham or indeed the person she married. It was left to Martina Anderson, who received an honours degree in social sciences from the Open University while in jail, to reveal that both she and Ella married at this time.

Martina Anderson's choice was Paul Kavanagh, a fellow bomber from Belfast. She was given special permission to marry him in Sutton Prison, close to York, where he was serving several life sentences. She was driven there under very tight security. To get permission from the prison authorities for the marriage of two Category A prisoners, she would have had to provide a detailed outline of the kind of relationship they shared. She would not have divulged IRA secrets about their past but would have been obliged to present a compelling description of where and when they met and how long they had known each other. In subsequent remarks to a Sinn Féin audience, she joked that when she arrived at his prison, they were allowed a few hours to 'get the job done', presumably a reference to consummating their union.

The fact that Anderson knew Kavanagh well enough to marry him offers an insight into her mysterious terrorist career in Britain before her Glasgow arrest. This was most likely the young man she met and fell in love with when on the run and being trained by the IRA in Donegal all those years before; some security experts wondered if Anderson was part of a Kavanagh–Magee unit between 1983 and 1984.

Kavanagh and an associate, Thomas Quigley, built and detonated a nail bomb at Chelsea Barracks in London on 10 October 1981. Their target was a bus full of soldiers, twenty-three of whom were injured. The blast killed two civilians and injured seventeen. It was a mass casualty attack and the nails, screw nuts and bolts in the bomb numbered 1,000 and caused immense physical wounds. One of the victims, fifty-nine-year-old widow Nora Fields, was killed when a large nail went through her body, piercing her heart. In 1985 the two IRA men received life sentences for murder and causing explosions, with recommendations that they serve no less than thirty-five years. It is not inconceivable that Anderson and Kavanagh worked with Magee and that they shared intelligence and safe houses with him. She is not saying and neither is Kavanagh.

Anderson, Kavanagh and O'Dwyer were all released in 1998, thanks to the Good Friday Agreement. It was on this release that the *Irish Independent* referred to Anderson as the 'former beauty queen'. O'Dwyer went on to publish a book and disavowed the use of violence to solve the 'Irish Question', while Anderson and her husband settled into a comfortable life in Northern Ireland, both pursuing careers in the political sphere, much to the anger and dismay of their critics and enemies. She was rewarded for her loyalty 'to the cause' when Martin McGuinness, her former IRA commander, persuaded her to build a political career.

Martina became actively involved at a senior level within Sinn Féin, as did Paul. In 2007, when McGuinness became Deputy First Minister of the Northern Ireland Assembly, she entered Parliament as a Sinn Féin representative for the Foyle constituency in her native Derry city. She was also appointed, bizarre as it may seem, as the first female Sinn Féin member of the Policing Board for Northern Ireland, a body comprised of ten Assembly members and nine non-political appointees. Its brief was to appoint the police top brass, hold the PSNI to account and discipline officers who transgressed. It also had to set targets for policing and investigate complaints against the force and individual officers.

McGuinness appointed Paul as one of his special advisers. John Radley, a former soldier who had four nails removed from his mouth when Kavanagh's bomb exploded outside Chelsea Barracks, expressed his anger at the appointment as follows: 'I'm a victim. I haven't got any chance of appealing my discharge. I lost my whole way of life, I lost my career, my whole life was ruined by this man. Why shouldn't he pay for that? Not just my life – twenty-three injured – two people killed.' Nails also pierced this soldier's head, neck and back. He testified that many of his colleagues were hit by spinning nails and bolts. His hand still has wires in it because he tried to shield his face from the blast, which also shattered his eardrum and left his nose half hanging off. He was subjected to thirteen hours of surgery.

In 2010 Martina Anderson lost her Foyle seat to Martin Durkan of the Social Democratic and Labour Party (SDLP) but Sinn Féin leader Gerry Adams later selected her to represent his party as a Member of the European Parliament (MEP). She lost this job in 2016 when the British government broke with Europe in what became known as Brexit. Undaunted, she returned triumphantly to local politics and again won the Foyle Assembly seat in February 2020. One could say that she was a consummate politician or that she was a woman with very important connections. Her motto in life, she said, was 'never give up'.

Paul Kavanagh lost his post of special adviser to Martin McGuinness when legislation was introduced banning anyone convicted of serious crimes from being in such a role. Sinn Féin later showed this former bomber some love when he was appointed to the Northern Ireland Education Authority Board. The party explained that he was given the job because of his 'wealth of experience in education, government and policy development'.

When I began research for this book, I was keen to talk to Martina Anderson, offering to let her help shape her own narrative so that readers would better understand her life. I explained that I was keen to know about her early life, the things she liked and disliked and the events which motivated her. She said that she would think about it but made it clear she had to consult Sinn Féin. I wanted to say to her that she was a sixty-one-year-old woman who could surely make her own choices, but I knew that it was not that simple. I advised her to talk to Adams, who knew me and my work. We had gone to school together.

Anderson subsequently emailed me that I should contact Sinn Féin and provided an email address for Sean Maguire. I did not have the opportunity to ask her if she had spoken to Adams. I presumed that she had and that he more than likely directed her to go lower down the Sinn Féin ladder. I wrote to Maguire and we spoke by phone. I explained to him that I was writing a book to focus on women who lived through the Troubles because there had been too much focus on men of the period. I told him that my book was not planned as a controversial work like *The Dirty War*. He laughed and said that all my books were controversial. He was correct, but I never saw this book in that mould. I explained how I hoped Martina would share her narrative. He suggested that perhaps she might want to write her own account of her life, something she had never mentioned when talking to me and she has had many years to do it. I told Maguire that I was somewhat dismayed by Sinn Féin's intervention in this matter and that I found it somewhat 'Kremlinesque' in character. My use of the word 'Kremlinesque' did not please him and he insisted that Sinn Féin was not a censor. We finished our conversation with him promising to talk to some colleagues in Dublin. He said that he would be back with an answer in a week, but I never heard from him, even though I tried again to contact him.

I spoke to fellow writers and sources whom I trust and they assured me that Sinn Féin continues to hold considerable sway over its members, the way the IRA always did. Sinn Féin is determined to shape its narrative of the past in ways that it hopes will eclipse any record provided by others. It is an effective way to bend and to kill the truth about the past. Rewriting history has always been the goal of demagogues and always has a negative effect on society.

It is unlikely Martina Anderson will be permitted to reveal the truth about her role in IRA operations in Britain and Europe. We can speculate about her motives, political views, influences and beliefs but until she shares her truths she will be confined to history as the 'beauty queen' bomber of a furniture shop. Like some other females who joined the IRA, she expected other people, many of them women, to pay a high price for her political ideals.

12

DEATH ON THE FRONT LINES

THE AVERAGE AGE OF YOUNG men serving in the Second World War was twenty-three; in the Vietnam War it was nineteen. Tracy Ellen Doak was just eighteen when she joined the RUC officer-in-training programme in 1982 and she became a fully-fledged officer within three years.

On the morning of 20 May 1985 Tracy was behind the wheel of her patrol car and her boss, recently appointed Inspector Billy Wilson, was beside her. At twenty-eight, he was considered an old-timer by the two male officers sitting in the back of the car: David Baird, aged twenty-two, and Stephen Rodgers, nineteen. Stephen may have been the only one among them familiar with the song topping the British Pop Charts that week, '19' by musician Paul Hardcastle, who was fascinated by the fact that so many American nineteen-year-olds had died on the front lines in Vietnam.

Inspector Wilson's presence impressed the others of the group in the patrol car. He was not one to sit behind a desk, convinced instead that he should spend time in the field getting to know his team and their capabilities. He was especially keen to observe the two young men in the car, since they were on their first station placement. In contrast, fresh-faced Tracy Doak was no rookie. She knew a great deal about policing. Her father, Beattie, had been an RUC constable for decades and her brother, Allister, two years older than her, was also a member of the force.

Now twenty-one, and having already served as an RUC cadet for two years before her officer training, she had a wealth of experience in policing and looked to have a very promising future in the ranks. A confidential report from her time on a cadet course in Cumbria praised her commitment and leadership qualities: 'Her confidence, commonsense and desire to do well made her an important member of the group of ten students of widely differing backgrounds and abilities. She showed organisational and leadership potential when given charge of a small group of students for a mountain walk.'

The report also applauded her concern for others and her commitment to hard work. According to her evaluation at that early stage in her career, she would prove to be a worthwhile member of the RUC, 'particularly in the current climate'. The reference to 'current climate' confirmed that the report's author believed this young woman would be up to the task of serving on the front lines in Northern Ireland. The report concluded: 'Overall, an excellent performance by a most mature and impressive young woman whom I assessed with considerable scrutiny against my own, not inconsiderable firsthand experience of N. Ireland.'

Tracy had dreamed of becoming a police officer from an early age even though she had the potential to follow an academic career. As a teen she was so attractive that some friends thought she might join a modelling agency. Her mother, Jean, remembers her being an energetic and athletic teenager who was a good hockey player. She was also adept at organising her brother and two younger sisters.

The Doak family was socially and politically moderate and very attached to their Ballywatt Presbyterian Church and its community in

Coleraine, despite living closer to Derry than Coleraine. A sign that the family was culturally progressive was that Tracy became a skilled Irish dancer and performed at many competitions. She also played piano and enjoyed singing in her church choir.

By any measure, she was an accomplished teenager and like many young girls of her age, she loved fashion. One of her favourite things was dressing up for fun. She would stride up and down the house wearing her father's police constable hat. It was not clear at the time if that was also a sign of a budding ambition to become a policewoman, but by the time she was sixteen, she had made up her mind about her future. She told her parents that she did not wish to pursue an academic career and then revealed how she had secretly investigated how to join the RUC cadets with the aim of becoming a police officer. Tracy was an independent spirit, determined to make her own choices and forge her own path in life.

Her parents respected her choice. From an early age, they recognised that she 'had a mind of her own', displaying a maturity beyond her years. She would live away from home for the next two years but kept in regular contact, writing letters to her sister Allison, knowing that, as the youngest, she missed the protection of her big sister. Each time Tracy returned home for short visits, she and her sisters would sit round the piano with Tracy playing while they all sang songs until late. Their mother remembers always making their favourite meal, lasagne, on those joyful evenings.

As a cadet, Tracy was expected to study, train and do social work. She spent time assisting elderly people in nursing homes and worked with mentally challenged and disabled children. When she reached eighteen, she was ready to begin her working life as an RUC officer-in-training.

She spent some time in the RUC's training centre in Enniskillen and was later transferred to Newry, a predominantly Catholic nationalist town where RUC personnel were not always welcome, especially in Catholic housing estates. Instead of settling down in Newry, she moved in with her maternal grandmother, who lived twelve miles away in Banbridge. Tracy bought herself a car and within two years was paying for work to begin on a new house for herself in Moira, a small, mainly Protestant village on the borders of Counties Antrim and Armagh. She had also met the love of her life, who happened to be another police officer, and they were planning to marry in September 1985.

When she got behind the wheel of her police patrol car on the morning of 20 May 1985, Tracy had not only chosen her wedding dress but had gone through several fittings and had booked a hotel for her wedding reception. She was, in her mother's words, always well organised. I suspect that Tracy possessed a stoic character. She accepted that her job carried serious risks but, nevertheless, she loved it and boasted about the friendships she made and the camaraderie she shared with colleagues. Tracy was hurting, though, even if she never really showed it. Things she shared with her mother confirmed that she was deeply saddened by the loss one of her best friends to terrorism: a young female officer, Constable Rosemary McGookin, who had only recently tied the knot.

The RUC station at Corry Square, Newry, most often referred to as 'the Base', was a prime target for the IRA's South Armagh Brigade because it ran operations against the Provisionals in the border region. It was a large police and British Army facility with a wide range of anti-terrorist staff and capabilities, housing British Military Intelligence personnel and members of RUC Special Branch. It was heavily fortified and ringed with sandbagged emplacements from which soldiers scanned the surrounding area for terrorist threats.

The South Armagh Brigade, along with a Newry IRA unit, spent months trying to decide how to attack the facility. One option was to drive a van containing a massive bomb to the entrance but this was considered impractical if not suicidal. Heavy security surrounding the base would never permit a van to approach the entrance and if such an attempt was made, the driver would likely be killed by British military snipers. The alternative and accepted plan was to lob mortars into the facility; they would be fired from tubes bolted onto the bed of a truck. Each mortar shell would contain 40lbs of high explosives. The risk that some of the shells might land in nearby homes did not seem to bother the IRA, who determined that the best place from which to launch the attack was Monaghan Street, about 250 metres from the Base, sending the shells over the roofs of intervening buildings.

At 6.35 p.m. on 28 February 1985, police officers were gathered in a Portacabin canteen on the base for an evening break when one of the mortar shells landed on it. Nine officers were killed and forty people, some of them civilian employees, were wounded. Others wounded were playing pool in a room adjacent to the canteen. Tracy was at home when the mortar attack occurred but was called to report for duty at the base afterwards. One of the dead was Tracy's friend Constable McGookin, who passed away as she was rushed to hospital minutes after the explosion. When it was time to go to her funeral, Tracy phoned her mum to ask if it was okay to wear a hat. She wanted to see her friend off with due respect.

Prime Minister Margaret Thatcher called the attack 'barbaric' while Taoiseach Garret FitzGerald promised that his security forces would help track down the culprits. The British press dubbed the attack 'Bloody Thursday'. The day after the attack, a United Press International report claimed that pro-IRA supporters drove past the bombed base honking their car horns enthusiastically. The IRA would carry out a similar mortar attack on the RUC training centre in Enniskillen in September that year, when thirty young cadets narrowly escaped death.

More than two months later, Tracy and her patrol team were tasked, as part of a two-car escort, with meeting a Brinks-Mat van carrying foreign currency. The van was on its way from Dublin to the border, shadowed by police from An Garda Síochána and Irish Army soldiers. After the van crossed the border at Killeen, facing a long stretch of open road leading north towards Newry, it became the responsibility of Tracy Doak and her two-car patrol to ensure it arrived safely in Newry. While this was a regular currency transfer, which usually passed without a hitch, it was the first time Tracy had been tasked with protecting it.

To this day, it is not clear how much attention was really paid by the police forces on either side of the border to this exchange, given it was happening in a dangerous part of Northern Ireland. Perhaps British and Irish police and intelligence agencies considered the exchange so routine that little consideration was paid to the risks RUC patrols always faced in that part of the country. According to some security experts, this was a major security failure by the RUC and gardaí.

The Killeen border stop and the rural roads leading from it were considered some of the most lethal parts of Northern Ireland because they were part of the battleground of the IRA's South Armagh Brigade. The area was dominated by IRA units from Dromintee, including a sub-unit from Crossmaglen and a unit from Silverbridge, who were all tied to the South Armagh Brigade and worked together when mounting large operations. The IRA in this part of Ireland may well have been the most effective terrorist outfit anywhere in the world at that time.

This was certainly the opinion of a senior, unnamed RUC Special Branch officer when later giving evidence to a public inquiry. He offered this observation: 'These people were very, very cautious. One of the reasons that they survived for so long intact and matured and developed into top quality – you know I hate to give credit to terrorists but they were formidable terrorists. They were very experienced terrorists and it wasn't simply the fact that the border was there, it was the fact that they were ultra cautious. And if they had seen one vehicle which they thought was out of place, they would have simply called an operation off because they would have feared it was the SAS or somebody like that. And their philosophy simply was we live to fight another day. They wouldn't just rush out on the word of somebody because they would fear they were going into some sort of trap. Now, they would never, for example, pull twenty weapons forward into a hide, into a single hide in the North. These boys, as I say, were ultra cautious. They wouldn't mount an operation on pure speculation, they would have needed to be certain, because every time they came together, especially with weapons, they ran the risk of being intercepted by – in that area particularly – by the army.'

Actually, the IRA had eyes and ears on both sides of the border and was even believed to have moles within An Garda Síochána, especially in its Dundalk HQ, which handled security on that section of the border. The area was truly the front line of a war and it was where Tracy Doak was now policing. Her father, Beattie, was aware of the risks his RUC colleagues faced in the Armagh area and was increasingly concerned about his daughter being based in Newry. He would later say that he regretted not using his influence to have her moved to another part of Northern Ireland. In truth, however, there were few safe places in the state for members of the RUC. Nevertheless, Newry and the border represented the place of greatest danger. This was brought home to him and the entire RUC on 28 February 1985 by the mortar attack on the base.

When the Brinks-Mat truck reached the border on the morning of 20 May, the two RUC escort cars, one driven by Tracy, took over as its security detail, with Tracy's car designated as the lead vehicle. Unbeknownst to the police, the IRA's C Team lookouts had eyes on the escort from both sides of the border. No one in the police cars paid any attention to a tractor-trailer parked on the road ahead, which had been driven there the night before from Newtownhamilton after the IRA took the family who owned it hostage. As Tracy's car was passing it, a 1,000lb bomb hidden inside was detonated by remote control from the Irish Republic. The target was not the Brinks-Mat truck's big load of currency but the members of the RUC who were safeguarding it. Tracy's car and everyone in it were blown to pieces. Minutes earlier, a bus taking handicapped children for a day trip to Dublin Zoo had passed the tractor-trailer.

'It is terrible to think that my daughter's remains were scattered across a field,' Tracy's mother told me. She applauded the RUC Chief Constable, Sir John Hermon, who later walked that field alone to honour Tracy and her three colleagues.

The first reaction of the gardaí to the explosion was to claim the bomb was detonated from the North but that quickly proved to be false.

There were rumours within the security forces and also in media circles that the IRA had advance warning of the truck's schedule from Dublin and its hand-off point at the border, possibly from an IRA mole within the gardaí. These were very quickly dismissed by the British and Irish governments and by security authorities in Belfast and Dublin, as even the suggestion of this could seriously damage relations between the police forces on both sides of the border. There had been an ongoing effort for years behind the scenes to ensure that smooth co-operation between the gardaí and RUC was maintained at all costs. Members of RUC Special Branch even privately referred to the Irish police as 'our sister force'.

But there was a secret hidden in the RUC's Special Branch Registry, which was so sensitive that very few ever had access to it. It was a file known as an SB50. It contained an allegation that Dundalk-based

Garda Detective Sergeant Owen Corrigan had links to the IRA's South Armagh Brigade. However, there was no data in the SB50 to support the accusation that Corrigan was an IRA mole and security experts from both the RUC and gardaí later placed little reliance on the file's significance for the murder of Tracy Doak and her colleagues. They argued that even if there was a mole, the IRA would not have needed assistance to plan this atrocity because the regular transfer of the Brinks-Mat truck at Killeen was obvious to many locals and therefore to the IRA. (The Brinks-Mat handover procedure ended after Tracy and her companions were murdered.)

Nevertheless, the presence of an IRA mole in the Dundalk gardaí – and possibly more than one mole – cannot be totally dismissed as a potential factor in the bombing that took the lives of Tracy and her team. An RUC Special Branch officer later conceded that when he mentioned Detective Corrigan's name to a senior colleague, he was told, 'Don't be so hasty, there's another boy,' meaning there was another IRA mole in the gardaí in Dundalk. Indeed, RUC Special Branch officers who had considerable experience of dealing with the gardaí believed in the existence of three moles in Dundalk.

Detective Corrigan had a reputation for falsifying logs, lying and being generally negligent about his duties as a police officer. He was known to be close to prominent members of the IRA's Armagh Brigade and his ownership of several houses heightened rumours that he was involved with the IRA in smuggling goods across the border. While some of his colleagues did insist that he was a good cop, according to other garda sources 'dodgy' was the word used when Corrigan's name was mentioned at the highest security levels in Dublin.

It seems that by the late 1980s many people were pointing an accusing finger at Corrigan, but this was well after Tracy Doak's murder and due in part to several factors. The first was an operation by the South Armagh Brigade, which was almost a re-run of the one that killed

Tracy and her colleagues. On 14 April 1987 one of Northern Ireland's most senior judges, Lord Maurice Gibson, and his wife, Lady Cecily Gibson, drove their car onto the Dublin to Liverpool ferry. Surprisingly, they had booked the crossing in their own names. This was careless because Lord Gibson was an IRA target and a controversial figure in the nationalist community. He acquired notoriety among republicans when he acquitted police officers who fired 109 bullets into a car that failed to stop at a checkpoint. The judge's home in Donegal was later fire-bombed, making it clear he was a marked man.

The couple returned to Dublin on 25 April. The RUC and gardaí knew their itinerary and two garda officers met the Gibsons off the ferry in Dublin and escorted them to the border, maintaining radio silence the whole way. At the Killeen border crossing, Lord Gibson stopped his car so that he and his wife could thank their escort. After handshakes were exchanged, the garda officers left. The arrangement was for the Gibsons to drive about 450 yards north where they would be met by an RUC escort to get them home to Belfast. Just before they reached the rendezvous, a bomb in a car parked at the side of the road was detonated by remote control, killing the couple. Three prominent rugby players travelling in a car close to the seat of the explosion were injured, though none seriously. Although the Gibsons had been careless in using their own names to book their holiday travel, the question remained: how did the IRA know where they were due to meet their RUC escort?

A similar trap on the same road was set for Justice Ian Higgins a year later. He survived because his flight arrived late into Dublin. Sadly the Hanna family of husband Robert (45), wife Maureen (44) and seven-year-old son David was slaughtered in an explosion when the IRA mistook their car for that of Higgins.

Then, on 20 March 1989, two very high-ranking RUC officers, Chief Superintendent Harry Breen and Superintendent Bob Buchanan, were killed after crossing the border when they were returning from a meeting with Garda Chief Superintendent Nolan in Dundalk. Despite deciding to divert along the narrow, rural Edenappa Road, with neither officer favouring driving through the Killeen border crossing where Tracy Doak and her colleagues, the Hanna family and the Gibsons had so tragically met their deaths, the IRA were waiting. Even had the officers chosen not to take Edenappa Road, the IRA had people in place to intercept them at the main Killeen crossing.

The two men were stopped by what resembled a standard British military checkpoint and gunned down by armed men in camouflage with their faces blackened. The double murder prompted lengthy inquiries into the possibility of collusion between moles in the gardaí and the IRA. While it was generally agreed that a mole facilitated the assassination of Breen and Buchanan, no one was charged with their deaths or the scores of other murders committed by the IRA's South Armagh Brigade. No mole was ever unmasked in Dundalk Garda HQ.

The Doak family, like others who have spoken to me for this book, feel that they have been denied justice. There are no known suspects for the attack on their daughter, though Special Branch files may contain the names of IRA operatives suspected of playing a role in the bombing by virtue of their links to the South Armagh Brigade's bombing specialists.

Tracy was killed on duty protecting the State. Although she was a young woman when she was murdered, she had achieved a lot in a life cut short at a time when she faced a bright future. Her family avoids discussing the complex security and political issues surrounding her death but they recognise that a lot of questions remain unanswered. Nevertheless, they are resigned to the fact that they will not get the answers they seek; a conviction shared by most of the people I interviewed.

'The parents of other victims are dying off without justice,' is how Tracy Doak's mum, Jean, puts it. When I asked her about the loss and the pain she continues to suffer, she replied, 'It is last thing at night and first thing in the morning. I wear it like a coat.'

After Tracy's murder, Jean and Beattie devoted a lot of their time to charitable works. They both participated in the work of the RUC George Cross Parents' Association, helping the relatives of murdered RUC personnel by addressing their welfare and health needs. The organisation plans social activities and assists families dealing with the pain of loss. Jean was also secretary of the Coleraine Irish Dancing Festival for twenty years. She received the British Empire Medal for her services to the community.

13

GRIEVING WITHOUT A BODY

We are running out of time to find the remains of my brother, Columba. It is my biggest fear. I am now seventy. I want this to happen in my lifetime. I want to bring my brother home. I don't want him lying in a cold, wet bog in Monaghan. I want to give him a funeral and give him back his dignity. This is what I call justice.

Dympna Kerr, née McVeigh, sister of Columba McVeigh, one of the IRA's 'disappeared' speaking to me on 4 January 2024

I HAVE A CONFESSION TO make. In my book *The Dirty War* there was a chapter called 'Secret Burials'. I revealed how the IRA interrogated suspected informers before killing them and secretly burying their bodies in remote rural areas near the Irish border. The IRA denied it, insisting that those who had vanished had left the country to work in England or were secret British Army agents. My source for this revelation about secret burials was the IRA's famous intelligence chief

Brendan Hughes. He named some but not all of the 'disappeared' after I began investigating the strange case of two young IRA operatives linked to an MRF 'sting' called the 'Four-Square Laundry', a bogus laundry service which operated mainly in Catholic west Belfast. The secretive MRF unit had recruited members of the IRA and the UDA into its ranks and was responsible for many assassinations. The laundry was a van that toured districts of Belfast and was rigged with surveillance equipment. Clothes from selected homes were forensically tested for firearms and explosives residue before they were returned cleaned and pressed.

Hughes told me that he had been involved in interrogating the two IRA figures I was concerned about. He explained that they were later taken to sites near the border where they were given the Last Rites before being shot and buried in unmarked graves. The initial assassins developed a friendship with one of the two young men, eighteen-year-old Kevin McKee, and informed the IRA leadership in Belfast that they could not bring themselves to shoot him. The IRA responded by sending two experienced gunmen from the Ballymurphy area of Belfast to kill McKee. They shot him, and I named them in my book, setting off a bitter feud between families in parts of west Belfast.

My story of secret burials soon turned into a search for the 'disappeared'. I subsequently discovered that the late Brendan Hughes had failed to reveal all his secrets about this IRA practice of 'disappearing' people. In particular, he did not admit that he interrogated Joe Lynskey, another figure killed by the IRA, whose remains have never been found, or that he had been present when Jean McConville was questioned and abused, before she was secretly buried.

Hughes told me the name of one 'disappeared' victim, nineteen-year-old Columba McVeigh, who had vanished a decade before. I explained to Hughes how I had investigated a British Military Intelligence sting involving McVeigh. I pointed out that both the

British Army and the IRA denied having any links to him, but I knew otherwise. Hughes said that McVeigh had been executed and buried on a hillside on a remote part of the border in the Irish Republic. The fact that he knew this suggested to me that the IRA's Northern Command, of which Hughes was a member, had ordered the death of McVeigh and the other 'disappeared' victims.

In the years since, I have questioned whether I had a duty to tell the families whose loved ones had been 'disappeared' that they were not missing; that the IRA had murdered and secretly buried them. Why did I leave it for families to learn this from my book? I really do not have an answer. When preparing this chapter about Columba McVeigh's family, I knew that I needed to discover what his sister, Dympna, his parents, Vera and Paddy, and his brothers had endured for decades while they were denied news of him and eventually were left without his remains to grieve over.

The pain Columba's mother suffered while she prayed every day for his return speaks to the horror of this cruel aspect of the conflict. One can only imagine how the family felt on learning in 1990 what I wrote about Columba in my 1988 book, especially the revelation that the IRA had murdered him.

In the 1980s Columba McVeigh's role as a British intelligence asset came to the attention of investigative journalist Duncan Campbell. He had received information about McVeigh from Fred Holroyd, an army undercover soldier and whistleblower. Holroyd believed McVeigh was compromised in 1974, a year before his disappearance, when he was roped into an undercover plot by a British Army intelligence officer, Sergeant Tony Poole. According to Holroyd, Poole hoped to infiltrate a Catholic youth into the IRA but his plan failed when he chose, as he called him, the 'woolly-headed' seventeen-year-old Columba McVeigh to be at the core of it.

According to Holroyd, whom I met and spoke to about this case,

Poole had decided that McVeigh should be encouraged to plant ammunition in his own home so that the army could raid the house and find it. McVeigh would escape and seek sanctuary with the IRA. Poole's ultimate objective was to use him to compromise a local priest he believed was running an escape route for IRA men fleeing Northern Ireland to the Republic. McVeigh's home was raided and, as arranged, he fled to seek sanctuary with the priest, expecting that he would be his conduit to the IRA. In the meantime, ammunition was found in McVeigh's bedroom and a warrant was issued for his arrest.

However, the priest dismissed McVeigh as a crackpot kid. After several days, with no place to hide, McVeigh turned himself into the RUC. He asked to speak to Poole but was told to go home. Instead, he spent another week with friends before he was finally arrested and charged with possessing ammunition. In court, he adopted an IRA posture of refusing to recognise the authority of the court. He was remanded in custody in the Provisional IRA section of Crumlin Road Gaol in Belfast.

In prison, the IRA was aware that he was not one of theirs. They accused him of being an informer and subjected him to harsh treatment. To save himself, he admitted that he was working with Poole and following his orders. The fact is, however, that before entering prison, Poole had met him and briefed him that when the pressure in prison became too much, he was free to admit to the IRA that he was an informer. He would then give the IRA the names of other informers. McVeigh supplied his IRA prison interrogators with a bogus list of informers, which included a local politician, a solicitor and his family's milkman. The IRA subsequently shot and killed a Protestant milkman but not the one McVeigh identified. The victim was doing relief work because the regular milkman was off sick. Holroyd saw the list of informer names which McVeigh provided and recognised it as a 'fabrication'.

Before the milkman's murder McVeigh was released from prison in 1975, having served several months in custody on a suspended sentence because the court had been assured that the bullets found in his home were 'duds'. As I wrote in *The Dirty War*: 'Because a suspended prison sentence did not reflect the seriousness of his offence, the obvious leniency of the court was a signal to the IRA that Columba McVeigh "had friends in high places". He left for Dublin and disappeared before the end of the year.' I added that he was executed and buried in the Irish countryside and that he fell foul of an ongoing atmosphere of paranoia and suspicion within the IRA.

The paranoia had its roots in a story Hughes told me about two young Catholic men, Vincent Heatherington and Myles Vincent McGrogan, who were trained by British intelligence to enter Crumlin Road Gaol in Belfast and feed the IRA prison leadership lists of bogus informers within the IRA ranks in Belfast. The aim was to create confusion in the IRA and the ploy succeeded. The two young men were later executed by the IRA. I believe that Hughes interrogated them and ordered their execution. When Hughes said that the IRA saw parallels between those two young men and McVeigh, I believed it was he who detected the parallels. Whether he ordered the subsequent murder of McVeigh I cannot know for certain, though I think it likely.

The IRA later claimed that McVeigh was one of theirs and his execution was held in secret to spare his family embarrassment. This was a lie. Fred Holroyd, the British Army whistleblower, subscribed to this falsehood based on things he overheard in his role as an undercover soldier. The claim about McVeigh being IRA was also made by Poole. I believe that this was to justify using a gullible young man in an absurd and dangerous plot.

Here is a far more powerful and truthful story about Columba from his sister, Dympna, who was three years his senior.

'He was not the full shilling,' she says of her brother.

When I asked her if she meant that he was naive, she agreed that this was a better description of him. It could, I believe, explain why Poole chose to exploit him. After all, he had called him 'woolly-headed'.

'Our Columba,' said Dympna, 'was the kind of kid that if he was about to throw a stone through a window and I said, "Don't do it," but a stranger said, "Do it," he would do it.' This suggested that he was a contrarian of sorts who was keen to impress others.

Columba was a boy who loved his mother and she adored him. He had three siblings: two brothers and his sister, Dympna, whom he related to most because she was closer to him in age than the others. Their parents, Vera and Paddy, were a traditional Catholic couple who lived in a small rural townland, Castlecaulfield, not far from Dungannon, County Tyrone. They had Catholic and Protestant neighbours and Dympna recalls there was harmony in the years before the Troubles.

'The only difference between Catholics and Protestants at the time was that Protestants went to church and Catholics to Mass,' she pointed out.

In 1971 the family moved to Donaghmore village, close to Dungannon. Paddy worked in a factory and Vera cared for the children. She was not strict but she had values which she expected her kids to adhere to; they included honesty and going to Mass and Confession. Dympna and Columba were members of the Donaghmore Youth Club. At a Youth Variety show in the mid-1970s, Columba dressed to impress, like he was taking part in a revue, with a hat perched to one side of his head – a photo of him wearing the hat was framed and his mother kept it in her lounge.

In 1973, when Columba was about to turn seventeen, he came to the attention of Sergeant Poole. No one knows exactly how this happened. I suspect that his friendliness and, as Dympna points out, the fact that he was gullible and 'easily led' may have resulted in him chatting with soldiers on foot patrols in his neighbourhood. In this way, his name would have been listed in the local army base as someone who might be vulnerable to recruitment as an informer. He had left school at fifteen, not having excelled at his studies, and worked construction jobs. He was a Liverpool FC supporter and enjoyed hanging out with friends. He had no association with the IRA.

At this time Poole was devising his absurd scheme to use a Catholic youth to infiltrate the IRA. It is conceivable that he may have asked soldiers patrolling Donaghmore if they had spotted a friendly face.

The McVeigh home was raided several times in early 1974, but it was assumed that this was part of army policy in Donaghmore. Columba's mother was upset when she saw him sitting and smoking with soldiers in a military jeep outside their home. She was also unhappy with her son's cavalier response to the raids. She warned him that his behaviour was reckless. If IRA sympathisers in the area saw him sitting in jeeps with British soldiers, they might think that he was a 'tout'.

The above incident is an example of Columba's inability to understand the reality of his environment. Dympna also tried to impress on him how it was unwise to be so friendly with soldiers but her efforts were ignored. 'As a Catholic girl I was aware that when soldiers whistled at you, which they often did, you ignored them,' she recalled. 'People knew that girls who associated with soldiers were tarred and feathered by the IRA so I was very careful to behave properly.'

She became concerned about her young brother when she came home late one night from a discotheque. 'When I entered the living room, I saw Columba on the couch, his legs crossed,' she remembered. 'He was juggling bullets in the air. On the arm of the couch was a Gold Bond cigarette packet.'

She asked him what he was doing with bullets and he told her to mind her business. 'I said to him that I hoped he was not gonna bring trouble to the family. I asked him to give me the bullets and I would go and throw then in the river but again he told me to mind my business. He said a wee man was gonna call for them. I told him again to give them to me and I'd throw them in the river. He told me to go to bed.'

Frustrated with his casual behaviour, she threatened to waken their mother. His response was that if she did so, he would tell her that Dympna was drunk. It was a cunning ploy, as Dympna even now acknowledges. 'Our mother would never tolerate women drinking,' she explained. 'She didn't have trouble with a man going to the pub for a few pints but a woman who drank was low class. We tried to explain to her that the world had changed and women could now have a drink socially, but she wasn't having any of it.'

Columba's threat was enough to send Dympna to her room. At dawn, she was wakened by loud banging on the front door. In the street outside were soldiers and armoured vehicles. She summoned her mother and they let in several soldiers, expecting that they would search the entire house as they normally did. Instead, one soldier went upstairs to Columba's room, opened the second drawer down in a cabinet and withdrew a Gold Bond cigarette packet, which Dympna recognised as the one Columba had when she saw him with the bullets. It quickly transpired that Columba had escaped through a downstairs backroom window and was now running through the back garden. She was surprised that the soldiers did not fire at him or pursue him. She was especially intrigued that they knew exactly where to find the cigarette packet with the bullets in it. They left the house immediately after, taking the packet with them.

McVeigh was now in the wind. His family next heard from him a week later when he announced in a call from the local police station that he had been arrested. His family did not know at that time that his actions had all been pre-planned on the instructions of his Military Intelligence handler, Sergeant Poole. What the family never knew, and Columba never told them, was that he had gone to the late Fr Denis Faul, a prominent justice campaigner who condemned all men of violence and whom Poole hoped to compromise. Columba had been sent packing. Some very prominent Catholics have tried to smear Fr Faul's reputation with no justification. Columba's mother admired him and he would visit her sometimes and sit down to a cup of tea and cake. She affectionately referred to him as 'himself'. 'He and my mother were the best of friends,' said Dympna, who never doubted that Fr Faul was non-sectarian. She knew that the IRA did not like him.

For reasons I cannot explain, Fr Faul never told Mrs McVeigh that Columba had been in touch with him. I wonder if it is possible that Columba spoke to him under the seal of the confessional when he was trying to entice him to link him with the IRA. This would have prevented the priest from discussing the matter. On the other hand, Fr Faul may not have wished to cause Mrs McVeigh undue worry. He may have dismissed the matter as the prank of a young man whom Dympna admits was 'naive – not the full shilling'. Dympna would not have expected Fr Faul to have discussed the nature of the episode with her mother, explaining that his focus was always on 'pastoral care'.

Did McVeigh tell Sergeant Poole about the family friendship with the priest? I am inclined to think that he did. When writing *The Dirty War*, I talked to Fr Faul and he was terribly saddened by way the British military exploited 'a vulnerable youngster' like Columba. He knew he was not a member of the IRA so I believe that when McVeigh came to him claiming, as Poole suggested, that he was on the run from the army and needed the protection of the IRA to get him across the border, Faul knew that this was nonsense. Contrary to what Sergeant Poole believed, Faul was not running an escape 'railroad' to help IRA men reach the safety of the Irish Republic. Instead, he was a thorn in the side of the police and military because he publicly hounded them for their brutality. He was also often no friend of the IRA and became a target of their anger, especially when he later tried to end the IRA hunger strike in the H-Blocks.

In 1974 the McVeigh family was faced with the unthinkable. Columba was charged with possessing ammunition yet no one in the family seriously believed that he was in the IRA. When he was remanded in custody to the IRA wing of Crumlin Road Gaol, the IRA recognised that something about him was amiss. They were determined to find out why he was in their midst and who might be 'running' him. Dympna and her parents, unaware of this, were upset when they visited him in prison and found he was 'black and blue' from beatings. He told his family that 'the screws' had assaulted him.

When he was released from prison in spring 1975, his mother's advice was that he had to leave Northern Ireland. Mrs McVeigh asked Dympna to persuade him to relocate to Dublin because she feared that if he remained at home, the army raids would start again and this was something with which she could not cope. McVeigh agreed to live with his older brother in Dublin until he could get a job and rent his own apartment. With money provided by her mother, Dympna took him shopping for clothes. She last saw him as he boarded a bus to Dublin. By Halloween 1975 he had a job, an apartment and a girlfriend. On Halloween evening, he left the apartment to buy cigarettes and vanished, never to be seen again.

Columba's family only learned that he was missing when his girlfriend in Dublin phoned them a month after Halloween. Her delay was strange and was never explained. The McVeigh family hoped that he would return, but years passed without any news. His clothes were sent from Dublin to his home in Donaghmore and his mother put them in a wardrobe in his bedroom. She expected him to walk through the door any day and give her a hug. On his birthday and at Christmas, as the years passed, she would buy him gifts of clothes and add them to the ones in his wardrobe. She would sit in front of the framed photo taken at the Youth Variety show years earlier and talk to him. At other times, she would say her Rosary in front of it, pleading for God to bring her news of her lost son. No one in the family gave up hope that they would see him alive again. No one had claimed his killing, which encouraged them to believe that he must be alive somewhere.

A decade later, when Dympna was living in England, her mother would phone her often to remind her to pray for Columba. 'She would phone and ask me if I had gone to Mass and lit candles for Columba,' Dympna recalled. 'I told her I prayed for him every time I went to Mass and that was five days a week. I would always light a candle for him when I lit ones for dead relatives. She told me never to do that. I should only include him when lighting candles for the living, as she did. She waited at home all those years for him to return. Her and my dad could not go anywhere together because she believed that there always had to be someone in the house in case Columba walked through the door.'

In 1990 Columba's younger brother, Oliver, then twenty-nine years old, bought a copy of *The Dirty War* and phoned Dympna about my revelation that Columba was 'disappeared' by the IRA. They agreed that they should not tell their parents. Then, in 1997, several months after Mr McVeigh died, Columba was named in a Sunday newspaper as one of the 'disappeared', quoting me. Mrs McVeigh's Sunday routine was to buy several newspapers after Mass, go home and read them while she enjoyed a cup of tea and a cigarette. This is how she learned what I had written about her son. She phoned Dympna and read from the newspaper but Dympna was quick with a reply.

'I'll never forget her call to my dying day,' Dympna told me. 'She had just read what Oliver had read years before in your *Dirty War* book. I had to calm her down and all I could say to her was that she could not trust reviews in newspapers, reminding her that this was a comment that she often made when reading the Sundays. I told Oliver not to reveal that we already knew what you had written. He calmed her down too. She continued to talk to the photograph of Columba, say her Rosary in front of it and she would cry in front of it too.'

Mrs McVeigh was reassured and continued to believe that Columba was alive.

From time to time, locals would claim that they saw McVeigh, with some saying that they spotted him in Dublin. These reports confirmed Mrs McVeigh's conviction that he was alive. I can relate to this. When my twin brother, Damien, left home for England in his late teens, he was gone for almost two decades before he mailed a note to my parents, proving to them he was still alive. During his absence, my mother prayed every day for news of him and lit candles, just like Mrs McVeigh. She would get depressed sometimes, imagining awful things that might have happened to him. I tried to reassure her that I would find him by seeking assistance from the Salvation Army's International Branch, which helps find lost people, but to no avail. In some respects, the fact that there was no news of my twin was considered good news by my mother.

Following the Good Friday Agreement, Mrs McVeigh was confronted for the first time about the truth of her son's disappearance when IRA representatives visited the families of the 'disappeared' to apologise and promise that information would be provided to enable them to locate the remains of their missing loved ones.

In 1999 the first search began for the remains of Columba McVeigh in a desolate site covering twenty-six acres of Bragan Bog in County Monaghan but nothing was found. In 2007 Mrs McVeigh, in her eighties, died without being able to bury her son. In December 2023 the search of Bragan Bog was ended. It is still not known if this is the site where the IRA actually buried him or if they had provided the family with false information. Had they really buried him in Wicklow, near Dublin, I often wondered.

What the IRA have failed to provide is their rationale for Columba's murder. The family, after fifty years of waiting, is entitled to know who ordered this, not necessarily an individual name but at least which section of the IRA made the decision to abduct him in Dublin and 'disappear' him. I personally believe that the late Brendan Hughes had the answer when he told me about secret burials and the murder of McVeigh. It is not unreasonable to conclude that Hughes was part of the IRA intelligence structure in the IRA's Northern Command in 1975 when Columba's fate was decided. If Hughes was able to tell me that McVeigh was abducted in Dublin, the family should have been informed why, by whom and the procedure used to kill him and to 'disappear' his remains. But the IRA preferred the easy way out by simply admitting he was one of the 'disappeared'. Was he interrogated by the IRA before they drove him to a lonely grave to be executed? Was he given the Last Rites? Why was he not permitted to write a note to his mother before he died? Why were his mother, her husband and siblings allowed to suffer for so long?

Until I wrote *The Dirty War*, the IRA seemed to have decided that the 'disappeared' should stay missing. I believe this decision was made by the most senior figures in the IRA's Northern Command, such as Martin McGuinness, and that this was shared with Sinn Féin's Northern leadership. Hughes suggested as much to me when we last met. It was at a time when I was seeking from the IRA its notes of the interrogation of several other men the IRA had executed as informers. Hughes had confirmed to me that the IRA kept the notes of pre-execution interrogations in 'special dumps'. The IRA's Belfast Brigade rejected my request for the notes, but this prompted me to ask Hughes who was responsible for withholding information on the 'disappeared' for decades. He was not entirely honest because he had withheld facts from me about his role in the 'disappearances'. Off the record, he remarked that I asked 'too many' questions and that I ought to be careful pressing some of the senior IRA figures for answers. He suggested that information on the matter of the 'disappeared' was held by a tight circle of people at the 'very top' in the North. He refused to divulge any more than what he had given me.

The IRA insists that British intelligence agencies, including Special Branch, should open their files so that families can learn the truth about collusion. This demand is hollow unless it is prepared to reveal what happened to the likes of Columba McVeigh when he left his flat in Dublin to buy cigarettes fifty years ago.

The McVeigh family made a plea to the IRA too, voiced for them by Dympna in January 2024: 'We want to take him back to where he was born and christened, and made his First Communion and Confirmation. We want to have a funeral Mass and put him in a grave beside his parents. People say, how do you now feel that you know he is dead? I can't think about him as dead. I just think of a body lying in a cold, wet bog. When you think of anybody dead, you think of a coffin. We have no coffin. He is lying in a bog. When we find him, we will give him a burial, and restore his dignity.'

* * *

Columba McVeigh was one of many teenagers recruited by British Army Intelligence, Special Branch and MI5. Another prominent name from among the 'disappeared' was Kevin McKee from the Ballymurphy area of west Belfast. He was very tall for his age with brown curly hair and a mischievous grin. He vanished on 2 October 1972, aged seventeen. Unknown to the IRA, his family and his closest friends, from the time he turned seventeen he was an informer and later a member of the MRF.

McKee was unmasked when Seamus Wright, another MRF asset, under IRA interrogation by Brendan Hughes, named him as an informer. The IRA interrogators were shocked because McKee was from a respected republican family. The IRA interrogation of McKee taught Hughes how the MRF operated. McKee probably thought that he had bought immunity, just as Columba McVeigh imagined he had, by giving the IRA important intelligence, but like young McVeigh he was misguided. After he was 'disappeared', McKee's mother suffered terribly as did his sister, Philomena. They searched Ireland for him.

A small number of people knew the whereabouts of the 'disappeared' and they kept this information to themselves. Hughes, before his death, when talking to prominent author-investigator Ed Moloney, claimed that Gerry Adams, who was a friend of the McKee family, knew about the secret burials, but Adams denied this, claiming the allegation had no foundation. Hughes felt guilty about his personal role in the 'disappeared' saga but not guilty enough to tell me the whole truth. He did, however, tell me enough to enable me, in 1988, to expose one of the IRA's grisly secrets of the Long War. In doing so he risked his life, assured by me that I would not reveal that he was my source. I kept this promise until after his death.

For decades the women of the McKee family pleaded for answers but to no avail. They had to suffer in silence while a young man in his late teens lay in an unmarked grave. They did not publicly admonish the IRA. I was told that they were consistently lied to by republican figures, including Brendan Hughes, whom they believed was a dear family friend. The McKee family declined to talk to me for this book.

14

MOTHERS AND EXECUTIONERS

IT TOOK LESS THAN A decade for the Divis Flats complex in west Belfast to become a concrete jungle, but it was not always so. In 1966, when construction began, it promised a new life for those who lived in the tiny two-bedroom houses like the one my nine siblings and I called home. By the time work started on the complex, with its centrepiece – the twenty-floor Divis Tower surrounded by twelve eight-storey blocks of flats, my family had relocated to a five-bedroom home in the Cliftonville area of north Belfast. It was as if we had 'moved up in the world' and in truth we had, because there was a cricket pitch opposite our home. Our address was not a street or a place, as in Ross Place where we had lived. It was a gardens – Chestnut Gardens. Having just returned to Belfast after years studying in a French religious order's seminary in Hampshire, I was impressed by the men in whites playing cricket just as I had done in the seminary. It was a new world, so unlike the grimy streets of the Falls area of west Belfast where I spent my childhood, but Cliftonville, with its fine homes and streets, would soon suffer its own decline as Belfast plunged into tribal warfare.

As a fledgling reporter I had reason to spend a lot of time in the war-torn streets of the Lower Falls and in the Divis Flats complex after hostilities broke out in August 1969. The novelty of the new Flats complex was quickly erased as the area became a battleground. Still, it must have seemed like a welcome haven to Jean McConville, her husband and their ten children when they found shelter there after she and her family were forced out of Protestant east Belfast. The irony was that Jean Murray, as she was known before her marriage, was a Protestant, but she had married a Catholic.

Jean and her husband had felt safe for years in Protestant east Belfast. He was, after all, a former British soldier, a fact that should have endeared him to their Protestant neighbours. But the sectarian atmosphere in 1969, when Protestant mobs burned whole streets of Catholic homes, infected life throughout Belfast. Suddenly, rampaging mobs raised the spectre of deep tribal fears. Layers of anger ingrained in the historical memory of the city from the 1860s were laid bare. In east Belfast Jean's husband quickly discovered that his religious affiliation trumped his past as a soldier of the British Crown.

Although she was physically unwell, the terror Jean and her husband felt at the possibility of being burned out of their home forced them to flee with their kids to the perceived sanctuary of the Catholic Divis Flats. It was 1971 but little did they know that a long war was on the horizon. There were now two versions of the IRA: the Officials and the Provisionals. The latter were the IRA newbies, dominating the streets of Catholic west Belfast. They were confronting the British Army and recruiting members at an ever-increasing pace. Jean saw how the Provisionals appealed to youth, presenting themselves as the protectors of the Catholic population. Many young people filled their ranks and they were the dominant republican force in Divis Flats.

Everyone was expected to play his or her part. If members of Cumann na mBan knocked on your door and asked you to hide guns, you refused at your peril. An X sign might be placed on your door. Suddenly, you were not in the IRA's camp. However, Jean had no desire to be a part of the conflict and, with her Protestant background, she had never been immersed in the folklore about the IRA being the patriotic protectors of the people. Her husband too, having been a British soldier, realised the futility of the IRA confronting the well-armed British Army. So Jean and her husband may have appeared aloof, somehow suggesting that they had other allegiances. It was a time when paranoia was endemic and those who did not share enthusiasm for banging the tribal drum loudly were regarded with deep suspicion. It led to some girls and boys being tied to lamp posts and tarred and feathered. Others were shot in the kneecaps or executed.

It was not long before the local IRA learned that Jean McConville was of Protestant heritage and that her husband had been a member of the Crown Forces. I am convinced that the whispered unease about this family of blow-ins from east Belfast took on a life of its own and it soon reached the ears of Cumann na mBan.

In 1972 Jean's husband died of cancer. Jean, a mother of ten, should have been embraced by her neighbours. Instead, she was shunned by some and found it tough to feed and clothe her kids. She had to deal with nasty slogans painted on her door, a sure signal that the whisperers were having an impact. Worse was to come when the family's two dogs were thrown down a rubbish chute and left to die, and one of her sons was beaten up at school, all because of the rumour that the family represented a threat of some kind and were hiding their Protestant background.

People who have never lived in a society with this kind of tribalism would find it hard to imagine the stress it can inflict on parents and their children. Jean looked tired and underweight, but she nonetheless tried to 'put on a good face', some friends later said. Her only form of enjoyment was to go to a local bingo hall, where she could relax, unaware that the eyes of Cumann mBan personnel were always on her. It is unclear exactly what their interest was in Jean beyond the fact that she did not seem to care much for the activities of the Provisional IRA and that her eldest son had joined the Official IRA and was now interned. There was great enmity at this time between the Officials and the Provisionals. After 1969 the slogan 'IRA – I Ran Away' appeared in Divis Flats and elsewhere in the Falls to signify that the old IRA – now Officials – had failed to prevent the burning of Catholic homes.

In 1972 a special unit was formed within the Provisional IRA and given the name 'the Unknowns' even though some of its members were known to Special Branch and British intelligence. It was a time when the dirty war – the war in the shadows – began to take shape and the Unknowns were to play a decisive role in it. Their job was to root out and deal with informers in IRA ranks because, even at this early stage in what would become 'The Long War', British intelligence agencies were using blackmail, intimidation and bribery to recruit both paramilitaries and ordinary citizens as informers and agents. These informer-agents included paedophiles, criminals, murderers and single mothers, who were easily pressured into reporting on the activities of terrorists in their neighbourhoods. For example, they could be given the promise of freedom from prosecution while they abused young men, in return for acting as loyal terrorist assets of the State. Men and women, young and old were recruited using the MI5 matrix MICE: 'M' stood for money, used as an inducement; 'I' represented ideology, as in a person who opposed the IRA and wanted to make a difference; 'C' was for compromise or, as the KGB termed it, *Kompromat* – the practice of finding compromising personal information on a person as a means of forcing him or her to spy on the IRA; 'E' was for ego. MI5 believed that some of their targets suffered from what was called a 'Bond' complex, meaning that they were types who wanted to become spies for the thrill they believed a secret life of spying for the British could offer them.

In the Divis Flats complex, and elsewhere in Belfast, British Military Intelligence used tactics straight from the playbook of the British military's counterinsurgency strategies in Kenya, Aden and Cyprus. They 'swept' men and women off the streets or snatched them from their homes. They took them to barracks near their homes and made them stand behind a blanket with holes in it suspended from the ceiling. They would peer through these holes as people were paraded past them. If they spotted someone who was a member of the IRA, they hand-signalled soldiers watching the exercise. Sometimes, those forced to undertake this task were driven slowly through their local streets inside armoured personnel carriers and told to look through slits to spot terror suspects. It was an effective tactic.

The Unknowns, a cell of thirteen operatives, working closely with the IRA's Belfast Brigade staff, were tasked with tracking down spies within the IRA's ranks or identifying ordinary citizens who were reporting IRA activity to the British military. The members of this cell were given specialist training in weapons and explosives at IRA camps across the border in the Irish Republic, often in Donegal. The most senior figure in the cell was a former British soldier, Pat McClure. Small, quiet and self-assured, McClure was ruthless and totally committed to the aim of the Provisionals to establish a thirty-two-county socialist republic in Ireland. He epitomised the kind of romantic Irish nationalist who took the stage when the Provisional IRA was formed in January 1970, dwarfing the Official IRA with its Marxist agenda and a commitment to ending armed struggle. The Officials wanted to forsake the cult of the gunman but they were not always successful in this aim.

Two known female members of the Unknowns were Dolours Price and her sister, Marian. They had been members of the students

People's Democracy (PD) movement, which was an element of the civil rights campaign for change in the late 1960s. In 1969, when Dolours was eighteen and her sister fifteen, their relatives were burned out of their homes in streets linking the Catholic Falls and the Protestant Shankill roads. Like Jean McConville, they experienced loss and terror and had to relocate. Dolours had graduated from St Dominic's Girls' High School and was studying to be a teacher. She was intelligent and articulate. Both sisters had grown up in a prominent republican family and by 1969 they were seasoned protesters. In November 1969, for example, they were on the ill-fated PD march that was attacked by loyalists and members of the B Specials at Burntollet Bridge.

Dolours Price shared her memory of the march with my fellow writer Ed Moloney, explaining how she and her fellow marchers were led into a trap set by violent loyalists: 'Everything was quite jolly and we came to a bend in the road where they had gathered and the police were there, so clearly the police saw them there and the police led us into the trap really, the police allowed us to parade into the trap and they came from the fields, the hills and we were being very badly stoned, so some of us leapt over a hedge to our left, which dropped us into a field and we thought we'd be safe there. We weren't because they followed us and we ran down the field to a river and they kept coming so we thought we'll go into the river because if we go into the river they won't follow us. We went into the river and they didn't come in after us but they stoned us from both banks and when eventually we came out of the river they were dancing around us like Zulus, beating whoever they could get at ... the police commissioner, the guy with the blackthorn stick, whatever rank he holds, eventually came down the field and ushered them away and I suppose he thought we'd had enough and escorted us out of the field and at the gate the women loyalists were waiting with their Union Jack aprons on and they were wanting to hang us, to kill us. You've got to remember, we were only kids.'

It has always struck me as somewhat strange the way Dolours ended her recollection with the line 'You've got to remember, we were only kids.' Yes, by most standards the Price sisters were still children, but they were also committed republicans. It was, one might say, baked into their DNA. Within two years, they were highly trained operatives in the Unknowns, capable of breaking down weapons, firing them and building bombs, as well as setting timers for them. According to Dolours, they were given SAS-type training by senior IRA figures, among them one of the IRA's best bomb-makers.

Another interesting fact which stands out in Dolours' memories is her description of the relationship she shared with her aunt, Bridie Dolan. I was familiar with Bridie's name from my boyhood in the Lower Falls where older people would talk about her in hushed tones because of what happened to her. When Bridie was a girl in her twenties, according to my late Uncle John Clarke, who knew her when he was an IRA operative in the 1930s, the IRA were storing gelignite under the floorboards of her bedroom. This would have been familiar to many women in that neighbourhood; when the IRA asked if they could store weapons in a home, no one dared deny them. My grandmother, Margaret Clarke, was angry the IRA did this but her view would later conflict with Dolours' account; she saw her aunt not as a victim but a type of revolutionary hero. The story put about by some that Bridie was a member of the IRA was discounted by others and was never resolved.

Gelignite can be very unstable and if not kept at the required temperature, it will 'sweat' and explode without warning. That is what happened with the gelignite left in Bridie's house in 1938 and I understood from my grandmother Clarke that poor Bridie had her hands blown off and was left totally blind. This was one reason my grandmother detested the IRA. The other was that her son, my beloved Uncle John who was in the IRA in the 1930s, was beaten by prison officers and was later lobotomised but IRA leaders never came to ask about his well-being. My grandmother portrayed IRA leaders of that period as self-serving and callous. The IRA's behaviour towards her son and what happened to Bridie spoke to her of the organisation's lack of humanity. In my grandmother's telling, Bridie was a victim.

When Dolours spoke to Ed Moloney of Bridie, she dismissed the myth of her being a victim, preferring to describe her as a martyr and an honourable member of the IRA. It is clear, however, that the words victim and martyr are interchangeable depending on one's personal perceptions. This is how Dolours remembered her aunt: 'Aunt Bridie at the age of twenty-five was in Cumann na mBan of course and in 1938 she went to Lipton Arms dump and the volunteer who was to lift the dump and she was to be his escort – [he] didn't turn up and she decided herself that she would lift the arms dump and she did and it exploded on her and her hands were blown off and her eyes were blown out and she was very badly mutilated, scarred. And she lived like that for the rest of her life … Bridie was a living martyr and as children growing up, we were always aware of this – very aware of, you know, the sacrifice that she had made because of her part in the struggle, which in 1938 was practically dead really with very few people keeping it alive.

'My Aunt Bridie was an inspiration to us because she was – I never heard her complain once. I never ever heard her complain about her afflictions and she was a very staunch and strong republican and you know she would not give the time of day to anyone she didn't think was a worthy republican, which meant she didn't like very many people who claimed then to be republican. She would come and stay with us in the summer sometimes because I had one aunt who looked after her all the time and that was quite a strain because you know if you've no hands, you know someone has got to take you to the toilet you know. It's really as basic as that and someone has got to feed you and she was a smoker and as children once you got to a certain age – once you got to 8 or 9 – you had to be able to give her a smoke and that would be to hold the cigarette for her and put it to her mouth and take it away and I hated the job. I thought it was the most awful job and I couldn't stand it, but I did it because it was Bridie.

'She was a living martyr and to not do it would have been a crime against the notion of republicanism practically and if you misbehaved she would call you over – you'd be summonsed over and she would say, "Come over here till I hit you," and you'd have to walk over because if you gave her the runaround and she had to come after you looking for you then your mother gave you a good wallop as well, so you'd go over to Bridie and she'd give you a few taps with the old stump. The stump of the hand. We used to play with her stumps; they were like little cats' paws – and she would say, "Aren't they like little cats' paws?" because you could see where her digits had been, you could see the little lumps where her digits had been and I would bring my friends in from the street to see her you know "Come in and see my Aunt Bridie."

'I would pick her dark glasses off to show that she had no eyeballs which people would just … especially kids. I used to think I should charge an entrance fee – charge them a penny to come in and see her!

'I believe Bridie did influence me enormously because I believe that in many ways I felt an obligation to carry on the struggle as they had started it way back in the '30s and they had continued it from the '20s from 1916 and as far back as they traced republicanism and I believe the fact that she was in the state that she was in and the condition that she was in obliged me in some way to continue the struggle because it validated her sacrifice and to ignore the struggle would have made her sacrifice futile, useless, and in many ways that's part of the reason and subsequently when I've … when I've analysed myself and I've wondered as to my involvement and, apart from internment and

'69 and apart from all of those influences, that was one of the strong influences, to make some sense of what she had suffered and to do it by being a good republican and by continuing what she had started; what they had all started.'

When one reads these admissions, one cannot but wonder about the impact Bridie Dolan's personal suffering had on Dolours Price and Marian, her younger sister. The fact that these words of Dolours were uttered decades later, after she had joined the IRA and become one of the Unknowns, raises the question of how callous and emotionally tough she must have been in 1972. After all, she had been trained to bomb, kill people and rob banks. It is impressive that she broke the IRA mould by insisting on leaving Cumann na mBan and joining the ranks of the men in the IRA. The Belfast Brigade's leaders were impressed by her intelligence and fearlessness and granted her wish to join their ranks. Her ability to transfer from the IRA's women's organisation paved the way for Mairéad Farrell and other girls to do likewise.

Dolours knew Gerry Adams and Brendan Hughes, the IRA's Belfast Brigade intelligence tsar, who helped brief and advise the Unknowns on how to unearth British moles in the IRA. She would soon get to know Jean McConville.

Early in 1972 McConville was abducted on her way home from bingo by members of Cumann na mBan and taken to a house where she was roughed up, questioned and released. It should be asked why, if she was a British intelligence asset, as the IRA would later claim, her British 'handlers' did not remove her from Divis Flats following this incident and resettle her and her kids in an English town. There is no definitive answer to this question or whether, indeed, she was an asset. If she was, her 'handlers' might have decided that the IRA threat to her had passed. They might have been keen to see what more she could achieve by keeping her in place. Moreover, assets were often left in place and sacrificed throughout the conflict because 'handlers' found them expendable and the risk of burning one might expose how British intelligence functioned and recruited local people.

Despite all the focus on the Jean McConville case over the years and the revelations by Dolours Price, it has never been clear how much serious journalistic effort, if any, was put into an investigation of the IRA's interest in Jean. It must be kept in mind when analysing her case that multiple people linked to this unfortunate woman have had reason to lie and to conceal their ties to her. It is best to start with what we really know.

Just before Christmas 1972 Jean was dragged from her flat with her children crying and clinging to her legs. They would later be placed in the care of the State and Jean was never seen alive again with no one willing to talk about what had happened to her. I was a reporter with the *Belfast Telegraph* when I received the information about Jean from the British Army press desk. Those of us who knew how the army functioned were aware that the press desk was linked to a disinformation operation as part of a Psy-Ops (Psychological Operations) strategy. I was told that a mother of ten kids had vanished and it was believed that the Provos were her abductors. It was an ideal story for the Psy-Ops 'suits' at army HQ to exploit to damage the image of the Provos. I went to Divis Flats and spoke to my Official and Provisional IRA sources and came away with no credible information about an abduction. Some people told me that McConville had fled. Others said that she had been taken by the army. No one suggested that the IRA had taken her.

This was a period when people vanished for a variety of reasons and locals preferred not to confide what they saw for fear of suffering a similar fate. There was a palpable fear in Divis when I raised the issue of McConville's disappearance with some of her neighbours. Some in the complex pointed an accusing finger at the British Army, claiming that people were being abducted by soldiers to act as 'spotters'. There was so much paranoia that it was difficult to make sense of the myriad stories in circulation about Jean and others who could not be traced. I subsequently learned that the paranoia and competing conspiracies served the purposes of both the IRA and its adversary, British intelligence. If it could be said of an asset that he or she probably went off to work in England, it meant the British could use this asset without having to release him or her back to their family. If the IRA 'disappeared' someone, they could spread a rumour that the person had left to work in England or America or that they were in the hands of British intelligence. The awful truth was that Jean was in the clutches of the Unknowns, in particular Dolours Price, Pat McClure and another female operative.

The claims subsequently made by the IRA, and especially by Dolours Price, who broke ranks before her death to tell my friend Ed Moloney her side of the Jean McConville story, need to be carefully evaluated. Dolours' account cannot be taken at face value because some of the things she said simply do not hold up to scrutiny. They appear, in most instances, to be self-serving.

If one is to believe Dolours, she received orders to deliver Jean McConville to an IRA unit in the Irish Republic: 'I knew nothing about her. She had been arrested by Cumann na mBan girls, questioned, and basically had owned up to what she had done.' But Dolours was a high-ranking member of a specialist cell. Is it conceivable that she knew nothing about this thirty-eight-year-old mother? What does she mean by saying that Jean had 'basically owned up to what she had done'? And was Dolours really the type to just follow orders without ever asking why she was tasked with doing something? From everything we know about Dolours, she was highly inquisitive. I think this post-facto explanation was her trying to shed guilt.

Dolours later appeared to know more than she first alleged. According to her, McConville, who was known to wear cheap tartan slippers, was working for the British. Several IRA members forced to take part in the blanket parade at Hastings Street Barracks, within sight of the Divis Flats complex, recognised the tartan slippers beneath the blanket as Jean's and claimed that it was her voice they heard behind the blanket. But how was this possible when people behind the blankets used hand signals to soldiers when they spotted members of the IRA? This claim and an unproven accusation that Jean had a transmitter in her flat to communicate with her British 'handlers' proved her guilt, said Dolours.

Two things about these allegations struck me as implausible. Why would Jean walk from Divis Flats to an army facility at Hastings Street wearing her shabby household slippers? And how many people would have been familiar with her footwear or her voice? Moreover, the IRA never produced a transmitter and her kids never saw one. I suspect that these allegations were only made after her disappearance as a storyline concocted by the IRA. It reminded me of a story I was told by Brendan Hughes, when writing *The Dirty War*, about a married couple executed by the IRA in west Belfast around this time who were also accused of having a transmitter. When I asked to see the transmitter or a photo of it, I was told this was not possible. If the IRA had found transmitters used by suspected informers, they would have held a press briefing and displayed them. If the transmitter claim against Jean can be dismissed, one is entitled to be highly sceptical about other evidence used by the IRA to claim that she was a British spy.

We know that after Jean was dragged from her apartment, she was taken to a house in the Leeson Street area of the Lower Falls where she was interrogated. We do not know if she was tortured, but I think that it was highly likely she was threatened and beaten. IRA interrogators were not known to be softies. Hughes told me that interrogations were 'not pretty'. Unfortunately, no one present at Jean's interrogation ever admitted to being a party to it. Were some of the Unknowns in attendance? If the IRA believed that they had a British intelligence asset on their hands, the interrogators would have wanted to know everything at any cost. Gaps in Jean's story, as widely reported, confirm that there are people alive with a lot to hide, some of them prominent IRA figures who later passed themselves off as members of the IRA's political wing, Sinn Féin, rather than admitting to IRA membership and being linked to this and other incidents surrounding the 'disappeared'.

With the help of Brendan Hughes, I was able, in 1988, to expose, for the first time, the fact that the IRA was 'disappearing' its enemies but he never mentioned two of the victims: Jean McConville and Joe Lynskey. Why did he tell me about the others, including one whose parents did not even know that he was dead until they read my book *The Dirty War*, but not them? I believe, having spoken to sources, that Hughes was present when Lynskey and McConville were interrogated. I later came to believe that Hughes must have had a deep-seated guilt about the murders of some of the accused, hence his reluctance to discuss their deaths with me. He was, for example, close to Kevin McKee's family, even though he had signed off on young McKee's execution and secret burial, and he respected Joe Lynskey as an accomplished intelligence officer with whom he worked from time to time. I also suspect that he was troubled by his role in the ghastly murder of Jean McConville and was unable to open up to me about it.

For her part, Dolours Price, in her confessions to Ed Moloney, glossed over her role in the murders of some of the 'disappeared'. She claimed, for example, that her first encounter with Jean McConville was at the interrogation house after she had received orders to pick her up and transport her to an IRA unit in Dundalk across the Irish border. Dolours never offered any information about Jean's state of mind; just that she had 'told everything'. Was Jean beaten and cleaned up? What threats were made to her to get her to talk? Dolours gave away nothing about her situation or what she admitted to having done. Like Hughes, who told me that Jean was a British spy, Dolours appeared to know nothing of McConville's alleged transgressions.

I find it incredible that no one would have explained to Dolours Price, Pat McClure and the other female IRA operative what Jean had allegedly done or whom she had compromised. The truth is, however, that this trio did not need to be briefed because they were in the house where Jean was being interrogated and were privy to what was being said and decided. Dolours knew when she laid eyes on Jean that other members of the Unknowns had already fed Jean a bogus story that three members of the Catholic Legion of Mary would be driving her to the Irish Republic. When Dolours and her two companions walked into the interrogation room, Jean thought they were the Legion of Mary crew who were taking her to the Irish Republic to start a new life. She was so sure that this bogus story was true that she asked Dolours if she would be given money when she reached her destination. Perhaps Jean was told that her children would follow later. I suspect that her interrogators, as they had done with others in this situation, convinced her that her punishment was being banished to live in the Republic. She was assured that she was not facing a death sentence.

If one is to believe Dolours Price, Jean was very talkative while they were driving her to the border. In recalling the journey, Dolours, who was twenty-one at the time it took place, displayed her cynical nature when she remarked how Jean 'talked a lot' and was 'arrogant'. Arrogant is a word no one else has ever used when describing Jean McConville. Did it not occur to Dolours that this mother of ten was terrified or perhaps even elated that she had seemingly escaped a ghastly fate? At one stage on the journey Jean called the Provos 'bastards', according to Dolours, who later felt justified in saying that she 'condemned herself out of her own mouth'. So was Dolours willing to take the life of a person simply because they dared to criticise the IRA?

I doubt if Jean McConville said any of the things Dolours accused her of, unless, of course, believing she was now in the hands of members of a respected Catholic charity, she felt she could sound off about her interrogators.

Jean was handed over to an IRA unit in Dundalk who had orders to kill and secretly bury her. After several days passed, they decided that they could not kill a mother of ten and they relayed this news to the IRA's Belfast Brigade. When IRA leaders in Belfast heard that Jean was still alive, Dolours, McClure and their female associate were told to go back to Dundalk, kill her and bury her in a grave already dug for the purpose.

It is hard to believe that by this time Dolours still knew nothing about Jean McConville's background and alleged crime, although she made no mention of these matters in her subsequent confessions to Ed Moloney. All she would later concede to knowing was that Jean was behind a blanket in Hastings Street Barracks identifying young IRA operatives from the Divis Flats. It is conceivable that McConville would have admitted anything given her circumstances and the threats she likely faced from Hughes and others. Dolours commented to Ed Moloney that if she had known Jean was the mother of ten, she would have suggested expulsion from Northern Ireland and not execution. But was that not what Jean was promised? I personally find Dolours hard to believe. Jean, when being driven to the border, must have asked Dolours what was going to happen to her children. She was, after all, a good mother and her children adored her.

Dolours' explanation of what transpired smacked of an attempt to conceal her true role in this shocking saga. Even when she eventually described the way Jean died, her recollection of the episode lacked specificity. It seemed like she had constructed a narrative to dismiss the matter as quickly as possible. She relied on an obscure use of 'three volunteers' when talking about herself and her two companions as Jean's assassins. It was her way of depersonalising their roles.

This is how she later recalled it to Ed Moloney: 'There had been a grave dug by the Dundalk unit, and she was taken by the three volunteers to the grave, and shot in the back of the head by one of the volunteers, and then the other two volunteers each fired a shot so that no one would say that they for certain had been the person to kill her. There was an equal chance that it was any one of the three. And she was left in the grave and the local unit buried her.'

Note her lack of detail and her attempt to distance the actual killers from the atrocity. And what about Jean? What did she say when the Unknowns trio reappeared as her executioners? Was she terrified? Did she cry out and beg for mercy? Did she ask about the fate of her children? Did she ask for time to say a prayer? Did one of the trio of killers say a prayer over Jean? No, she was disposable in their minds. They even left it to the Dundalk unit to fill in the grave.

When Jean McConville was being executed, two or possibly three members of the local IRA who dug the grave and filled it in after her murder were also at the graveside. One was an informant for the local police force, An Garda Síochána, and he was also the son of the IRA's commander in Dundalk. It is not unreasonable to assume that this informant confided his role in the Jean McConville murder to his handlers, but we cannot know this for certain. After her murder, the informant was eventually unmasked as a traitor by the IRA, but, unlike others who betrayed the organisation, he was permitted to leave Ireland and settle in America. Was he pardoned because of his father's seniority in the IRA, or were other factors at play?

Before she died Dolours Price confirmed the presence of the others at Jean's death. It is horrific to imagine this frightened mother, standing or kneeling in a cold, dark grave with five people standing over her. None of them ever broke ranks to tell us what Jean said in the final minutes of her life.

What the gardaí knew about this murder and those of other

'disappeared' is a question that requires answers. The IRA's leadership, and its killers and gravediggers who were involved in disappearances throughout the Troubles, benefited from silence.

Patrick Radden Keefe, in his book *Say Nothing*, named a person he claimed was the second female shooter of the trio who murdered Jean McConville. I did not find any evidence to support his assertion that the person he named was indeed the second female shooter, although I was the first investigative journalist to expose the IRA practice of secret burials in 1988 in *The Dirty War*.

Dolours herself made many claims linking the Sinn Féin President, Gerry Adams, to the murder, and to the formation of the Unknowns. He has consistently denied the allegation and has dismissed claims that he was ever a member of the IRA. This is not the topic of this book and has been covered by other writers, especially by Ed Moloney, whose film *I Dolours* is an important piece of evidence for any student of the Troubles, as are his books on various aspects of the conflict. I wanted to focus on women's roles linked to this exceedingly depressing episode.

Later in life Dolours suffered from PTSD, due in part to being force-fed for six months in a British prison in a manner even some Guantanamo terror suspects did not experience. She also had to deal with her own personal demons linked to Jean's murder and the fate of other victims she helped disappear. Among them was her friend and mentor, Joe Lynskey, a former monk who was an intelligence officer attached to the Belfast Brigade. Lynskey made the mistake of ordering a failed murder attempt on an IRA officer. The motive for the murder was that Lynskey was having an affair with the officer's wife and wanted her husband killed. He had been using the officer's home as a bogus safe house while the officer was interned and it was then the affair began. Brendan Hughes found out about Lynskey's role in the attempted murder and recommended that he be court-martialled.

Lynskey was a highly regarded operative who worked closely with the Unknowns. The trio who shot Jean McConville were also involved in the murder of Lynskey. He made no attempt to escape on a car ride to the border or when he was handed over to his executioners. During the journey, he was seated in the rear, clutching a little overnight bag. He was a small, balding man who maintained a low profile. His secrecy gained him the moniker 'the mad monk' but in fact he was highly educated, studious and respected by those close to him. He tried to explain to Dolours on the journey what he had done to place himself in such a predicament, but she told him she did not want to hear what he had to say. She, nevertheless, admitted that she later felt a great deal of regret about leading a friend to his death.

Brendan Hughes had many regrets too. He broke with the Adams–McGuinness faction that moved to end the conflict, arguing that they sold out those who died for the cause. Dolours felt likewise and held a deep resentment of Gerry Adams. Towards the end of Hughes' life, as he was dying of cancer and drinking heavily, he was holed up alone in a flat in the Divis complex. I once asked him what it was like to look into the eyes of someone he knew was about to be executed. He replied that it was 'like staring into the recesses of a dark cupboard'. This was a terrifying, macabre statement. Was it what Dolours saw that drove her to become a drug addict, leading to her death?

Jean McConville's body was discovered in 2003 at Shelling Hill Beach on Carlingford Lough. I have been asked many times if I believe that she was a British intelligence asset. I cannot rule out the possibility, but in any respected court of law the evidence used to warrant her death would have been tossed away. The British authorities claim that she never worked with them, but this is an equally meaningless assertion since they have never been a reliable source on most matters linked to the dirty war.

Was it possible that Jean, lacking money to feed her kids, was bribed and pressured to work for British Military Intelligence? Yes, but even if it were true, she did not deserve to be murdered and 'disappeared'. My personal instinct is that Jean was not a spy, but I cannot fully discount the possibility that she was coerced by the British military into providing information on the local IRA. Given the lack of evidence that she was an informer, I am inclined to think that she was a victim of paranoia in her neighbourhood because of her reluctance to support the Provisional IRA.

The IRA's 'disappeared' policy, or what I called 'secret burials' in a chapter in *The Dirty War*, was described as a war crime by Dolours Price before her death. Sadly, the murder of women like Jean McConville did not end in 1972. It is difficult to write about Jean without mentioning the shameful killing, two decades later, of Caroline Moreland by the IRA's ISU.

Every time I look at photos of Caroline, I imagine her at home in her kitchen in 1994. The radio is on and she is swaying to the song 'Love Is All Around' by Wet Wet Wet, while her auburn curls caress her face with every movement of her body. Caroline, a thirty-four-year-old mother of three young children – two boys and a girl – was at home when IRA 'heavies' abducted her on 2 July 1994. It was eight weeks before the IRA ceasefire that led to its declaration of an end to hostilities.

Like Jean McConville, Caroline was always short of cash but her kids loved her because she did her best with what little she had. She would make them sandwiches for day trips to the seaside or to parks. She was a loving mother dedicated to her children. Rumours later claimed that she had been a member of Cumann mBan and my research shows that she used her nursing skills to patch up IRA personnel injured in operations in Belfast. On this basis alone, I believe that she was an active member in the women's branch of the Provisional IRA.

After her abduction, no one heard anything more about her, in the same way locals appeared to know nothing when Jean McConville was dragged out of her home, her little ones screaming at her abductors. Caroline was now in the clutches of one of the most ruthless IRA units, known in local parlance as 'The Nuttin' Squad'. It was the successor to the Unknowns and its modus operandi was to shoot its victims through the head after they had been tortured. Those who fell into this squad's hands rarely lived to tell the tale; one exception came in 1990, when an IRA officer, Sandy Lynch, who was a British intelligence asset, escaped from a house where he was being beaten and interrogated.

After Caroline Moreland was abducted, MI5 and Special Branch knew that the IRA had seized her. After all, the IRA's Belfast Brigade was riddled with informers. I was told by someone I considered a reliable source that Frederick Scappaticci interrogated Caroline immediately after her abduction because his handlers were keen to know what she might reveal to the IRA and the IRA wanted to know what she had told their enemy. This was not only incorrect, it was part of a campaign of deception to blame everything on Scappaticci, who was branded 'Stakeknife' by my late former colleague, Liam Clarke. What Liam failed to grasp, as did many of us then and since, is that the moniker Stakeknife was part of a clever ploy. Stakeknife was not an individual. It was a code-name for a British intelligence project. In other words, Scappaticci was not the only 'Stakeknife' agent within the IRA's ISU, which was interrogating and killing people judged to be IRA traitors. By making Scappaticci the one and only Stakeknife, the FRU leadership was able to deflect attention from its other Stakeknife agents embedded in the IRA's ISU for more than a decade. This issue impacts the truth about the murder of Caroline in ways I could never have imagined until I began writing this book.

Special Branch, from its own sources in the IRA, discovered very quickly that Caroline had been held in the Andersonstown area of

Belfast before being moved, within forty-eight hours, to the border area. The IRA taped an interrogation of her in which she admitted to being an informer. Snippets of her admission were played for the media. She was heard to say that she wished that she had not been involved with British intelligence, who coerced and threatened to send her to prison and to take her children from her if she did not do their bidding. There is no evidence that she was physically abused while in IRA custody or forced to make the statement of guilt. Perhaps, like others before her, she was promised immunity for her honesty and was convinced that she would be returned to her children.

When I first learned of Caroline's story, I initially assumed she was pressured to hide guns for the local IRA unit, a practice the IRA had of forcing on single mothers because they were easy to intimidate, but the truth was that she was an active member of the IRA. She first came to the attention of Special Branch in 1992. They ordered her arrest but after questioning she was released. The Branch had an agent in the IRA who had marked her for his Branch handlers as someone who could be recruited to operate at a high level within the IRA's Belfast Brigade. During a second arrest in 1994, Caroline broke under the pressure of a sustained interrogation, during which she was threatened that she would go down for decades and lose her children. Her interrogators were in the unique position of being able to pile on the pressure because they knew so much about her IRA activities from one of their own agents within the organisation. A source who saw her sitting alone in an interrogation room during this second arrest said she was crying and appeared emotionally broken. By then she had agreed to become a Special Branch informant.

It is unclear how the IRA discovered months later that Caroline was a Special Branch asset, but she would undoubtedly have been under scrutiny by the IRA's ISU operatives after being interrogated by the Branch and released without charge. I learned that after her second release, she was questioned by members of the ISU. Special Branch had briefed her on how to convince the IRA's spy hunters in the unit that she had not broken down under Branch interrogation, but some ISU personnel were not entirely convinced by her explanation of how she resisted intense pressure from Special Branch detectives.

We do not know exactly what led to her being abducted by the IRA four months later and handed over to 'The Nuttin' Squad'. This time she told her ISU interrogators that during her time in police custody, she had been subjected to tremendous emotional pressure by Special Branch whose detectives knew a great deal about her ties to the IRA. She described the terror she felt when her Branch interrogators threatened her with losing her kids if she did not become an agent of the State, while assuring her that they alone could protect her. Caroline became a pawn in a dirty war riddled with spies, double agents and callous IRA spy hunters.

Fifteen days after her abduction, an elderly woman walking her dog found Caroline's body on a rural Fermanagh road. She had been made to kneel and had then been shot three times through the head. It was overkill. Was it a trio of Unknown types who had been briefed to use the same tactic employed in the murder of Jean McConville, each one firing a bullet into Caroline's skull? Caroline's daughter, Shauna, later remarked that at least the IRA had not 'disappeared' her mother like they had done with Jean McConville. Caroline was subjected to a violent end, never to see her little ones again. The IRA dispensed its form of justice not caring that she was a mother of three.

Caroline's murder leaves us with many unanswered questions and her family is anxious to see them resolved. There are people in west Belfast who laid hands on this young mother and they should tell us the truth of what happened to her throughout this awful episode. The most cynical aspect of the murder was that it occurred just before an IRA ceasefire and a subsequent IRA declaration of an end to hostilities.

I asked several former IRA figures to identify who in the IRA's Northern Command gave the order to kill Caroline. They all agreed that, due to the politics of the time, it was a decision that would have been handled by Martin McGuinness who was on the IRA's Army Council. McGuinness also dealt with everything north of the Irish border.

One of the men I spoke to said that it would not have been a matter for McGuinness alone. According to him, 'The fact the IRA was about to make a major pitch about a ceasefire and ending the war would have made the killing of this poor woman a big issue. McGuinness would have had to discuss it with the Belfast Brigade and the Sinn Féin leadership, as well as his buddies on the Army Council. The Brits would not have attempted a rescue of her because they knew the IRA was about to capitulate and you don't upset the apple cart when it's full of apples. I am sure McGuinness, who was top dog, made the decision to kill her but only after he consulted one other figure in the North who was also a member of the Army Council. There were several stakeholders in making the decision to kill her. Ultimately, the Sinn Féin leadership had a say in ordering her execution. This was all about saying to the rank and file that anyone who betrays the IRA dies no matter if a ceasefire is in place. There was no need for it. It was cruel. They could have made an exception because the war was effectively over. But they did not want to be seen to be soft. They wanted to be seen to be in control as a warning to others who might be inclined to betray them. She was sacrificed to make a point.'

Caroline's death demonstrated that both sides in the war were equally vicious and cynical. It was particularly poignant and shameful, mirroring that of Jean McConville. The fact that the decision to kill her was made by IRA leaders who were about to end the war is a deplorable example of cynicism and cruelty. The identities of those who abducted Caroline, the ones who interrogated her, those who transported her to the border and her killers have been known to the authorities for years. Privately, the reason given that no one has been charged with her murder is that investigators lacked the intelligence to bring the guilty people before the courts. It is difficult to initiate murder charges or secure convictions without credible witnesses or forensic evidence. Nevertheless, it would be good to know how many of those known to be linked to this shameful murder were arrested and questioned and if any among them were State assets.

This is where I might have left Caroline's story had I not decided there were some aspects of it which still confused me. I had been assured, for example, that Scappaticci interrogated her and was involved in the decision to kill her. This was a lie. He was in Britain when she was murdered. So, if Scappaticci was not a prime mover in her murder, who was? Who was so powerful within the IRA that he could persuade the Army Council to risk a historic deal with Britain to end the war by slaughtering a young mother weeks before the IRA laid down its arms? Who could convince IRA leaders that Caroline was such a threat to the IRA that she had to be executed on a lonely country road?

It was at this point that I learned that Caroline had a lover who was a very senior IRA figure. Could this man have been responsible for her death? Did he ensure that at no time in IRA custody was she physically abused by interrogators during the fifteen days they held her? There was no evidence of abuse in her medical post-death records.

The fact that Caroline had a secret lover, one never mentioned in all the stories about her, alters the trajectory of her demise. This lover's identity is known to British intelligence. He was another Stakeknife agent. By encouraging the media to make Scappaticci the scapegoat in all the Stakeknife murders, British intelligence has been able to hide and protect all its other killers within the IRA's Internal Security apparatus, including Caroline's lover. He cannot be named for legal reasons but he had the motivation to kill Caroline if she had learned during their secret love affair that he was a double agent. Only a person with her lover's unassailable reputation within the IRA could have advocated for her execution and succeeded in getting Army Council approval for it. We can only speculate what he might have told the Army Council. Could he have suggested that she knew the identity of a major IRA figure involved in negotiations with the British who was a traitor? If she divulged his name, it had the potential to jeopardise support for a peace deal within the IRA's ranks.

There was always something highly suspicious about the IRA's decision to murder Caroline. She was a perfect example of a victim of the dirty war. In this case, the IRA needed to protect one of its own who was at the apex of decision-making at a critical time in the final stages of the peace process.

An unresolved question was why Special Branch did not launch an operation to rescue Caroline, just as they had done when Sandy Lynch was in the ISU's clutches and mere minutes before he was about to be shot. The answer, according to a retired British intelligence source, was that 'orders came down from the top not to rock the boat'. Talks with IRA leaders were at a delicate stage and it was 'imperative' that no one jeopardised them. A rescue operation might have led to a gun battle and the deaths of IRA personnel. Such a scenario had the potential to encourage the IRA rank and file to reject any forthcoming deal with Britain.

Did the order from the top originate with MI5? The source did not believe so: 'It came from above, as far up the Intelligence chain as it gets, and it applied to everyone, including MI5, Special Branch and Military Intelligence. I suspect the matter of this poor lady was considered the IRA's business and not ours.'

When one thinks of the top of the British intelligence chain, one must consider the Prime Minister's Office, their Director of Intelligence and a joint intelligence committee representing the various branches, including MI5 and MI6 as well as Military Intelligence.

Caroline's daughter, Shauna, ignored my requests to speak to her about the stresses caused by her late mother's murder, but her brother Marc has launched a legal case for a review of the murder with the assistance of his lawyer, Kevin Winters. In his request for an independent inquiry into the killing, Marc accepted that his mother had been 'an informer for the security services'. The use of the phrase 'security services' was, I suspect, intended to mean Special Branch and MI5.

The basic aim of the legal strategy was to point out the failure of the RUC to conduct a thorough inquiry into Caroline's death or to examine the role of someone referred to as 'Stakeknife' in respect of the activities of the IRA's ISU. The legal review acknowledged that two persons were arrested and questioned about her murder, but no one was brought to justice. I was intrigued by some aspects of this review document, not because of what it stated but what it deliberately left unsaid. It mentioned a person named Stakeknife but did not specify that this individual was Frederick Scappaticci. One has to wonder if Marc's lawyer had bigger fish to fry by not naming Scappaticci as Stakeknife. Was his aim to seek a broader investigation into the role of all agents within the IRA's ISU? It is important to note that British agents within the ISU were either former British soldiers or the likes of Scappaticci and Sandy Lynch who were IRA officers recruited by Special Branch. The Stakeknife agents were controlled exclusively by the FRU, and Special Branch ran its own agents whom they refused to share with British Military Intelligence.

Until there is a thorough, unimpeded investigation into the IRA's ISU, the FRU's Stakeknife Project and the role of Special Branch agents within the IRA, secrets surrounding murders like Caroline Moreland's will not be fully understood nor will the perpetrators be prosecuted.

15

A POLITICAL FIREBRAND

PART I

IN THE EYES OF HER contemporaries, she will always remain the small, frail, miniskirted student in a leather jacket and boots standing on a barricade in Derry's Bogside in 1969 shouting through a megaphone at lines of policemen.

Across the Atlantic in Woodstock, Joe Cocker was singing the Beatles song 'With a Little Help from My Friends', and the 1967 hippies of Haight Ashbury were flowing into New Orleans. In Derry people were marching and singing 'We Shall Overcome', the chosen anthem of the Northern Ireland Civil Rights Association.

The girl on the barricades in the autumn of 1969 was twenty-two-year-old Bernadette Devlin, a Queen's University student who had become the symbol of a new generation of young, educated Catholic activists. In 1968 they had taken to the streets to ask the British government to grant Catholics the same civil rights as people elsewhere in the United Kingdom but no one in the corridors of power in London was listening. For decades, successive British governments had abdicated their constitutional duty to Northern Ireland, allowing Unionist governments in Belfast to gerrymander constituencies and to treat

Catholics like second-class citizens by denying them fair allocation in jobs and housing. The political dam keeping Catholics hemmed in politically and socially was bursting, yet in Britain no one cared.

Bernadette looked more like a high-school girl than a university student with a smile accentuated by a cute gap between her upper teeth and dark-brown hair flowing to her shoulders. She was the icon for a generation that mimicked the tactics of the 1965 black marchers in America who trekked from Selma to Montgomery to demand an end to segregation and the right to vote. Like their brethren in the US, Northern Ireland's civil rights campaigners were deemed a threat to the State. Bernadette and her fellow protesters, such as Eamon McCann and John Hume, would be beaten off the streets by the police and its paramilitary arm, the B Specials.

Standing on a barricade in the Catholic Bogside in 1969, Bernadette demanded that the RUC leave the area. For some, she had swapped protest for confrontation. She was articulate and her fiery rhetoric quickly made her a hated figure in the unionist community. In contrast, some nationalists saw her as their Joan of Arc: unafraid, committed and determined. When I first saw her in my early reporting days, I was impressed by how resilient and tough she seemed.

Before she stood astride Bogside's barricades, Bernadette's life had been transformed in ways that even she could never have imagined. The year 1969 was singularly defining in her life. In spring she became a Member of the British Parliament for Mid Ulster, making her the youngest MP of her generation. No one in her family expected her to rise to such heights. Also in that year, when she was in her last year of a psychology degree, Queen's University refused to let her sit her finals, thereby expressing their opposition to what they called her 'extra-curricular activities'. It was an appalling decision by the main centre for learning in Northern Ireland, which had well-established ties to the unionist hierarchy. Queen's political linkage to unionism remained in place throughout the Troubles. No apology was offered to Bernadette Devlin for what was a bigoted decision to cancel the last two months of her scholarship. It remains a stain on the history of the institution, though she was not the only female to be treated in this fashion by Queen's.

Josephine Bernadette Devlin, born on 23 April 1947, was the third-eldest of the six children of John and Elizabeth Bernadette Devlin. Catholic families of that generation in Cookstown and nearby Dungannon survived on social security benefits. Her father, who held republican views, was a big influence on her childhood but he died when she was nine. Like many young girls, she had to help her mother around the house and tend to her younger siblings. She was considered industrious and studious, traits that were evident when she was in her teens attending St Patrick Girls' Academy in Dungannon. She would later admit that even though her father had talked politics to her, it was not until she became a civil rights protester that she realised how many of the complaints he made about their society and its treatment of Catholics were accurate. The sudden realisation that he was right all along struck her in 1968 when she witnessed policemen with batons beating peaceful protesters on the streets of Derry.

It is important to note that Bernadette's politics in the late 1960s were focused on social issues and did not embrace the republicanism of her father or those senior IRA figures clearly present in the ranks of the civil rights struggle. The prospect of using violence for political ends was anathema to her and to many student marchers. At Queen's she was one of the founders of the PD protest movement, many of whose members were Protestants. Whether you like, disapprove of or detest her, she is a remarkable figure. When I interviewed her for a BBC television documentary, she did not shrink from answering all my questions, a trait which was not evident in interviews I conducted with other political figures.

As the youngest MP, Bernadette's maiden speech in the hallowed halls of Westminster stands as a testimony of who she was at that time. On 22 April 1969, aged twenty-two, she revelled in the opportunity to speak to the British Parliament in a chamber filled mostly with men. I suspect that there were few females of her age who possessed the candour and courage required for such a moment. She was the youngest woman elected to Parliament and was seen by many in republican circles to be following in the footsteps of Constance Georgine Markievicz, the Irish revolutionary and suffragist who had been a member of Cumann na mBan and James Connolly's Irish Citizen Army. In the latter role, Markievicz took part in the 1916 Rising in Dublin. It is believed that on the first day of the Rising she fought in St Stephen's Green, where she shot a policeman who later succumbed to his injuries. The playwright Sean O'Casey, a Citizen Army volunteer, later recalled how she displayed courage 'in abundance' and 'wore it like clothing'. Unlike Bernadette, Markievicz was born into wealth, which she gave to the poor before her death in 1927, and, also unlike Bernadette, she did not take her seat in Westminster. It meant that she was denied the right to deliver a maiden speech

Comparisons were quickly made between the slightly built girl from Cookstown and the tall, striking aristocrat whose father, Sir Henry William Gore-Booth, was an Anglo-Irish landowner and famous Artic explorer. In case the parliamentary audience in 1969 missed the link between these two women, Bernadette reminded them at the outset of her address: 'I stand here as the youngest woman in Parliament, in the same tradition as the first woman ever to be elected to this Parliament, Constance Markievicz, who was elected on behalf of the Irish people.'

The words in her speech echoed many of her late father's opinions: 'There is no place in society for us, the ordinary "peasants" of Northern Ireland. There is no place for us in the society of landlords because we are the "have-nots" and they are the "haves". In asking her fellow parliamentarians to address inequality in Northern Ireland, she claimed to speak for Protestants and Catholics who, she said, lived under 'landlords' who even held fishing rights and owned the land on which people had lived for generations. 'This is the ruling minority of landlords who, for generations, have claimed to represent one section of the people and, to maintain their claim, divide the people into two sections and stand up in this House and say that there are those who do not wish to join the society,' she continued.

After lecturing her fellow parliamentarians about social injustice in Northern Ireland, she gave them a taste of what she had witnessed on the streets of the Bogside: 'I saw with my own eyes 1,000 policemen come in military formation into an oppressed, and socially and economically depressed area – in formation of six abreast, joining up to form twelve abreast like wild Indians, screaming their heads off to terrorise the inhabitants of that area so that they could beat them off the streets and into their houses.' She added that the Honourable Members might find it amusing that she had helped to build barricades in the Bogside in the early morning hours. As, a person who believed in non-violence, it was her only option, she assured them.

No one escaped her criticism, including British Tories, Northern Ireland's Unionists and even the government of the Irish Republic, which she defined as 'capitalist like the Tories'. It was a speech that the British and those on the left in Irish politics surely applauded and there were some important truths articulated. She spoke of underlying problems in Northern Ireland and the dangers ahead and warned that leaving the Unionist government at Stormont in charge of Northern Ireland would solve nothing. She would be proved right about this. These Unionists were incapable of delivering proper reforms.

Leaving them in power instead of abolishing Stormont after the tragic events of August 1969 would prove to be a fatal error. They were left in charge of the RUC, which desperately needed to be reformed, as well as the paramilitary B Specials and even the British Army after it arrived on the streets of Belfast and Derry. One of Bernadette's final pieces of advice to the British Parliament on this day, four months before Northern Irish society plunged into a tribal chasm, was her caution to those who thought sending troops to Northern Ireland would solve the issue. In a line like a Cassandra echo, she said, 'If British troops are sent in, I should not like to be either the mother or sister of an unfortunate soldier stationed there.'

One wonders if taking her seat in Westminster would have garnered the approval of her father, had he been alive. After all, she was thumbing her nose at Irish republicanism which had historically promoted political abstentionism. Her heroine, Markievicz, refused to take her seat when elected to the British House of Commons. Bernadette also did something Markievicz would have considered heretical. She took the oath of allegiance to the British Crown, a requirement for her 'to be seated' to make a maiden speech.

As she left Parliament on that historic day, the Beatles 'Get Back' was about to dominate the pop music charts. If she heard it, would she have imagined it held a message for her to return to where she really belonged?

Once back in Northern Ireland, she was on the radar of the RUC and the excessively armed B Specials. Her criticism of them in Parliament had not gone unnoticed. During what would become known as the Battle of the Bogside in August 1969, the RUC got its revenge by arresting Bernadette for inciting a riot. By then, a bonfire of suspicion and sectarian hatred had exploded in west and north Belfast leading to the arrival of British soldiers with fixed bayonets, ready, it seemed, to protect the Catholic population. I saw them, four abreast, striding through the Lower Falls, arriving close to the Clonard area after loyalists burned all the houses in Bombay Street behind Clonard

Monastery. The soldiers, mostly young men aged between eighteen and twenty-five, looked confused, as soldiers do when they lack a defined enemy and no one has fully explained their role to them.

Bernadette was released after serving a brief prison sentence and afterwards flew to America where her notoriety led to her appearance on the top-rated *Johnny Carson Show*. She would quickly demonstrate that controversy followed her and she welcomed it. She had moved to the left politically, further away from the republicanism of her father. She was now attracted more to socialism, which was at the core of international protest movements. In part she mirrored many political activists of her generation, whether they lived in Belfast, Alabama or Paris. She disliked the traditional Irish-American attachment to republicanism, preferring to compare the problems in Ireland with issues facing blacks in America. Those parallels were not necessarily perceived as accurate or politically appropriate by many white Americans and Irish-Americans, a considerable faction of whom were historically racist. Bernadette did not seem to understand the complexity of American politics. For some observers, she exuded a naivete which Irish-American leaders were quick to identify. She failed to grasp, for example, that while the civil rights marchers in Derry knew the words of 'We Shall Overcome', most of white America, including many Irish-Americans, refused to identify with this protest song.

For all her experience on the streets of Derry, this twenty-two-year-old had yet to acquire a depth of knowledge of a wider world. While it did not limit her intellectually, she lacked the political and social experiences to address many and varied complex issues. When she was handed the key to New York City, she arranged for it to be given to the Harlem chapter of the Black Panthers. Whatever her goal, this was considered an offensive gesture and a sign of her political naivete. It is questionable how much she knew about the Black Panthers, and whether, in fact, they were truly representative of the civil rights cause of most African-Americans. Unlike Martin Luther King Jr, the Black Panthers did not exclude the use of violence. They allied themselves with international liberation movements and adopted a form of Marxist-Leninist economic doctrine. They were, nevertheless, a significant component within the US civil rights struggle. In some respects, they reflected aspects of the republican element within the Northern Irish civil rights movement.

After her US visit Bernadette began adopting a republican socialist doctrine, very much in keeping with James Connolly's socialism and the ideas which had defined her heroine Markievicz. In 1971, still single, she gave birth to a daughter, Róisín.

The year 1972 was a defining one in the Troubles. Internment without trial, introduced the previous August, was in full force. It confirmed that Bernadette Devlin was right when she warned in her maiden speech about the dangers of leaving the Unionists in control of Northern Ireland. They had persuaded Edward Heath, the British Prime Minister, that a British military solution was possible. The result was that elements of the British military and political apparatus were reaching back into a dark colonial past for answers to what was a political and not a military issue in Northern Ireland.

On Sunday, 30 January 1972, about 10,000 people assembled in Derry for a march to protest internment without trial. The outcome was tragic. Members of the British Army's Parachute Regiment, which had recently shot innocent people in the Ballymurphy area of west Belfast, turned their guns on innocent protesters in Derry's Bogside. Twenty-five paratroopers fired their weapons, all of them using live rounds. They killed thirteen people and injured fifteen others. Subsequently, they claimed that they had been shooting at IRA gunmen. The British government spread the same lie and launched an inquiry under the chairmanship of Lord Widgery in an effort to whitewash what had happened. The atrocity became known as Bloody Sunday.

According to Derry politician Mitchel McLaughlin, Bernadette Devlin was a British military target on that fateful day. As a witness for the Saville Inquiry, a second British inquiry into Bloody Sunday which began in 2000, McLaughlin recalled being at Free Derry Corner in the Bogside on Bloody Sunday listening to Bernadette talking to a small crowd. Suddenly there were several cracks, which he realised were shots from automatic rifles of the self-loading type (SLRs) used by the British Army. Like most people living in Derry or Belfast, or reporters like me who witnessed gun battles, the sound of a discharge from an SLR was distinguishable from the rattle of a Thompson sub-machine gun, a Sterling sub-machine gun, a pistol and a .45 revolver. His memory of that moment was vivid, as he told the inquiry: 'I saw a bullet hit the wall above Bernadette Devlin's head. Brick-dust flew out as the bullet made contact. Bernadette Devlin was still standing up at this time, although she may have been in the process of bending down to take cover.' In the chaos, Bernadette was unaware of having cheated death.

There is no longer any doubt about what transpired on Bloody Sunday or the British military cover-up which followed. It is surprising, however, that a few authors who should know better have continued to promote conspiracy theories about the events of the day. A favourite lie in Parachute Regiment ranks is that the IRA had a makeshift hospital in the Rossville Flats of the Bogside and that dead IRA gunmen killed by Parachute Regiment snipers were ferried across the border and secretly buried. The reality is that the Paras deliberately opened fire.

The day after the massacre Bernadette was in the British House of Commons, due to speak as an MP, but she was denied the opportunity. In her anger and frustration she slapped the Tory Home Secretary,

Reginald Maudling, across the face after he said that the British Paratroopers only killed in self-defence in Derry. Prime Minister Edward Heath later declaimed that she had really planned to physically assault him but her arms were not long enough, so she laid into Maudling. He described the incident as the 'Honourable Lady' launching herself from the opposition benches at him like she was crazy and had the intent to murder him.

Field Marshal Lord Michael Carver, who provided me with damning classified information about Heath when I was making my Channel 4 documentary *The Last Colony*, told me that Heath hated Devlin. He was not sure why she topped his list since there were many other people in Ireland for whom he had absolutely no respect. Carver put it down to Heath's general dislike of women, even Margaret Thatcher. He said that after the Commons episode when Bernadette struck Maudling, Heath told friends that it would have been better 'if she had been born dead'. The venom in Heath's words shocked Carver, though he pointed out that Heath was a 'very strange fellow'. He did not elaborate on what he meant by this description, but it was clear that he and the other generals, like Harry Tuzo and Frank King, who spoke to me privately and damned Heath, considered him arrogant and untrustworthy; a man who would sell the British Army down the river to protect his own backside. He had lied to them about internment and 'his other grandiose schemes'. They all agreed that, even after Bloody Sunday, Heath wanted the army to shoot protesters on the streets of Northern Ireland. Perhaps, if Bernadette had known about this, she would have reached for Heath even if it had meant leaping over Maudling.

Bernadette probably did not imagine that her 'Maudling slap' would deliver her some musical fame, albeit in the world of anarchist punk. The band Chumbawamba was so impressed with her that it dedicated its fourth album, *Slap*, to her. The seventh track on the album, also named 'Slap', referenced her assault on Maudling 'whose policies towards Northern Ireland contributed to the Bloody Sunday incident'.

Maudling hated visiting Northern Ireland. On his first visit to Belfast, he was so depressed and disheartened that when he sat in the plane to return to London, he called a stewardess with the demand, 'Get me a large Scotch! What a bloody awful country.'

In 2003, two years before he died, Edward Heath was forced to appear before the Saville Inquiry. During his testimony, he had to address issues I had raised with him a decade earlier when I was making *The Last Colony*. I had challenged him over outrageous things he had said behind closed doors in No. 10. In response to my questions about him telling the British Army it could legally shoot protesters on the streets of Northern Ireland, he ordered me, my executive producer, Ian Kennedy, and our camera crew out of his home in Salisbury. He subsequently refused to speak to the media about the Troubles until he was called to appear at the Saville Inquiry. During his testimony he was asked to respond to all the matters I had put to him a decade before.

On her twenty-sixth birthday, in 1973, Bernadette Devlin married 'the love of her life', Michael McAliskey, who was a teacher. The tabloid hounds wanted to know if he was the father of her child born out of wedlock.

Sometimes I think of Bernadette as a human version of the Duracell battery. Over decades, she was always charged, ready for the next protest or challenge, yet there was potential for chaos while she navigated the ever-changing highways and byways of the Irish political landscape. Her flirtation with socialism led her into the world of older republicans who claimed to be the driving force behind the civil rights movement beginning in the mid-1960s. They claimed the socialist mantle of James Connolly but also tinkered with Marxism, which they had studied while languishing in prison in the 1950s during the failed IRA border campaign. My late Uncle John became a devotee of Marx and Lenin following spells in prison, which compelled me to conclude that many of the IRA men of his generation underwent that transformative political experience. Those who subsequently perceived advantage in the civil rights struggle had by then embraced Connolly socialism, not always realising its roots were in anti-imperialism. They emerged from prison at the end of the 1950s determined to jettison the cult of the gunman and replace it with social action. Their rejection of traditional republicanism, with its attachment to the Catholic Church in Ireland, set them on a collision course with republican traditionalists. Within a decade, this would lead to the split in the republican movement; the result was that, in January 1970, two separate IRAs had emerged. The Connolly socialists became known as the Officials, or 'Stickies', and the traditionalists became the Provisionals.

Within the Officials' leadership there were two factions, one led by Seamus Costello, who, at the formative age of seventeen, was involved in the IRA's border 'war' in the 1950s. He performed so well that he became known as 'the Boy General'. He was born in the Irish Republic but had close links to IRA figures in the North. He promoted a leftward political trend in the IRA using his influence with senior figures in Dublin. Costello was almost a decade older than Bernadette; he nevertheless admired her and she him. They bonded politically because of a shared desire to establish a new political party based on republican socialist principles.

In December 1974, at a press conference in a Dublin hotel, Costello launched what would soon be called the IRSP, with himself as chairman. He neglected to mention that, like the Official and Provisional wings of the IRA, the IRSP would have a military wing, the INLA. Former Official IRA members joined his new military wing, some bringing with them arms belonging to the Officials, a move that led to a bitter feud which would lead to the loss of lives on both sides.

Bernadette McAliskey was in the leadership of the IRSP but there is no evidence to suggest that she knew about Costello's secret military group. Some might wonder how she could not have known, but what is clear is that she was never a member of it. People who knew her well agreed that she would not have wanted to play any part in a military set-up. She was on record telling people for decades not to join paramilitary organisations. Yet, while she had never shown any desire to support IRA violence, when her name was attached to a party with an armed faction, she was quickly accused of INLA membership. Within a year, she had resigned from the IRSP after it failed to bring the INLA under its political control. Close to 50 per cent of the membership of the IRSP political leadership followed her out the door. Costello was assassinated three years later by a member of the Official IRA who was then killed by the INLA. Bernadette's foray into the machinations of Costello, a man steeped more in a traditional IRA military history, was another example of her political naivete. She was too often willing to take people at face value, ignoring the contentious, bitter and conspiratorial nature of republican politics down the decades.

While 'the Boy General' Costello created the INLA, the one fighter in its ranks who came to symbolise its military ruthlessness and effectiveness was Dominic McGlinchey, to whom the British tabloids gave the moniker 'Mad Dog'. McGlinchey, who had once been a leading Provisional, was not mad but he was ruthless. While the INLA was small compared to the other militant republican groups, it attracted attention for carrying out some of the most high-profile assassinations of the Troubles, such as the killing of Airey Neave, and using for the first time a mercury-tilt-switch bomb. It was also involved in mass murders.

Much of the INLA's business revolved around bitter internal shootings and feuds with the Official IRA. When McGlinchey became chief of staff of the INLA, he ran it like his own fiefdom. It was during his time at the top of the organisation that it began to fragment into groups fighting to control their own turf. It was responsible for sectarian murders, not necessarily ordered by McGlinchey, and in Belfast petty criminals joined its ranks and used their guns to carry out robberies for personal gain. It suffered its greatest losses from internal feuds, which led eventually to the assassination of McGlinchey. Before an assassin got to him, his thirty-one-year-old wife, Mary, was targeted. In 1989, when she was bathing her two young sons, aged nine and ten, in her home in Dundalk, two gunmen wearing balaclavas entered her home. They beat her and dragged her away from her sons as she pleaded with them for the lives of her boys. They took her to the bathroom where they shot her nine times at close range in the head, neck and chest. The killing was the result of an internal INLA feud, but the lack of a proper investigation meant it went unsolved and led some to believe that the authorities knew who was responsible and had prior knowledge of it. Dominic McGlinchey had a list of over ten members of the INLA he blamed for his wife's murder and his aim was to kill every one of them. He survived various assassination attempts by enemies in the INLA but was eventually killed in front of his son as he made a call from a public phone kiosk in Dublin. His murderer, armed with a shotgun, was a member of the Official IRA. By then, McGlinchey had left the INLA and had made this public, but he had many enemies. One of his last comments was that he would be remembered for nothing.

Bernadette had her own brush with death, years before the McGlincheys were murdered. It was 1981 and she was again a prominent voice on the airwaves and in the streets, campaigning for IRA prisoners involved in the 'blanket protests' and later the dirty protests inside the Maze Prison. She had found her voice again and when the hunger strikes began in 1980, she was prominent in the 'Smash-The-H-Blocks' campaign. She, her husband, Michael, and their three children – Róisín (9), Deirdre (5) and Fintan (2) – were all at home in their remote farmhouse near Coalisland at 8.30 on the morning of 16 January 1981 when her would-be killers arrived. The McAliskey children were in their bedrooms and their parents were in the kitchen, unaware that three gunmen had just cut the telephone cable outside their home.

Bernadette and her husband only realised that they were in imminent danger when one of the gunmen began knocking down their front door with a sledgehammer. Michael ran to the door, hoping to draw the intruders outside, and shouted at Bernadette to hide. He met three assassins, armed with pistols, as they pushed into the house and forced him into the kitchen, where they shot him twice at close range. Bernadette had run to the main bedroom, but the gunmen were methodical in their pursuit of her. Without saying a word, they followed her and shot her eight times. One bullet missed her heart by a centimetre. They then strolled out of the house.

Shortly after Bernadette and her husband were shot, soldiers of the 3rd Parachute Regiment who had been patrolling nearby arrived outside her home. One came inside and saw her and her husband lying in pools of blood on the floor. She told him to see to her children. His companions made no effort to enter the home to offer first aid, instead remaining outside for thirty minutes until medical help arrived. Bernadette felt that they were hoping she and her husband would bleed out. Meanwhile, the three assassins were apprehended driving back to Belfast. Bernadette and her husband survived, but I have learned from talking to survivors that even though bullet wounds heal, the mental pain and fear generated by facing death remain. In some cases, the body suffers too, with lagging aches and horror etched into it. 'No one ever feels the same or even looks the same after staring at death,' my late friend Detective Inspector Jimmy Nesbitt used to say.

Bernadette's memory of the assassins was that they were cold and 'methodical', suggesting that they had done this before. There is little doubt that they had carried out due diligence, because they knew how to cut the telephone wires to the house before gaining access. They were members of the UDA's South Belfast Battalion. At this time, UDA hit squads such as this one were under the control of UDA chief John McMichael. A year before the attempt to kill the McAliskeys, he warned that the UDA might have to send hit squads into nationalist areas to take out 'the leaders of the revolt'. When asked what this meant, he replied, 'Eliminate them!'

At that time, the UDA was riddled with British agents, mostly members who had been encouraged or blackmailed into working for Special Branch, MI5 or elements of British Military Intelligence, such as the FRUs run by Colonel J. (Brigadier Brian Kerr) in the 14th Intelligence Company. Within this decade, 14th Intelligence would have its own soldier-agent, Brian Nelson, running UDA hit squads and providing them with details on republican targets to be eliminated. Some targets were not at all republican, like the prominent Catholic lawyer Pat Finucane. Bernadette believed that the British authorities had prior knowledge of the threat to her life and her family but allowed the attack to proceed. There was no evidence of a special British military operation in the area before or after the shooting, yet it appeared the army was close by the McAliskey home at the time and was able to find and arrest the gunmen when they were making their escape. The episode in some respect mirrored the events leading to the murder of Rosemary Nelson. The army had been in the vicinity of Rosemary's home in the days before her murder but it was pulled out just before her murder. I have no doubt from my enquiries that elements of the British intelligence apparatus knew about the UDA plan to kill Bernadette.

Dominic McGlinchey had stared down the grim reaper several times. Maybe that was why Bernadette formed a close bond with him in the 1980s and kept the friendship up to his death in 1994. In dealing with dissent in the INLA, McGlinchey was ruthless, but this side of his character was never referenced in her approval of him. Despite her opposition to violence, she carried McGlinchey's coffin, as did her daughter, Róisín, along with Provisional IRA leader Martin McGuinness. Bernadette said this of McGlinchey: 'He was the finest republican of them all. He never dishonoured the cause he believed in. His war was with the armed soldiers and the police of this state.'

Such praise might, for some, befit a towering historical figure like Michael Collins but hardly a republican militant such as McGlinchey, who was vicious with his own when they betrayed him and even more brutal with his perceived enemies. He was not Costello who, for all his perceived flaws, was a serious political thinker, albeit one who was narcissistic. Bernadette had a shrewd mind, so to have heaped this kind of praise on McGlinchey, she must have had long and detailed political discussions with him. A source told me that it was Bernadette who persuaded him to abandon the gun and leave the INLA before he was killed.

I suspect that she must have seen something of herself in him. She defended him by insisting that he 'bore no resemblance' to the person portrayed by the media. In her opinion, his thinking was 'fundamentally democratic'. In furtherance of her defence, she praised his intellect and told David Sharrock of *The Guardian* that he was 'the greatest republican of his generation'. In making such a comment, she redefined republicanism as a 'secular egalitarian democracy'.

On choosing these words, she was really referring to her and Costello's aspirations in a language never publicly associated with

Dominic McGlinchey. This was the language of James Connolly's brand of socialism, not of republicanism in an Ireland context. McAliskey had always advocated for the protection of the freedom and rights of citizens, irrespective of their social or religious attachments, and for the fair distribution of wealth and natural resources. She advocated for the rights of everyone, Catholic and Protestant, to shape society through the political process. Like Connolly, she believed in secularism, having decided that religion in the political and social sphere, especially where the Catholic Church in Ireland was concerned, was a negative element.

When I hear Kris Kristofferson singing 'The Pilgrim', I am reminded of McGlinchey. He, too, was a walking contradiction, but so was Bernadette at times. On the other hand, she was a potent symbol of her generation, whether you approve or not of her methods, principles and associations. Had she been born in Paris or Alabama I have little doubt that she would have pounded the streets in protest as she did in Northern Ireland. She would have stood atop barricades and confronted the powerful. She was a young woman when she was thrust into the maelstrom of Irish–British politics. It was a critical time in history, yet she had the courage to deliver a maiden speech in the British Parliament much like a seasoned politician would have done. Bernadette McAliskey was a bright beacon of her generation, when females were trying to escape the narrow confines men had established for them, especially in the social and political spheres. She did not advocate for militant Irish republicanism, though she flirted with ideas that were promoted by some of its more prominent figures like Costello and McGlinchey. It is true that she lost her way at times but rarely her political compass. She is both a victim of the Troubles and one of its most prominent figures. She paid a terrible price for her political activism.

PART II

When your mother is Bernadette McAliskey, it is to be expected that your life will be different from that of your contemporaries. When you choose to carry her name and live in the society where your mother was such an iconic figure, people expect you to be a political firebrand as well.

Róisín was only nine years old when she stood over the bullet-riddled bodies of her parents. She grew up resembling her mother in appearance and, by all accounts, she has the same forceful personality and a consuming interest in social issues. In the public eye, she was tainted with her mother's political past after the British tabloid media photographed her carrying the coffin of Dominic McGlinchey.

Róisín emerged from childhood suffering from frequent joint pain and asthma attacks, which left her frail for weeks at a time. Nevertheless, the pain and discomfort did not deter her from a busy work and activism schedule. Like her father, she became a schoolteacher, and like her mother, she developed a keen interest in community issues and was frequently critical of British policy-making. The fact that she was the daughter of Bernadette Devlin ensured that she was often in the spotlight. Following in her mother's footsteps, she constantly highlighted social inequalities, the plight of women in the home and in the workplace, and the failure of the British government to address the problems facing men and women, Catholics and Protestants in Northern Ireland's prisons.

In 1996 she was living with her boyfriend, Sean McCotter, in a house close to her parents' home in Coalisland. Sean was a young man who had served six years for an IRA bombing, but he was no longer connected to the IRA. His uncle was Seamus Twomey, one of the founders of the Provisional IRA. This shaped some negative perceptions of Róisín but as someone later pointed out, falling in love with a former IRA man was not a crime in itself. Critics, nevertheless, saw it as a cause for concern. At the start of November she was three months pregnant but even that did not slow her down. However, things were about to change.

On the morning of 20 November armed police and soldiers stormed into Róisín's home, seized her and drove her to the Castlereagh Holding Centre in Belfast. Although called a holding centre, this was in fact an interrogation centre where detectives, members of Special Branch, Military Intelligence and MI5 observers managed and oversaw the interrogation of terrorist suspects. You could be held for seven days without legal representation and without visits from relatives.

Until its demolition in 2005, Castlereagh was a very secretive establishment beyond the scrutiny of the law and where torture had taken place. It was effective because many people were so terrified when they arrived that they soon coughed up information. Suspects held there were blackmailed and coerced into working for the security forces. The RUC considered it a powerful tool in combatting terrorism. It had a sterile environment through which tens of thousands of suspects were processed.

In 1977 the late Senator Edward Kennedy wrote a personal letter to police surgeon Dr Robert Irwin, in which he praised him for his courage in breaking ranks to expose police brutality at centres like Castlereagh; Irwin had recorded at least 150 cases of prisoners who had been physically abused:

> As my brother Robert Kennedy once told the students at the University of Cape town in South Africa on his visit there in 1966: 'Each time a man stands up for an ideal, or acts to improve the lot of others, or strikes out against injustice, he sends forth a tiny ripple of hope, and crossing each other from a million different centres of energy and daring, these ripples build a

current which can sweep down the mightiest walls of oppression and resistance.'

Róisín McAliskey was not told why she was driven in a police/military convoy from her Coalisland home or where she was being taken. But once she was escorted into Castlereagh Holding Centre, she must have been somewhat frightened. She was aware of its notoriety. It had a medical facility, as is customary in most interrogation centres, including Guantanamo, where doctors essentially abandoned their oaths to do no harm and oversaw extreme interrogations. Loyalist leader and hitman Billy Wright once told me that when he was young, he was interrogated at Castlereagh. During one questioning session, he was bent over a desk and a pencil shoved up his anus. Róisín was subjected to no such treatment because she was a high-profile suspect and the RUC had a foreign extradition warrant for her arrest. Nevertheless, for a young woman, pregnant and prone to asthma attacks, Castlereagh would have been a scary place.

For the first five days of her stay, Róisín was held without legal representation under the Prevention of Terrorism Act. She was not informed of the foreign warrant for her arrest or what it accused her of doing. This was a tactic to allow interrogators to assess her and to question her about matters not related to the warrant. They wanted to know how mentally tough she was, whether she would talk about her boyfriend and about people they both knew or about IRA activities to which they were seeking to link her.

On day six Róisín was finally told that the German government had issued a warrant for her arrest, tying her to the mortar bombing of a British Army base at Osnabrück four months earlier, on 26 June. On day seven in Castlereagh, she was taken from the facility and flown to London, where she was remanded in custody based solely on the German warrant. Her life was about to get much tougher.

In a move that contravened international law, Róisín was sent to Belmarsh men's prison, where she was listed as a Category A high-risk security prisoner. She was highly stressed, underweight, almost four months pregnant and was suffering from a range of ailments. The Category A designation meant she faced a very strict regime. Male prisoners jeered her and she was ordered to clean excrement from the walls of her cell. She spent one week in Belmarsh during which she was sick and did not eat for days.

By then, she was being represented by Gareth Peirce, one of Britain's most accomplished lawyers. Peirce had her transferred to London's Holloway women's prison. But even there, life was no bed of roses. Her Category A status remained in place, requiring her separation from other prisoners. She was strip-searched, often twice daily: early morning and late evening. This was a deliberate tactic that had been used on female republican prisoners in Armagh, who later pointed to the practice as a reason for launching a dirty protest. She was permitted limited visits, called 'closed visits'. Even though she was not allowed to touch anyone during the visits, she was still strip-searched after them. Major human rights organisations, including Amnesty International, branded strip-searches 'inhumane and degrading'. They were part of a deliberate British government policy to criminalise and humiliate 'political' prisoners and took on a much more permanent form under Margaret Thatcher. The strip-searching of Róisín McAliskey after visits was manifestly intended to punish her because there was no obvious security component which required it. She would eventually be strip-searched seventy-five times throughout her pregnancy.

No matter how you feel about her or her mother, these tactics contravened basic principles of law and decency. Even if this could be explained away as merely a security strategy, what was the purpose of the prison staff turning her cell light on and off every hour during the night or sometimes leaving it on all night? Anyone with common sense would know that the obvious reason to do this was to create stress and tiredness. The fact that the recipient of this regimen was pregnant made it particularly cruel and could have damaged the baby she was carrying. It was obvious that orders had come down from British intelligence to weaken her resolve so that she might start talking.

The prison authorities at Holloway, as part of the effort to keep her isolated from others, refused to let her exercise in the prison yard. They left her with no option but to drag herself, pregnant and tired, up several metal staircases to a small roof covered with wires, meaning that she did not see much sunlight and had little space to move around.

Her lawyer and Amnesty International made her plight known to the public. By February, when she was six months pregnant, there was some relaxation of the rules, but she still could not exercise with other prisoners and spent most of her days in her cell. Gareth Peirce and Amnesty decided that the prison regime was having a detrimental effect on her physically and mentally.

It is worth noting that the plight of women in prisons across the UK was horrendous. By the 1990s there were more females than males in prison but fewer prison staff and decrepit institutions with poor pre- and post-natal care. In a report into the detention of Róisín McAliskey, Amnesty made these powerful points about the failures of the system:

> On 20 February 1997, the Chief Inspector of Prisons, Sir David Ramsbotham, published three reports which reportedly revealed unacceptable conditions in three women's prisons: Risley in Cheshire, Holloway in London, and Low Norton in County Durham. Women in prison are being severely

affected by shortages of space and lack of staff. Consequently, the number of hours women are spending locked up in their cells has increased significantly. In addition, the length of time prisoners are allowed to associate with one another is being reduced. In some instances, women are not receiving adequate medical attention. In general terms, women are facing harsher detention conditions which, in some cases, may amount to cruel, inhuman, or degrading treatment prohibited by treaties to which the United Kingdom is a party. The government claims a lack of resources as a justification. However, the current emphasis in policy is to make the whole system more harshly punitive rather than constructively remedial.

In Holloway, for example, Róisín McAliskey was strapped into a wheelchair to travel to bail hearings and only after February 1998 was she allowed, supervised by prison officers, to be in the exercise yard with other female prisoners. Most inmates were denied enough exercise time and proper or sufficient medical care. Róisín later told friends that, in many respects, her case served to highlight the punitive character of the system as it affected all females behind bars in Britain.

The biggest issue facing her lawyers was that the international extradition system did not require the German authorities to share with them the information underpinning their warrant. Consequently, Gareth Peirce had to hire a German lawyer to chase down this information in Germany through its courts and security authorities. Germany was demanding that the British government simply hand over Róisín for questioning about an IRA mortar attack on the British military base at Osnabrück, claiming that she was part of a five-person IRA unit which was responsible.

In the 1990s the Provisionals had units operating across Europe, which comprised male and female operatives. One unit of five operatives, three men and two women all in their twenties, was tasked with carrying out bombings and assassinations in Germany, where there was a British–North Atlantic Treaty Organization (NATO) military presence. The IRA had arms dumps in Germany and Holland, containing weapons, explosives, timers and mercury-tilt-switch devices. The unit's members would travel separately in twos, a male and a female, pretending to be a young married couple on holiday. They would drive a car or a Ford transit-type vehicle onto the Cork to Roscoff ferry and then to Germany via France and Belgium. With the EU's open borders, it was easy to navigate to most European cities. The terrorists varied their routes as they saw fit.

One of the members of the unit which attacked the Osnabrück base was a former British soldier, Michael Dickson, who had served with the Royal Engineers. He later claimed he had no explosives experience but he was able to construct a launch platform for mortars. There was also twenty-eight-year-old James Anthony Oliver Corry from the New Lodge area of north Belfast. He was a trained IRA operative who knew a lot about weapons and explosives and later admitted the purpose of the mortar attack on the British base was to kill soldiers and demonstrate that the British Army was not safe anywhere in Europe.

The mortar attack, like other bombings on the British mainland at that time, was part of an IRA strategy to put pressure on the British government to let the IRA's political wing, Sinn Féin, be a part of any talks leading to a peace process. The IRA had walked away from talks because the British government rejected the idea of negotiating with Sinn Féin. It wanted to deal with what a senior British politician told me were 'the real men', meaning only the IRA's Army Council leaders and not political figures like Sinn Féin's president, Gerry Adams.

There is a curious aspect to this, which involved me personally. I met British Prime Minister John Major's adviser, David Davis, who asked me privately on Major's behalf if the IRA would ever do a deal with the Tory government. Would Adams be amenable to talks to end the conflict? I pointed out that Adams probably would like to go down in history as the man who brought the war to an end but he could not act alone. He would need the support of Martin McGuinness to convince the IRA to come on board if a peace deal was to be struck. McGuinness would have the means to keep Adams safe if talks with the British government were to happen. In other words, he would have to keep Adams alive if a section of the IRA decided to rebel. But, as things stood, Adams was not going to be able to engage in talks, since he had always denied that he was a member of the IRA. This was a problem. He was, by his own admission, only president of Sinn Féin and it was the IRA to whom the British government wanted to talk. John Hume had adopted a similar policy when I brought Adams and him together in a public forum, namely a BBC radio debate I produced. Hume, like Major, had said to Adams: 'Why should I talk to you? You are only a message boy. I want to talk to the real men.'

I believe that the IRA pulled out of peace process talks in the early 1990s because Adams, as president of Sinn Féin, was being denied a place at the negotiating table. The British side was adamant that he could not be a part of any conflict negotiation. It had to be the men who were running the war on the IRA's Army Council. Only they could discuss ending the conflict. It was only after IRA bombs exploded in Britain, especially the truck bomb at Canary Wharf, that the British were forced to change their stance and Adams became one of the chief negotiators of the peace process.

After the mortar attack on the British Army base on 26 June 1996, James Corry, the explosives expert of the IRA unit, left the IRA to support the peace process. A least, so he claimed when later apprehended and questioned about the attack. He said it was designed to kill soldiers but 'not too many'. He attributed his membership of the

IRA to seeing a woman shot dead by the British Army when he was a child playing in the street. He also said that during five arrests he was subjected to psychological torture. His statements about why he joined the IRA were only made after he was caught and tried for the Osnabrück bombing.

Corry's job had been to set up three mortar tubes in the back of a Ford transit van, which he then parked at the side of the base. The mortars would be set to prime and fire after thirty-five minutes. There would also be a small bomb in the van, timed to go off later to destroy any forensic evidence in the vehicle. His plan did not go as he hoped. One mortar landed inside the base and exploded, causing a huge bang and damage to parked cars, but no one was injured. Two other mortars launched but failed to reach the perimeter fence. The van was destroyed but not its number plate. This helped investigators trace it back to the Cork–Roscoff ferry.

Corry and Michael Dickson, the man who built the platform for the tubes and bolted it into the van, were critical players in their unit. Dickson had served several tours at British Army bases in Germany. But they had three other companions who were also crucial to IRA operations in Europe. Two of those were lovers: Donna Maguire and Leonard 'Bap' Hardy. They fell madly in love when they met at an IRA training camp. She was a vivacious convent schoolgirl from Newry while he was a tough, cunning operator from County Louth in the Irish Republic. Maguire was high on a British intelligence wanted list, which named her 'the angel of death'. She had been dispatched to work with an IRA unit in The Hague as early as 1989, when she turned twenty-two. Like Mairéad Farrell, she was fearless and resourceful. By 1996 the British and European authorities wanted to interview her about IRA operations across the EU.

A story which speaks to Maguire's conniving personality, and her willingness to make money no matter the method, relates to an episode in January 1996 when she won a settlement of £13,500 from Newry Council. She claimed that she had tripped on a broken pavement eleven years earlier. It did not, it seems, stop her running around Europe but, according to her, she was forced to give up swimming, as well as dancing and jogging, which she loved. Her ankle, she insisted to a court, would swell up. To make matters worse, she could no longer wear high heels.

Before the Osnabrück attack, this IRA unit had rented a holiday property for two weeks at Hatten, almost 100km from their target. The owner of the property, Manfred Schmidt, later recalled that five young people stayed at his cottage. The lease was signed by a person he identified from police photos as Michael Dickson and a girl called 'Beth'.

One month after the attack, Maguire married her lover, Hardy. But within five months, the focus was not on this couple or on Dickson and Corry, who were in hiding, but on Róisín McAliskey. According to the German authorities' warrant, she was 'Beth', the fifth member of the unit who had signed the cottage rental agreement. Manfred Schmidt and his wife confirmed this, hence the arrest warrant.

Róisín's lawyer, Gareth Peirce, was highly sceptical about a German claim that Schmidt and his wife had been shown photofits of Róisín and Michael Dickson provided by the RUC and had identified them. When the German warrant for Róisín's arrest arrived in London, it contained the claim that Schmidt had several times picked her out as 'Beth'. The evidence looked cut and dried but this would prove to be no ordinary case. When a German news crew tracked down Schmidt and presented him with photos of Róisín, he was shocked and said he had never identified her as 'Beth'. Mrs Schmidt, who had more interactions with 'Beth' than her husband, also said she had never identified Róisín as 'Beth'. Manfred Schmidt added a curious observation that while Róisín McAliskey did not look like 'Beth', they shared 'a shy look'.

The German case was fraying at the edges but there was the matter of forensic evidence allegedly linking Róisín to the attack. According to the German warrant, fingerprints tied her to it. Much to Gareth Peirce's surprise, the Germans themselves were confused about this evidence. First, they alleged that Róisín's prints were found on foil from a cigarette packet at the cottage rental. The German investigators and their legal advisers could not, however, seem to agree on where the foil was found, with three potential sites identified. This was not only sloppy; legally it was not the kind of evidence that should have been used to underpin a warrant calling for the arrest and extradition of anyone. Peirce insisted that with such legal confusion, the Germans were obliged to send her their fingerprint evidence so that it could be examined by a senior British forensic expert. The Germans refused to do so.

The German case took two more hits. Their claim that a Rover car, which Manfred Schmidt allegedly saw the IRA unit driving, travelled from Roscoff to Cork by ferry on 30 June after the mortar attack, with all five members of the unit on board, was proved impossible because there were no sailings from Roscoff on that day. Then there was the handwriting sample they believed they could link to Róisín McAliskey. It was on a piece of paper given to them by Schmidt whose young daughter had been given it by the mysterious 'Beth'. According to Mrs Schmidt, their daughter got on well with 'Beth' and the two exchanged addresses. It transpired that the address 'Beth' provided was fictitious and written in capitals. A handwriting expert could not tie it to Róisín nor could he rule her out because anything written in capitals is impossible to link with any reasonable degree of accuracy to a sample of a person's normal writing style. This was the last legal flourish by the Germans and it had collapsed their case, or so it seemed.

Meanwhile, Human Rights Watch and Amnesty International continued to warn that Róisín's prison regime was subjecting her to inhumane and degrading treatment. She was in danger of losing her baby. By now, the controversy had made its way into the US media and the halls of Congress.

Writing to friends from her prison cell, Róisín bemoaned the fact that there were no young or old people in prison. There was no real laughter, innocence, wisdom or a need to care for or comfort others. It was now April 1997 and she was heavily pregnant. Her bail applications had all been rejected. There was no case to fight so she could not go before the courts or even offer an alibi, and her lawyer said that there were plenty of those.

A month later, in a London hospital, she gave birth to a baby girl weighing almost 6lbs, whom she named Loinnir. For her family and supporters, there was more good news. She would not be returning to Holloway. She could go home to Coalisland with her baby. The British Labour government announced that it would not be extraditing her to Germany. There was no apology nor was there an admission that the German case against her was based on a false premise. She was, however, released.

Would Róisín have been released if Margaret Thatcher had been prime minister? Probably not. It later transpired that the Labour government was warned by senior party figures that the German case was deeply flawed. It would not meet the criteria to secure a conviction in the UK. If it went ahead, it would be a public relations disaster for the new Labour administration, which had returned to power under Tony Blair in 1997. There was, nevertheless, almost a PR disaster when Labour Home Secretary Jack Straw announced that Róisín was going home because the medical evidence would make her extradition 'unjust and oppressive'. Within twenty-four hours, under pressure from a wide political constituency, he had to eat his words, replacing them with this statement: 'I applied myself as I am required to do by law to the facts of the case and the evidence before me, and I took no other considerations into account whatsoever.'

This was Straw reversing course, pointing out that the legal facts of the case and not her medical condition guaranteed her release. He had already been told by a former Labour solicitor general, Lord Archer of Sandwell, that the British Crown Prosecution Service would have thrown out such a case. 'In an English court, evidence obtained as this appears to have been, almost certainly would be ruled inadmissible,' Archer had warned Straw.

The Germans disagreed. In 2007 they reissued a warrant for Róisín's arrest. She appeared before a court in Northern Ireland, where her lawyer expressed incredulity that after a decade and the fact that the British government had dismissed the last warrant, Germany was still behaving in a ridiculous fashion. The late Martin McGuinness accused the German government of being 'petty and vindictive'. But was it just the Germans pressing for her arrest? I have spoken to people whose links to this matter span several decades. Two of them suggested to me that there were those within the security architecture in London who had argued for a 'go-around' by the Germans. In other words, they favoured launching another effort to prosecute Róisín. One of my sources felt that this was petty and time-wasting, rooted in deep-seated anger towards Róisín's mother.

'There were some left-overs from the Thatcher era who hated any mention of Bernadette and it was her links to the IRSP and the INLA which did not sit well with them. It goes back to old resentments following the death of Maggie's close friend and hero, Airey Neave. He was loved by many in the shadows of power in London. The Irish have long memories but so too have we Brits. Things happened in the Cold War which some still remember vividly,' claimed one of my sources.

In November 2007 the Belfast Recorder, Judge Burgess, finally brought the saga to an end, relying on the British Home Secretary's decision of 1999 and adding that, given the time which had elapsed, it would be 'oppressive' to accede to the German warrant for Róisín's extradition. Bernadette described the post-traumatic stress her daughter had suffered from childhood. No mention was made of the nine months Róisín had spent at the Maudsley Hospital in London to treat her for postnatal depression. She was never given an opportunity to present the alibis her lawyer, Gareth Peirce, had assembled, showing that she could not have been in Germany at the time of the Osnabrück attack. Four members of the five-person IRA unit in Germany were located and each served several years. Donna Maguire and her husband 'Bap' later made headlines after they were arrested in Spain in an alleged money laundering sting. 'Beth', the mysterious fifth member whom the Germans believed was Róisín, was never identified. Those who know 'Beth's' identity have never broken ranks on the issue.

Róisín suffered from poor mental health yet she was interrogated in Castlereagh and subjected to degrading and inhumane treatment in prison, living with the fear of being extradited during her pregnancy. Her pain was compounded by the fact that from childhood she was already suffering with PTSD. Her mother fought to prove her innocence and in the aftermath of the collapse of the German case, she said that her daughter was scared for life and her physical condition had deteriorated while she was in custody.

Mother and daughter paid a terrible price for being political activists in a conflict not of their choosing. They epitomise the emotional and physical pain many women suffered during and after the Troubles.

16

THE CENOTAPH MASSACRE

ENNISKILLEN, A PICTURESQUE NORTHERN IRISH town, was the scene of a shameless act of IRA brutality on Sunday, 8 November 1987, while people were commemorating the dead of two world wars. At 10.48 on that morning of remembrance, a Provisional IRA bomb exploded near the town's war memorial, the Cenotaph, killing twelve people and injuring sixty, some of them seriously. One of the injured victims died after spending eleven years in a coma.

Stella Robinson was at home in Enniskillen when the bomb went off but she thought it was a neighbour slamming a garage door. Her parents, Bertha and Wesley, had always attended the ceremony and, on this Sunday, they were accompanied by her sixteen-year-old brother, Julian. Her parents would never come home but Julian would miraculously survive, with small cuts to his face and leg.

The horror of the day would remain fixed in Stella's memory forever because two people she adored were cruelly snatched from her and from her three sisters and two brothers. Loss is something most of us cannot fully grasp until it alters our lives ineradicably, wrenching from us something we cannot replace. It leaves us with acute emotional pain, forcing us to rely solely on our memories to compensate for lives lost. Memories of the good times are all that can fill and bridge years of emptiness as we age. Stella and her siblings had to rely on their recollections to survive and carry on the legacy of their parents.

In 1955 Stella was the first of five children born to Bertha, *née* Houston, and Wesley Robinson. Wesley, born in 1925, was seven years older than his wife. They were very much a traditional churchgoing couple, both Methodists. Wesley was very attached to his religion and would attend services several times a week, including on Sundays. As the years passed, he became involved with Methodist Missions and held weekly Bible classes in Enniskillen.

Wesley was not considered a political person and he rarely expressed opinions about Northern Ireland's tribal issues. Nevertheless, he was a member of the B Specials, the exclusively Protestant paramilitary force feared by Catholics. It had some of the largest arsenals of weapons of any paramilitary police force in Europe. Joining the B Specials was like a rite of passage for many young Protestant men in rural areas of Northern Ireland close to the Irish border. Fear drove many of them, who lived on insulated farms or in small, isolated townlands, into the ranks of the B Specials.

After leaving the Specials, Wesley joined the RUC police reserve. Stella remembers her father polishing the buttons on his uniforms. He always made sure the boots or shoes he wore shone brightly. 'My father loved dressing up,' says Stella. 'He just loved uniforms. When I grew older, he insisted on me and my two sisters wearing black patent shoes to school or church. He would polish them like his own. The same with my mum's.'

He was a fastidious, strict father who taught his children how important it was to be mannered and kind to others. He was a country boy, deeply attached to the land and this was evident in his love of gardening. He and Bertha had a small patch of land at Lisbellaw, a few miles from Enniskillen, where they kept hens, ducks and some sheep. He had a large vegetable garden and shared the produce with neighbours. They were also free to take what they wanted if they were in need. It was an idyllic environment for Stella and her siblings in the 1960s: feeding the animals, bringing in the hay and helping their mother cook. Bertha ran the small farm because Wesley worked for a time in cattle sales before joining the ranks of the Northern Ireland Customs Service. The job required him to stand guard at British customs posts in places like Pettigo, Belcoo and Belturbet, adjacent to the border. As a customs officer he was unarmed but he wore a fine tunic and Stella remembers how much he admired it. In the 1960s customs officers like Wesley were authorised to prevent people smuggling goods and animals from North to South and vice versa. Generally, a British customs post would be separated by several hundred yards from one on the Irish Republic side of the border.

Customs staff on both sides knew and liked each other and this was how Wesley built friendships with his counterparts in the Irish Republic. He would often take Bertha and the kids on trips to beaches in Donegal, Mayo and Sligo in the Republic, where he taught the children to swim. Bertha would prepare for their trips by baking cakes and buns the night before and making flasks of tea and loads of sandwiches the next morning. It was a time of joy and innocence. Wesley liked visiting County Mayo because his brother was a Methodist minister in Ballina, one of the biggest towns in the west of Ireland.

With the advent of the Troubles, life changed dramatically in areas close to the border in County Fermanagh, with Enniskillen at his centre, and in County Tyrone. The family moved closer to Enniskillen because Wesley sensed pressure building along the border. Sometimes he was the lone customs officer at a remote post but he never expressed fear in front of his children. Still, something would soon happen which would trigger fear in him.

During his years as a customs officer, he struck up a friendship with a Protestant couple, Thomas and Emily Bullock, who lived in a farmhouse in Aghalane, a small townland on the outskirts of Derrylin. Wesley was often on duty in a customs post near their property and was appreciative when they visited him and brought him tea and sandwiches. Thomas was a part-time member of the UDR, the British military force that replaced the B Specials in 1970. Membership of the UDR meant that Thomas could continue to keep a weapon at home, a security measure he considered necessary living within sight of the border. His wife used to say, 'They will have to come over my dead body to get to my Tommy.'

On a dark night in 1972 two IRA gunmen arrived at the Bullock home. It is not clear if Emily knew or recognised them, though the fact that she opened the door suggested that she knew who they were. They shot her dead at point-blank range, stepped over her body and sprayed the living room with bullets as they entered it, killing her husband. Detectives suspected that the gunmen were locals, otherwise Emily would have greeted them with a gun. Tommy always had his gun ready for such an emergency but he didn't have time to use it. This was the only occasion when Stella heard her father talk about the Troubles.

'My father was very fond of Emily and Thomas,' says Stella. 'They were so kind to him. He found it strange that Emily used to boast that killers would have to get over her dead body to kill her husband and it is exactly what they did. I realise now how much this must have bothered my father, but my parents tended to shield us from dreadful events.'

By 1987 Wesley was no longer working on the border and he and his wife had moved to Enniskillen. Stella, now a mother of three children, lived there too with her policeman husband, Kenneth. Her brother Julian was the only sibling still living with his parents. He liked watching football with his dad and Stella visited them often. She was very close to her mother, who loved to spoil her grandchildren.

Stella vividly remembers the day she went with her parents to Belfast before Christmas. It was Thursday, 5 November 1987 and her parents wanted to shop early for gifts for their children and family friends. In a shop, her father took her aside and asked her to persuade her mother to accept a gift of a skirt and blouse he wanted to buy her. Stella found this amusing, since he also insisted on buying a new hat for her because he loved women wearing hats.

Two days later, on Saturday 7 November, Wesley and Julian watched a football match before the annual television event Wesley never missed. It was the Royal British Legion Festival of Remembrance, broadcast by the BBC from the Royal Albert Hall, London. The event commemorates all those who have fought and died in conflicts, especially in the two world wars. A smaller event known as the Armistice, or Poppy Day, ceremony was scheduled for Enniskillen for the following day. Traditionally people would gather round the Cenotaph in the town centre for a ceremony attended by local people, members of the security forces and Church dignitaries. The Cenotaph was a distinct bronze statue of a soldier, his head bowed, on a stone plinth dominating a space at the junction of Belmore Street with East Bridge Street and Queen Elizabeth Road.

Sadly, most Catholics and their political and religious leaders boycotted these annual commemorative events even though tens of thousands of Catholics throughout Ireland fought and died in both wars. Some attributed Catholic indifference to the anti-British feeling following the Rising in Dublin in 1916 and others to Irish President de Valera's neutrality policy in the Second World War as well as his decision to sign a condolence book commemorating Hitler in the German legation in Dublin at the end of the war. Others rightly noted the IRA's close links to the Third Reich and a meeting in Germany between an IRA leader Sean Russell and Nazi military leaders, among them Joachim von Ribbentrop and Admiral Canaris. De Valera did not attend the Irish National War Memorial Service in Dublin in 1939 and it should be noted that even *The Irish Times* had ceased reporting on the annual War Dead Commemoration in Dublin by the mid-1940s. Irish republicanism was at the root of the Catholic rejection of the public honouring of the dead of the world wars.

One event was about to change this and Margaret Thatcher would call it 'a blot on mankind'. 'Every nation', she would tell the BBC, 'should honour its dead.'

Stella was at home looking after her children on that fateful morning of 8 November. She expected her parents to be on their way to the town centre. Her father would have made sure that his shoes and those of his wife, Bertha, were polished to shine. People familiar with the ceremony knew that the best place to view it was on the pavement running along the gable wall of the Reading Rooms owned by St Michael's Catholic Church. Over time the Reading Rooms, which had once been a school, had become the local community centre. The upper floor was unused but the ground floor had bingo sessions and the basement was a social club where men played snooker and card games. A sign of the character of Enniskillen was that both Catholics and Protestants used the facility, often for social gatherings and community events. Its gable wall faced the Cenotaph directly.

Bertha and Wesley, their son Julian between them, were standing with their backs to that wall, across from the Cenotaph. Wesley had been at that same spot every year. Near him on this Sunday was sixty-seven-year-old John McGaw, a well-known Enniskillen personality. If his past behaviour was anything to go by, he would have greeted Wesley and his wife warmly.

'Everyone knew John,' says Stella. 'I remember how he would give me a big hug and it was like he was going to squash me. He earned what little money he had from painting, decorating and odd jobs in town. People liked and respected him because he was generous with his time. He used to visit people in hospital or in nursing homes, no matter their religion. He would spend time with those who were lonely and always had a chocolate bar for them. He was such a character and a constant fixture of the social life of the town. He did not have a car so he walked everywhere. My mother used to say to him, "I'm going to find you a good woman," and he would laugh and reply, "As long as she's not the cross type."

The Honour Guard of soldiers who were due to parade around the Cenotaph had not yet arrived when a 40lb bomb exploded without warning, blowing out the gable wall of the Reading Rooms, collapsing the building. The blast sent huge chunks of masonry into the assembled crowd. Some parts of the wall crushed people, killing them instantly. Minutes after the blast, RUC officers, ambulance crews, soldiers and locals began pulling people from the rubble, but in some instances, rescuers were unable to reach people trapped underneath because of the weight of the pieces of masonry; instead they had to wait for heavy machinery to assist them.

An RUC reserve constable, who had been standing beside the gable wall, later remembered seeing Johnny McGaw to his left when the bomb went off, sending debris down on top of him and pinning him under it. The reserve constable was eventually freed by firemen and treated for multiple fractures.

Stella learned about the tragedy from her sister-in-law and rushed to the local Erne Hospital. As she began searching for her parents and brother, she heard someone say that Johnny McGaw was dead. Minutes later, she found her brother, Julian, in a room where he was being treated for cuts and bruises. He described standing between their parents when the bomb exploded. Somehow, neither the blast nor large pieces of debris had touched him.

'I asked him if Mum and Dad were alive,' recalls Stella. 'He said Mum was probably dead. He saw her face and it was like when you squeeze a rubber doll. He tried to remove a big piece of masonry on Dad's chest but it was too heavy to shift. Nevertheless, he thought Dad might still be alive.'

Soon after, Stella's husband, Kenneth, arrived with the sad news that Bertha and Wesley were both dead. A temporary mortuary had been set up at Enniskillen Territorial Army Base and he offered to undertake the onerous task of identifying the bodies.

In the hours after the explosion, Provisional IRA leaders were scrambling to come up with an explanation for the atrocity caused by their no-warning bomb. They saw the global outrage on television newscasts and were especially concerned by the expressions of condemnation and horror from across the political spectrum in the United States and the outrage in Ireland. Alan Dukes, the opposition leader in the Irish Parliament, referred to the IRA as 'these rats scurrying for cover in the sewers of their own violence'. Musicians and artists also denounced it as a violent act of terror. U2, the Irish rock band, were on tour in the US and its leader, Bono, interrupted a performance of their song 'Sunday, Bloody Sunday', to condemn the barbaric attack. He said: 'Fuck the revolution! Where is the glory in bombing a Remembrance Day parade of old-age pensioners, their medals taken out and polished up for the day?' Chris de Burgh, a famous Irish singer-songwriter dedicated his song 'At the War Memorial' to the victims of the Enniskillen bombing. His words expressed the hurt people felt across the world: 'People getting ready there are waiting for the bands. / And old men with their memories of comrades gone away.'

There were, I was told, frantic calls between Provisional IRA and Sinn Féin leaders in Northern Ireland and Dublin in the hours after the bombing, but it would take another ten years before the IRA would issue a hollow apology. Six hours after the blast, it instead came up with a bunch of lies in a phoned message to the BBC in Belfast. The message began with a statement of regret and a claim that the bomb had been 'aimed at catching Crown Forces personnel on patrol in connection with Remembrance Day services but not during it'. But here was the biggest lie of all in the IRA's faux apology:

> The bomb blew up without being triggered by our radio signal. There has been an ongoing battle for supremacy between the IRA and British Army electronic engineers over the use of remote-controlled bombs. In the past, some of our landmines have been triggered by the British Army scanning high frequencies and other devices have been jammed and neutralised. On each occasion we overcame the problem and recently believed that we were in advance of counter measures. In the present climate, nothing we can say in explanation will be given the attention the truth deserves, nor will it compensate for the feelings of the injured or bereaved.

This verbiage only appealed to ardent IRA supporters. By the time it was delivered, a forensic expert had already discovered that the Enniskillen bomb was triggered by an electronic timer, a microswitch and a battery. There was no evidence of a remote-control device, as the IRA had claimed. The thoroughness of this forensic examination was confirmed days later after skips full of debris from the bomb site were transported to a forensic laboratory and examined in minute detail.

The only reasonable conclusion, given the bomb was on a timer and not remotely controlled, was that it either exploded at the exact time the IRA had planned or it exploded prematurely. Given that the IRA wanted to kill a lot of members of the police and military, the most likely scenario, because only civilians were murdered, is that the bomb exploded prematurely. However, it must be stated that either scenario confirmed the IRA was prepared to kill civilians, considering them collateral damage, and it was going to be a mass casualty event.

I have always felt that there was something missing in the coverage of the Enniskillen tragedy and I believe there is a matter worth considering. The British and Irish governments have been sitting on highly classified papers related to the bombing. One concerns the fact that after the atrocity, a member of Britain's MI5 who was closely connected to secret operations against the IRA, particularly the running of agents within the Provisionals, broke ranks. He complained that his agency knew, as it did about many IRA operations, that the attack on the Cenotaph was planned. He went further, making a claim which, if aired publicly in the aftermath of the bombing, would have been political dynamite. He claimed that MI5 tampered with the bomb's timing mechanism, determined that the explosion would devastate the IRA's public image. One must treat a matter like this with considerable caution. Was the MI5 agent a disgruntled figure? Was this a bogus story concocted to damage the agency? I spoke to several sources I trust and I can confirm that the British and Irish governments have concealed this document. One retired intelligence figure told me that he had heard there were files 'scrubbed' in the wake of the bombing and that a 'matter arose which muddied the waters in the intelligence corridors' in Northern Ireland, specifically about the running of agents. Perhaps the governments have been unable to untangle or address this issue. If they did so now it would imply that they deliberately buried it for decades. The truth is not easy to locate in the intelligence world, but there is sufficient evidence to suggest that we do not and may never know the whole story of the Enniskillen bombing.

Not in doubt is the fact that the IRA planned an attack on the Remembrance Day parade. However, I have always suspected that State assets were a part of the planned bombing in Enniskillen. As for the bomb's timer being altered by MI5, it is likely to remain a mystery unless the IRA offers for interview the bomb-maker and that is unlikely.

An even bigger atrocity was planned for the same day, twenty miles from Enniskillen in the townland of Tullyhommon, beside the Irish border. Police were notified by the IRA about this bomb, which was five times the size of the Enniskillen one. An IRA spokesman warned that there was an unexploded bomb at Tullyhommon, but it took two days to locate it. Why? We do not know. The bomb's firing pack was subsequently recovered by the Irish police but they lost it, thereby making it impossible to determine if the IRA deliberately abandoned the bomb or if the bomber had tried to explode it but it had failed to go off. This remains an unresolved mystery.

In the aftermath of the murder of her parents, Stella and her siblings felt confused. There were so many unanswered questions. Stella was somewhat relieved when Catholic nuns from a local convent who had tended to the injured at the Cenotaph came to her home to say they had done as much as they could. She was also impressed by the wreaths and messages of sympathy from many people and organisations in the Irish Republic, proving how many friends her father had made during his years as a border customs officer.

Stella says that in the wake of the bombing, many who lost loved ones felt a mixture of fear, pain and confusion. People did not really know how to react and it took a long time before they found the courage to demand answers as to why such an atrocity happened. In the years after the bombing, most victims like her 'kept their dignity' and remained silent. It was a reaction I encountered when talking to the victims of similar tragedies. I tend to think that the advent of victims' groups such as the SEFF gave victims the means, cohesiveness and tenacity to advocate for action, whether this was demanding police investigations or a focus on the plight of those who had suffered quietly for years after losing their loved ones. After the Enniskillen tragedy, none of the victims was offered counselling or any other psychological assistance.

One person appeared to define the victim response to the Enniskillen loss of life. He was Gordon Wilson, who had a draper shop in the town. Like Stella's father, Gordon was a well-known member of the Methodist community and was considered, like others in his religious fraternity, politically moderate. On the day of the bombing, he was standing near the Cenotaph beside his twenty-year-old daughter Marie, a student nurse. Both were buried under rubble. He held her hand tightly and her last words were 'Daddy, I love you very much.' She was unconscious when the two were rescued and she died a short time later.

Within four hours of the explosion, Gordon Wilson granted the BBC an interview and his words quickly found their way around the world. The media fixated on them to define the tragedy. 'I have lost my daughter and we shall always miss her but I bear no grudge. I bear no ill-will,' he told the BBC, as he described his daughter's last minutes holding his hand.

His sentiments were quickly translated by the media into the motto, 'The Spirit of Enniskillen'. He became the epitome of forgiveness and reconciliation; the face of reason to emerge from decades of violence. In that bleak moment, he was plucked from obscurity as a local shopkeeper and brought into the limelight as a man of courage, ready and willing to talk to the men of violence on both sides. He was internationally applauded as a peace-maker. According to him, the Enniskillen bombers should be punished but he personally bore them no ill-will or hatred. He was not interested in revenge.

Gordon Wilson's calls for forgiveness found their way into the peace process in the 1990s. He received accolades from governments and peace organisations worldwide. When he died in 1996, aged sixty-seven, *The New York Times* recalled the words of former Irish

Taoiseach Albert Reynolds, who appointed him to the Irish Senate and credited him with 'personifying peace and reconciliation on this island'.

Not everyone saw the world the way Gordon Wilson did and not all the families of the victims were ready to talk about forgiveness. Their emotional wounds were too raw for many to start forgiving the IRA or to begin making overtures to paramilitaries on both sides. Most of them had yet to fully process how they felt about the tragedy they had gone through. Most wanted answers for the rationale behind this gruesome act of terror and some could not understand how Gordon Wilson was prepared to throw a mantle of forgiveness over the atrocity.

According to Stella, the families of the dead and injured were not asked their opinions. Gordon Wilson did not call upon the survivors or ask if he could represent them. Though it may have been his intention to do so at the outset, he did not and he quickly became the 'Voice of Enniskillen'. Survivors were not angry about this, nor did they feel any antagonism towards him, but some felt that he should have stopped to ask others how they felt about him appearing to speak for them.

Stella learned that Gordon Wilson's thirty-year-old son, Peter, did not share his father's opinions. He visited Stella and her family and apologised for his father, saying that he was the kind of man who would go to the ends of the world for an interview. This is how Stella felt in 2023, reflecting on Gordon Wilson's prominence: 'We fell into the trap – whatever Gordon must have said at the time, everyone assumed that all the families felt the same way. We were not of a mind to speak out, anyway. We were not thinking the way he was thinking. It was a total shock ... but his son came round to us and he was the same age as me and he said ... he kind of apologised for the way his father was talking on the TV and he didn't want us to be ... and I remember the day ... the night he came round. He was such a nice fella. He's dead now. And he said, "Can I come in?" and he said, "My father will go from one end of the earth to … and he loves speeches and always did" and he says, "I don't know how me father did all that." And he said, "I just want to let you know that just because my father says it, I am not the same as my father. I am not."'

Peter's criticism suggested that his father had become a willing media creature. It may appear a cruel thing to say about a man who was offering forgiveness to his daughter's killers, four hours after she took her last breath, but it must also be considered in the context of the time. The traumatic experience of the explosion and losing his beloved daughter in the way he described must surely have had a major impact on him. Within hours, it transformed him from a quiet, unknown shopkeeper into a man in the maelstrom of Ireland politics and an international celebrity. Gordon Wilson died a short time after Peter was killed in a road accident.

Stella believes that one of the outcomes of the public discourse driven by Gordon Wilson at the time was a perception that the people of Enniskillen were 'not bothered' about issues like having a major public inquiry. 'We did not have a voice. It was other people speaking and making decisions for us,' says Stella.

The most immediate question facing her and the other victims, which they did not articulate loudly, was how such an atrocity could have happened in their town. While the media continued to focus on Gordon Wilson in the immediate aftermath of the bombing, *The Irish News* dismissed one of many conspiracy stories that were surfacing. It was claimed that Enniskillen's Catholic parish priest, Monsignor Sean Cahill, had blocked the RUC from searching the Reading Rooms before the parade at the Cenotaph. The Monsignor denied this, telling reporters that he would willingly have acceded to any police request to search the building but that no such request was made. The RUC issued its own statement, confirming that it had never asked for access to the building. This bogus story was being fed to the media by people determined to create division between Catholics and Protestants in the town

Nowadays Stella lives with dreams of what might have been had her parents lived to see their grandchildren growing up. Sometimes there are moments when she is reminded what a wonderful person her mother was. One day, when she was talking to a lady who worked with Bertha in a local bacon factory, she learned how caring her mother was.

'My mother used to help in the factory canteen in the evenings when there were staff shortages. Some of the men were poor and could not buy desserts, so my mother used to bake cakes, bring them to work and give them slices with their tea.'

For Stella, stories like this make her loss less painful but she still feels betrayed by the failure of the authorities to find the perpetrators and punish them. She is not consumed with revenge but, like so many victims, she hoped for answers and above all else for justice for her mum and dad and all the dead and injured of the Enniskillen atrocity. In her heart, she knows that justice is a concept, rarely a reality.